Questions of Rhetoric and Usage

KENNETH S. ROTHWELL
University of Vermont

Questions of Rhetoric and Usage

SECOND EDITION

 Little, Brown and Company
BOSTON   TORONTO

Library of Congress Catalog Card No. 73–20935

THIRD PRINTING

Published simultaneously in Canada by
Little, Brown & Company (Canada) Limited

PRINTED IN THE UNITED STATES OF AMERICA

The author is grateful to the following sources for material reprinted in this book:

John A. Allen. For his satirical letter on fraternities.
American Heritage Publishing Company. For entry "version" from the *American Heritage Dictionary
of the English Language.* © Copyright 1969, 1970, 1971 by the American Heritage Publishing Co.,
Inc. Reprinted by permission.
Appleton-Century-Crofts. For excerpts from *Shakespeare's Principal Plays.* 3rd Ed., edited by
Tucker Brooke, John William Cunliffe, and Henry Noble MacCracken. Copyright, 1935, by
D. Appleton-Century Company. Reprinted by permission of Appleton-Century-Crofts.
Basil Blackwell, Publisher. For an excerpt from Thomas Hobbes, *Leviathan,* edited by Michael
Oakeshott.
Cambridge University Press. For an excerpt from G. S. Kirk, *The Songs of Homer.*
Car and Driver. For excerpts from "Six Car Comparison Text," *Car and Driver* 18 (January 1973)
p. 32. © Ziff Davis Publishing Company; and from "Lotus Elan Sprint," *Car and Driver* 18
(January 1973) p. 79. Reprinted by permission.

For SOOKAMLS

Preface

To the Student

     You should be told at once that this textbook does not claim to provide all the answers for success in written expression. As probably everyone knows, no set of formulas will magically produce an effective writer. Writing involves much more than mere skills — "correct" grammar, punctuation, sentence and paragraph structure, and attention to mechanics; it involves the whole personality. The way we perceive reality, the books we've read, the conversations we've had, the life style we've chosen, the spoken and unspoken philosophies we've committed ourselves to — all these enter into the creation of a written style. A textbook cannot take all those variables into account. It must limit itself to that body of knowledge and theory which is fairly well known and agreed upon, and which can be gotten across in a classroom.

     None of this is to say that the textbook does not have its place. It does, however, need a teacher to go with it. Only an experienced teacher is equipped to help you explore those elusive areas of inspiration and imagination where theory and rules cease to be helpful. The textbook is not truth itself, but a guide to truth. If you are committed to improving your control over standard written English, your own energy, your teacher's advice, and this text will provide mileposts along the way.

To the Instructor

A major change in the second edition is the incorporation of prose models from contemporary writers to underscore the point that the timeless patterns of written prose remain timely. A distinction has also been made between style as artifice and as function, a definition that should be valuable to those faced with teaching students who demand "practical" English — whatever that is. New student themes have been drawn from the author's classrooms of 1973, and the usage section has been revised to take into consideration rapidly changing standards of usage in high-level journalistic writing. The section on the research paper now caters to the student interested in writing for a course in the social sciences, though its methods are also applicable to the literary research paper. A section on writing a film review has been added, as well as material on writing the essay examination, and the chapter on logic has been redesigned to come closer to the needs of student writers. The latest editions of standard college dictionaries are discussed in chapter eight, though unhappily the 1973 edition of the *Random House College Dictionary* did not appear in time to be included.

Depending on the students in the course, you should probably first assign the introductory chapter for discussion of aims and goals in the course (in the full expectation that you will end up taking issue with much of what I say). I always like to get a class theme the first week of the semester as a guideline for diagnostic procedures and for comparison with the final theme assignments at the end of the course. Then you could go to chapter two to explore the case history of a student theme and the nature of outlining. Next you could move to the sections on paragraphing and sentence structure, in that order. My experience has been that the sections on style as artifice require students who have become fairly sophisticated about writing, and should for that reason be put off until the end of the semester. Chapters on the dictionary, and on logic, should be made as special assignments, coming near the beginning and end of the course. The sections on writing the research paper, writing about film and literature, and writing the essay stand in the wings, awaiting their cue. The materials on usage and grammar should be referred to continually. You may use the book's numbering system for referring students to the appropriate sections by simply jotting the right numbers down in the margins of themes.

Acknowledgments

Along the way, many people have generously offered advice for improvement of the first edition. I am especially obliged to the following: Grier Nicholl, Ada E. Leeke, Joseph F. Dunne, William J. Hofmann, Robert L. Keefer, J. Robert Leach, George Gleason, Clayton E. Hudnall, Janice Wilson, Catherine K. Rosenbaum, Patricia Piety, Renee C. Crauder, Holly Castle, Robert Francis, and

Patricia Burnes. Even lengthier commentaries came from Nancy Deane, Richard S. Beal, and Alton Seidl. In my own department, Littleton Long and Virginia Clark gave valuable advice on the research paper and on matters of modern grammar and usage. Students from my English 1 class, Written Expression, at the University of Vermont, were especially helpful in shaping the main directions of my revisions. Special obligations go to Jean Heath, John Snow, Scott Whitted, and Arnold Fertig for allowing me to publish their papers.

At Little, Brown, Charles Christensen continued to preside over the text's career; Deborah Otaguro handled production; and David W. Lynch undertook to teach the writing teacher to write — with notable results I think. Bart Casey has faithfully assisted me throughout the entire enterprise. Victoria Osborn and Laurie Ginter helped out in many chores, and Evelyn Kyle did the typing, with her usual skill. As always, my wife and children patiently endured the unendurable. To them, much thanks.

K. S. R.

Contents

Questions of Rhetoric and Usage

Part One   RHETORIC

Rhetoric may be defined as the faculty of observing in any given case the available means of persuasion.
ARISTOTLE, Rhetoric ca. 335 *B.C.*

A hearer, then, is included in the very idea of preaching; and we cannot determine how in detail we ought to preach, till we know whom we are to address.
JOHN HENRY CARDINAL NEWMAN, The Idea of a University, 1873

1   Introduction

1.   What Is Rhetoric?

The Greeks called it *rhetoric.*[1] It was the art of effective and persuasive speech, of translating thought into language, of getting the point across to an audience that might be indifferent or even hostile. In the *Art of Rhetoric,* Aristotle described the best means available for being persuasive in courtroom, council, and occasions of ceremony. The Athenian lawyer found it a storehouse of hints for accusation and defense (forensics); the politician, for debating the good and expedient (deliberative oratory); and the public speaker, for praise and blame (declamatory speech). Today the word *rhetoric* is applied to written as well as spoken expression, prose as well as oratory, and more often to style and organization than its original goal, persuasion. But it still is the art of planned utterance, aimed at uncovering the best strategies for reaching into the hearts and minds of others. It is writing not just for oneself but to others.

Modern abuses have twisted the meaning of the word to suit its worst rather than its best users. Television and radio have assaulted the eyes and ears

---

[1] In the Greek "rhētorikē" [ῥητορική], which means literally "the art of" (*ikē,* or "ique" as in "techn*ique*") the "orator" (*rhētōr*).

of mass audiences with appeals to prejudice, snobbery, greed, fear, and insecurity. Never before have so few done so much to debase the taste of so many.
The hidden persuaders make automobiles into sex objects; airline travel into
airborne seduction; housewives into beaming plastic dolls; and cigarette smoking
into a symbol of virility. Politicians fear more for their "image" than for the
truth. The packaging is more important than the contents. No wonder mass
man has either rejected all propositions as false or succumbed to the torpor of
the tube.

Persuasiveness has been oversold, damaging rhetoric's own image.
Phrases like "mere rhetoric," "that's just a lot of rhetoric" (substitute *hot air!*),
and "rhetorical balderdash" show how low a proud scholarly tradition has fallen.
It is not, however, rhetoric that is at fault but the *abuses* of rhetoric. Rhetoric
can serve honest or dishonest ends just like any other manmade instrument.
As a result, people mistakenly identify it with ambulance-chasing lawyers,
oily politicians, glib salesmen — unscrupulous persons bent on twisting words
to suit their own ends. A rhetorician "wins friends and influences people" to
line his own pockets. Or he is brother to the wicked sisters in Shakespeare's
King Lear, outrageously flattering their father to gain property while the virtuous
sister, Cordelia, is mute.

So long as collecting and arranging proofs to defend an honest thesis
is still a part of the human enterprise, rhetoric will have much to offer. For
defending truth remains a major end of rhetorical training. Rhetoric, by training
human beings to choose among alternative patterns of words to expose a false-
hood or defend a truth, is far more than a mere skill, like welding. Thought
and language cannot be as easily disconnected as many think. We cannot have
bright ideas and hire a flunky to write them out for us, as though language
were a cosmetic. The way we write implies more than a commitment to words;
it also demands a commitment to truth. This moral intention in rhetoric, calling
for truth and rightness, was deeply rooted in the minds of students at the medieval universities, and can be felt in our own colleges. In medieval universities
the "trivium," grammar, rhetoric, and logic, was the heart of the curriculum.
Today the composition course carries on this humanistic tradition, preserving
something of the moral ideals that Greek and Roman scholars first gave to
humanity.

Language, like every other part of our culture, is undergoing the "future
shock," the numbing brought on by our startlingly changing time. The atmosphere is clouded by *anomie,* rootlessness and alienation from traditional values,
exposing all authority to attack. Because it stresses planning and craft, rhetoric
is thought to emasculate creativity and spontaneity. It is said that the student
left alone to do his own thing will eventually discover a method of expression
satisfactory for him. Theoretically too, a dozen apes left alone for a century

in a room with twelve typewriters might eventually type out *Paradise Lost.* But what inefficiency! The theory behind a rhetoric course is that if you consciously mimic patterns of written expression proven effective through centuries of trial and error, you will learn more than the self-taught, self-discoverer will by the unconscious mimicry he puts himself through. How many people want to spend thousands of dollars on a college education only to realize in middle age, like Monsieur Jourdain in Molière's play *Le Bourgeois Gentilhomme,* that they have been speaking prose all their lives! Yet rhetoric is not a conspiracy to kill spontaneity and creativity. Aristotle devoted a good share of his *Rhetoric* to ingenious strategies for responding to many kinds of arguments. He also gave many hints for finding the best means of persuading others. We might describe rhetoric more clearly as a way of encouraging controlled and efficient spontaneity. It is best to leave nothing to chance in a written argument. Plan for all contingencies. At the same time, if chance or inspiration — "the divine muse" as it was once called — unexpectedly knocks at the door to offer help, never spurn her either.

It is easy to be frightened about a writing course. The first results may be discouraging, as with tennis or golf lessons. You have after all been writing all your life. What can a teacher possibly tell you? The self-taught tennis player who suddenly decides in middle age to take lessons goes through the same wringing out. His game has been adequate; now suddenly, after the pro has dissected his forehand and backhand, he can barely hit the ball. But with patience and practice, the lessons gradually make themselves felt in steady, over-all improvement. So it is with writing lessons. Frustration must be expected. But several months of systematically analyzing others' styles and comparing them with your own will bring improvement. The day may even come when you will be horrified to stumble on college graduates who have not had this kind of training in the use of language.

2. Why Write?

A major weapon for survival if you don't live alone in a jungle is the ability to persuade others that what you think is right. True enough, the decent and honorable are usually proven to be right, but history also shows that the decent and honorable cannot always sit back smugly waiting for the world to acknowledge their rightness. Action helps. Action with words. Almost anything written down on paper is an attempt to persuade, or convince, others — to read it, to think about it, to act on it, or to learn from it. The study of rhetoric thus makes a vital addition to the composition course.

The strategies outlined here are designed for the kind of prose written in college and university work. This is not the same as spoken language, nor does it bear much resemblance toward other special kinds of written dialects, such as those of underground presses, and of emerging American subcultures. The kind of written dialect dealt with here reflects conventions that affect most of the factual, informative, helpful prose written in America in the 1970's. Anyone unfamiliar with these conventions, which are informally watched over by editors and journalists and teachers, loses an important asset of persuasion: credibility. The audience will simply think the writer is an ignoramus, though his "originality" may impress them.

Has the electronic culture, with cassette and tape, made writing less important? Probably not as much as people think. The intellectually inert are satisfied sitting back absorbing reality from the packaged sounds and images of mass culture. And certainly the galaxy of audiovisual aids that technology has brought even to the study of the humanities — film strips, tapes, movies, closed-circuit television — is a blessing, not a curse, when properly used. Remember, however, that material programmed into these gadgets had to be composed, planned, or blocked out by a writer. Even in the "post-Gutenberg age," as Marshall McLuhan labeled the period in which electronic gadgetry has challenged the printed page for supremacy, leadership will remain with writers, not watchers and listeners.

In the mundane world, however, writing remains a necessary chore in business and the professions. Informative prose, the kind we are dealing with here, appears daily in the newspapers, with their stories of politics, sports, business, and society; in business, with its annual financial reports, its house organs, its sales appeals, its letters; in the academic world, with its learned journals; and in community life, with its constant demand for PTA reports, church financial canvasses, Boy Scout activities, and charity drives. Rare indeed is the college-trained man or woman who can escape the need to put thought on paper.

3. The Writer's Questions

"What am I really trying to say?" "How am I going to say it?" "Do I really know what I'm talking about?" "How can I best convince them I'm right?" "Have I done my best on this job?" Such questions crop up when we try to put thoughts on paper. They signal that the writing grows out of an internal dialectic, a dialogue with oneself, and are the reason for this book's title. Raising questions, all kinds of questions, sharpens thinking and shapes answers. And the questions need not be merely technical ("How shall I support this proposition?"), they can be moral ("Is this proposition honest?"). Our choice of words "gives us away" because they mirror our innermost selves. "Fool, look into your heart and write," said Sir Philip Sidney. No one knew better how difficult this simple advice could be.

Question-asking invites decisions. It makes us into "perturbed spirits" forced, like Hamlet, to make choices, though perhaps unwilling to do so. Making choices, being for or against something, opens us up to doubt, anguish, turmoil, complexity, uncertainty, strength, and knowledge. It takes us from childhood to adulthood. The struggle of a hard-working writer for perfection is the loneliness of the long-distance runner, not the camaraderie of football. "Between the idea / And the reality . . . / Falls the Shadow," wrote T. S. Eliot. Anyone who has struggled to get thought on paper knows the truth of his insight. And anyone who thinks he may have succeeded also knows the joy of having reached the top of the mountain. Writing therefore deals with asking questions and making tough decisions. What could be better training for life itself?

We may insist as often as we like that man's intellect is powerless in comparison with his instinctual life, and we may be right in this. Nevertheless, there is something peculiar about this weakness. The voice of the intellect is a soft one, but it does not rest till it has gained a hearing. Finally, after a countless succession of rebuffs, it succeeds.
SIGMUND FREUD, The Future of an Illusion, 1927

First, as Cicero saith, it helpeth greatly to teach plainly to define, and to make things that be compounded, intricate, or confused, to appear simple, plaine, and certaine: Secondly, by dividing things orderly into their parts, it greatly helpeth memorie: and thirdly, it helpeth to amplifie any kind of speech, and to make it more copious.
THOMAS BLUNDEVILLE, The Art of Logicke, 1599

2   The Writer's Materials:

Thought and Action

INVENTION AND CREATIVITY

4.   How Do I Get Started? The Four I's

In front of Philosophy Hall on the campus of Columbia University is a full-sized casting of Auguste Rodin's statue *The Thinker.* Chin on palm, he is trying, a teacher said a long time ago, to think of a theme topic. He could have said more accurately that the thinker was busy inventing ways of approaching a theme topic. In academic life as well as "real" life, writing assignments grow out of the specific occasions that already have at least a rough outline. The challenge then is not what to write about, but how to find the ways of approaching, defining, stating, restating, focusing, limiting, and amplifying the topic. The means of expression, not the subject itself, create the difficult questions. If you are clever and know your own feelings, you can always treat a subject interestingly. Your job is getting from topic to theme.

Asked to write a paper on a personal experience, some students sit hopelessly paralyzed in front of a typewriter for hours, unable to put one word on paper. Others have no problems; their copiousness resembles Niagara Falls as the words tumble out one after another. Why should this be so? Chances are the inarticulate student is afflicted with one of the four "I's": Inexperience, Indifference, Insecurity, and Insensitivity. Because none of these is programmed into the human mind, each can be conquered.

4a.   A Handicap: Inexperience

Some theologians believe the universe was created *ex nihilo,* from nothing. Probably not very much else springs from nothing, least of all effective writing. The equivalent to nothingness is inexperience. And inexperience about life is bound to generate very little of interest to an audience. Words spring out of our actions and our thoughts. The worker on the assembly line lives a life unreal to those who have never spent an endless day of noise and dirt, or who have not seen Charlie Chaplin's satire of the assembly line in the film *Modern Times.* Pollution may seem remote until you have canoed down a New England stream in August, and the anxieties of struggling for a place in a profession remain outside the imaginations of those who have never felt them. Effective *pro* and *con* arguments on birth control, the rights of American Indians, teacher accountability, collective bargaining, and the rights of women cannot come from a vacuum. A commitment in our own lives encourages us to discover the right words. Experience — all we learn about ourselves (our inner life) and all the knowledge we gather about things outside ourselves — shapes our attitudes and opinions and gives us the richness of ideas from which we can draw something to write about. Without this experience we stumble against the black terror that is called "writer's block."

4b.   A Problem: Indifference

Writing blocks are also built of the wall that indifference puts between us and the world around us. Like inexperience, this obstruction can grow out of sloth, or simple laziness. Not finding the energy to use the mind, we are too weak to listen to others, to inquire, to read, to meditate, to analyze, to form opinions.

Minds as much as bodies need exercise to stay in shape. Addled prose from undisciplined thought is the intellectual equivalent of a flabby waistline from overingestion and underexertion. The alarming percentage of citizens who volunteer "No Opinion" on any subject of consequence in public opinion polls consists mostly of people who have lost interest in all but their own immediate affairs. We can almost stand back and watch those who do have the energy to develop opinions move into the vacuum to shape opinions for them. You can work up training sessions for the mind: give unrelenting attention to public affairs as reported in good newspapers and magazines such as *The New York*

Times, Atlantic, or *The New Yorker;* attend plays, concerts, and recitals; listen enthusiastically to lectures and discussions; get into conversation with people who know a great deal about their subjects; examine the politics in local and national government; and selectively scrutinize the best programs on commercial and educational television. These prescriptions are a partial antidote to the flat prose ground out by the writer who cannot figure out his own attitude toward his subject.

4c.   A Threat: Insecurity

If you get over the walls of inexperience and indifference, you may, like many among us, end up on the rim of the chasm *insecurity.* There the spectres leap at us from every side, and they are familiar enough even to professional writers. The dreaded "writing block" may grow from anxiety about correctness, making you distraught over whether to use *who* or *whom,* and stopping the pen. Many writing teachers play down formal instruction in usage and grammar to dodge this bugbear, though they all see the peril in carrying that policy too far. Fear of not being able to produce, of "drying up," can cause mental paralysis, even for the beginner. The dreadful sense that there is really nothing worth saying left to be said on the subject also congeals the ink in the pen.

Short of seeking the advice of a psychiatrist, what can be done? An exercise in automatic writing is one way to break down this block. Writing out every thought that pops into your head for ten minutes may give a sense of the resources hidden in the depths of the mind. The millions of cells in a brain store away astounding masses of data — details, anecdotes, stories, memories. Illiterate persons in primitive societies perform prodigious feats of recall, mainly because their culture relies on speech, not writing. Primitive bards in Kirghiz, Siberia, improvise long epic poems called *Manas,* partly from memory and partly by on-the-spot improvisation. Some otherwise ill-informed Americans can spout baseball statistics from a World Series of nearly prehistoric times. Obviously the "uneducated" have enormous potential for verbal fluency.

What bizarre faces, weird costumes, grotesque encounters, brilliant speeches, great music, epic quests fill our nightly dreams only to evaporate by midmorning! The raw material of dreams, sufficient to make a Balzac out of every man, slips into oblivion (though we can salvage some of it simply by writing down regularly the remnants of dreams that stay with us when we wake up). And what happened to the lost fantasies of childhood that let us create imaginary empires in which we ruled supreme? They are locked into the brain's immensely compact computer, awaiting rediscovery — a potentially priceless means toward vivid self-expression.

The narcotics craze of the Sixties tempted the unwary to explore hidden recesses of the psyche with powerful, and destructive, drugs. Psychedelic effects trickled into, indeed almost overwhelmed, art forms, including literature. But long before that questionable chapter in American cultural history, psychologists and poets had known about the associative powers of words — such as earth, air, fire, and water — for releasing verbal fantasies from the subconscious. Experiments in writing classes have shown that the word *water* suggests floods of ideas that can be turned into interesting papers. The many great "sea" stories, from Homer's *Odyssey* to Melville's *Moby Dick* to Hemingway's *The Old Man and the Sea* prove that the sea, like the sun and the wind, arouses primordial responses in the human mind.

4d.   A Barrier: Insensitivity

A fourth threat to effective expression is insensitivity. In this context, "sensitivity" is not mere squeamishness unfitting one for the realities of the workaday world. It involves the mind's and the body's sensory capacity — the ability to see, feel, touch, taste, smell, and hear. Being sensitive to the external world means being able to translate perceptions into words. The poet Gary Snyder defined poetry as "riprap on the slick rock of metaphysics," which instantly makes sense when you understand that this kind of "riprap" is "a cobble of stone laid on steep, slick rock to make a trail for horses in the mountains." This is real coordination of eye, ear, and mind.

Another kind of sensitivity makes the writer conscious of his selfhood, his inner motives and psyche, his personality. Few essays disguise the evidence if the writer has not come to grips with his own identity, explored his own consciousness, and defined his way of seeing his universe. How do his ideas and values compare and contrast with those of others? And yet the self dwindles in importance as the subject gains it. Some subjects are so important they at once obliterate the writer, but others, such as personal essays, allow the writer to intrude, show off, dazzle his audience. To write an effective essay requires more than merely being a liberated person with knowledge of self, just as to compose great love poetry demands more talent than merely being a great lover. Self is more likely to be defined by engaging in actions, relationships with others, and experience than in isolated brooding. And the relevance of self-knowledge to effective expressions depends on the subject and audience. An audience interested in getting a good analysis of a war may find the reporter's asides about his own feelings intrusive, and an audience interested in autobiography may want even more personal insight.

4e.   How Can I Plan without Panic?

The problem of selfhood is so complex that the preliminary step in writing, the "pre-writing phase," as it is often called, might logically deal with less cosmic questions: (1) *What* shall I write about? (2) What *materials* will I use in the discussion? (3) What *form* should the materials be put into? And (4), what *effect* do I wish my words to have on the audience? Raising these questions naturally leads us to think about the *motive* behind writing, *selecting* a topic, the raw *materials* for building it up, the *form* of the materials, and finally the *effect* on the audience. These questions may work in isolation or in any combination. If you think deeply, about effect on an audience (question 4), you will find yourself agreeing with Edgar Allan Poe, who said in his "Review of Nathaniel Hawthorne's 'Twice-Told Tales,'" that all a fiction writer's energies go into establishing a "single effect." Poe believed that "in the whole composition there should be no word written of which the tendency, direct or indirect, is not to the one pre-established design." Questions about motivation, choosing materials, shaping those materials, and effect on audience will face the writer struggling to move from preliminary to final stages of composition. Other questions that will come up are whether the ultimate goals are praising, blaming, informing, delighting, teaching, or soothing the audience.

5.   How Do I Convert Topic into Theme?

Assuming you believe in what you are saying and that you feel therefore that you must do a good job, what is the next step? Let's analyze an assignment that a student, Jean Heath, was given in a composition class and her activities, step by step. Following that, we'll look a little more closely at some of the specific methods, such as outlining and formulating a theme, that go into writing.

An instructor may assign a theme topic on a subject of contemporary interest to connect the college writing course with the realities of the modern world. It is probably not going to be entirely open (that is, "write 500 words on *any* subject you can think of"), but will be half-limited already, such as something about university life, aging in America, or, as in the hypothetical paper we are about to explore, women's liberation.

If the topic is unlimited (write on any subject you can think of), you can run through several check systems to spring loose an idea. What is your attitude toward major components of society, such as automobiles? Or mass transportation? Television soap opera? Commercials? Laws against pot? The draft system for pro football? Your feelings, measured against those of others, will often generate steam for a paper. That failing, try ransacking newspapers and encyclopedias for subjects (articles, not words). Examine subject headings in the *Reader's Guide to Periodical Literature* (see page 257). Find some interesting people to talk to. If all these aren't fruitful, contemplate the advice of the great eighteenth-century man of letters, Dr. Samuel Johnson: "A careless glance upon a favourite author, or transient survey of the varieties of life, is sufficient to supply the first hint, or seminal idea, which enlarged by the gradual accretion of matter stored in the mind, is by the warmth of fancy easily expanded into flowers, and sometimes ripened into fruit."

On the other hand a topic may be totally limited, such as a "A Comparison of Hal and Hotspur in Shakespeare's *1 Henry IV*," or "John Dean's Role in the Watergate Affair." But even a limited topic often requires further pruning and cutting to make it focus. Hal and Hotspur in which *scenes* of the play? John Dean during what *phase* of the scandal? And so forth.

5a. How Do I Select a Topic?

With these principles in mind, Jean Heath ponders an assignment: write a theme on the general subject of women's liberation. Being female, she has had first-hand experience with the problems of women and she is therefore well within her competence in choosing this subject. The consciousness of the ways in which society has defined her role and that of other women without consulting them has been growing. She knows, or believes, that it will be more difficult for her to get into graduate school than for a man. She rather resents, or thinks she does, that she cannot have free choice to enter such professions as engineering, airline piloting, surgery, and even building construction. Male taboos, she feels, have already unfitted her psychologically to compete. She has also been able to discuss these problems with members of a local women's consciousness-raising group. She has, finally, read widely in the works of Germaine Greer, Simone de Beauvoir, and Betty Friedan, acknowledged experts on the subject of women's liberation. She has accumulated enough practical and theoretical experience, having crumbled the wall of indifference, to undertake an essay without too much straining.

5b. How Do I Limit the Topic?

First, however, Heath must limit the subject to manageable size. She begins by making a part-whole analysis that gives her not only a tentative statement of her thesis but also an enumeration of ideas.

> THEME: How Does Society Treat Women?
> Women in industry: underpaid piece workers
> Women in the home: fettered to children and routine housework
> Women and childbearing: the world is overpopulated anyway
> Women and professional status: not much
> Women and mass media: constantly made to look stupid
> Women and politics: real breakthroughs have been made but there are more to come
> Women and education: their training has made them what they are

> Women as wives: too often they are mere behind-the-scenes counselors to husbands of limited ability
>
> Women and economic discrimination: Where should I begin? How many women are corporation vice presidents?

As you can see, from her reading and discussion Jean Heath has already developed a formidable list of possibilities for a theme. As she looks at this list she realizes that almost any topic can be developed into a full-length paper. Which provides the special "angle" as newspapermen (or better yet in this context — newspaper*persons*) used to say? Which will best open up the topic, convert it into an interesting paper? As Jean looks over the list, she realizes that her own choice of topics reveals much about the kind of person she is. She has gone through introspection and self-discovery as she has defined herself by determining what her attitude is toward a subject of importance to human beings. We discover ourselves by being ourselves and by talking to ourselves and to others — a continuing dialogue — not by waiting passively for lightning to strike. She further realizes that she is somewhat aggressive, but paradoxically reluctant to speak out publicly about her feelings, and yet impatient with people who cannot see the world as she sees it. At the same time she is wise enough to realize that these characteristics can be strengths or weaknesses depending on how she exploits them. As she goes through the list, she tries to think how each topic would appeal to the kind of audience she is writing for: a class of indifferent women and possibly hostile men.

Wanting to show proof of both credibility and logic, and eager to avoid being charged with feminine emotionalism, she determines to take on a part of the subject that will best fit those goals. She discards the idea of "women in industry" because she lacks first-hand experience. Not having been locked up in the home with children, and realizing that many of her classmates see this as a privilege, not as bondage, she scratches "women in the home" too. Her expertness as a wife is also in short supply because she has not been married. Lack of experience that will make her statements credible also leads her to drop "women and professional status" and "women and politics." As for "women and childbearing," she cannot discuss so controversial a topic as abortion because she has mixed feelings about its morality.

That leaves two: "women and education" and "women and the mass media." They both interest her; she knows quite a bit about them from experience. Could they be combined? How, she asks herself, have the educational system and mass media handled women? What has been women's fate in the hands of these two systems? This question unlocks the floodgates of her mind and the answers come flowing out. Jean knows perfectly well how she *feels* about this issue: her attitude toward the whole question is one of righteous indignation. She also *knows* a lot about the subject from first-hand exposure to the educational system and mass media. Can she put the thought and feeling together in a readable way?

5c.   How Do I State a Thesis?

Jean Heath now knows that she needs to turn her ideas into some kind of a thesis about the problems of women. She really wants to write an argument (to persuade the reader, see page 16) although veins of exposition (to inform the reader, see pages 38–39) will have to mingle with the argument. Because the instructor, for this first assignment, has not limited the means of expression to either exposition or argument, Jean does not really need to worry about the problem. She therefore jots down a preliminary thesis and outline to focus her thoughts.

> THEME: Males have succeeded all too well in their subtle plot against women's rights.
>   I. Most girls grow up intimidated by masculine rules.
>   II. Girls are systematically trained to live not for themselves but for men.
> III. By comparison, men learn to live for themselves primarily.
>   IV. The product is an American woman who has lost her own sense of identity.
>   V. Conclusion: Awaken women to the existence of this tyranny.

This inner struggle, this turmoil, has now given her a theme: a recurring, unifying subject around which to build her paper. The word *plot* reveals her own innermost feelings on the subject. You may not think that men have plotted against women. I may not think so, either. But Jean thinks so, and that commitment will determine a great deal of what she says and how she says it. Her examples, illustrations, comparisons, metaphors, and even the choice of her verbs, will grow from that vision of reality. Yet she does not wish to sound like a paranoid — a person who feels pursued by persecution; hence, she decides to sugar over some of the bitterness with a bit of humor, just to let the reader know she's aware of her audience.

5d.   How Do Questions Determine Structure?

As she shuffles her materials around to get the best order, and tries to think of supporting proofs (examples, comparisons) for her argument, she realizes that the paper's structure will also be determined by the kinds of questions she asks herself. If she asks "In how many ways are women exploited?" she will find herself enumerating and perhaps classifying. If she asks how industries treat women, she will end up comparing and contrasting. If she asks "What is the real reason men exploit women?" she will inevitably build the essay around the principle of "eliminating alternatives," which John Stuart Mill, a nineteenth-century philosopher, called "the method of residues" (see page

170). Asking the right question at each new part of the outline remains the crucial act in discovering workable organization.

5e.   Person and Audience

Jean is also troubled, as everyone is, about knowing whether to use the first, second, or third person. The first person "I" suggests a chattiness and familiarity unacceptable in a legal or technical document but perfectly all right, desirable even, in an informal essay. Third person "he," "she," and "one," have a clear place in objective, impersonal, writing where information, not feelings, is being transmitted. Using those, she can be sure she will be unable to insert herself into the dialogue; on the other hand, they can make the tone of an informal essay stiff and wooden, wholly inappropriate.

The second person "you," once universally banned by composition teachers, can offer some intimacy between reader and writer, though "you" may signify almost everything from "you yourself" to "mankind in general." The second person "you," unless overworked — and the whole art of writing is never overworking anything — like the first person plural "we," is a way around the modern dilemma over the allegedly sexist use of "he." The women's consciousness movement in the past few years has made the use of "he" as a generic way of talking about mankind (and womankind) a sensitive issue in some quarters. Of course many languages long ago arbitrarily designated words as masculine or feminine without much regard to their meaning. The German word *Macht,* meaning *power,* is designated as feminine. Unhappily, however, a writer who attempts to avoid the male chauvinist pig label by substituting "he or she" for "he" soon wears out his typewriter ribbon. If you are writing for an audience sensitive to this issue, or if you really believe third person "he" is part of a male linguistic plot called "Manglish," you may be well advised to get around it with circumlocutions: "you," "we," and "one." At least until the English language accepts a pronoun designating both sexes.

For Heath, however, most of these problems fell into place when she asked a simple question about the assignment: What are the best means for taking a stand on an issue in an informal, personal kind of essay? The material itself suggested that third person would work best for the dominant descriptive, analytical passages; and first person for the subordinate personal opinion sections. She may also have sensed that she was writing for her classmates — persons much like herself. This audience was neither inferior nor superior in expertise; it could be neither condescended to nor deferred to. Other writing situations — addressing a specialized paper to experts, or preparing an instruction manual for home hobbyists — may call for a different tone altogether. Jean has valid reasons, however, for using the third person, lapsing occasionally, unobtrusively, into the first person.

5f.   How Do I Approach My Audience?

Jean Heath also knows that she can begin with an assertion and then offer proofs to support it, or she can offer examples and then generalize from them. Writing the first paragraph, she determines to follow the latter road as a way of enticing her reader into the subject. She also ransacks her mind for suitable examples (or "proofs") to bolster her thesis. At the same time she senses that a hostile audience, as hers is likely to be, cannot safely be assaulted head-on. It is the rare Demosthenes who can win over a roomful of enemies without making concessions to them. She therefore decides to be persuasive without being abrasive.

5g.   The Theme Appears

Having gone through this spiritual wrestling match and electing to scramble the original train of thought into a different order, Heath plunges into the first draft of the paper. After much revision, the paper turns into a fairly sophisticated mixture of description, exposition, and argument — all organized around the principle of effect and cause, with a dash of climactic order thrown in. First Jean shows the effects of a system, and then the cause; at the same time she saves her most telling point for the very end to achieve climax. Heath has used all these rhetorical devices without knowing it. She is instinctively a resourceful rhetorician. And why not? Clever people do use these strategies instinctively by unconsciously mimicking experts. But not all of us are equally clever. And besides it is satisfying to see how one's own mind works — also called "insight."

MALE CHAUVINISM EXPOSED: WOMEN AS PEOPLE

I. The female side.
A. Opens with implicit theme statement.

B. Specific examples lead up to full thesis statement.

C. Rhetorical questions.

D. Full statement of thesis.

"When I get married I'm going to be in sad shape. I don't know how to cook, sew, or clean." So states one worried freshman girl to a group of other coeds sitting about the lounge of Struthers Hall. All eight girls, intelligent young American females, confirmed the essential truth of this lament with piteous cries of agreement. And yet why this chorus of approval for a slave mentality? Why do so many young women in our society feel this way? Surely it is not demanded that as soon as a woman marries, she must abandon all pretense to brains, character, intelligence, career, and settle into the type of a contented housewife. Apparently some males have succeeded all too well with some females in their subtle plot against women's identity.

From our earliest years we females are brainwashed into believing that the major goals of life are to entrap a male and raise a family. Toward this goal, we are indoctrinated in subterfuges, snares, traps, dirty little secrets. A chorus of clichés assails our ears. Slimness above all; no one likes a fat girl. Watch out for eyeglasses ("Boys never make passes at girls who wear glasses"). Be a five-star chef, for "the way to a man's heart is through his stomach." And be the good housekeeper for "cleanliness is next to god-liness." Don't go out for the team; even if you can run rings around most boys, be a cheerleader instead. In short, most of adolescence passes in learning conformity to the prevailing rules of a male-dominated society.

Now, I ask, in the meantime how is our male counterpart being indoctrinated? He is learning how to avoid entrapment by females because their goal of matrimony is essentially at odds with his goal of masculine liberty. He is learning that the little woman will take care of his needs in the event that he does marry. He is learning that it is, as it was his father's, the divine right of males to slouch, undershirted and beer-canned, a TV freak, in front of the tube while the women drudge and slave in the kitchen. He is also learning that as "the breadwinner" his education is of prime importance, far more so than the education of any girl. He is therefore treated to a handsomely endowed professional education, while his sister is packed off to the local community college, if she's lucky. It's always possible of course that at the university of his choice he will meet an educated female suitably trained as a life companion. His sister must settle for what she can find at the office.

Obviously these two well-defined sex roles have evolved over centuries, but in America they take a particularly virulent form. Every vestige of our culture shouts that women have less to offer than men. Television commercials portray housewives as nitwits obsessed with the fear of using the wrong laundry detergent, worried sick that the neighbors will glimpse yellowing floors and greyish window curtains, or, worse yet, "ring-around-the-collar." Women's magazines make the center of life kitchen and children. Employers back away in fright when a woman asks for a job beyond the level of clerk. Is it any wonder that a girl grows up convinced that housewifery is her only role? To ask for any other job is to arouse suspicion of some kind of moral disorder or unspeakable "queerness." After all, mother (who is sacred) was this way too, wasn't she?

III. Conclusion.

A. Women must assert their rights.

I think the way to fight back against this subtle tyranny is to expose male dominance at every turn. Women must assert their right to enter professions, to work at men's jobs (whatever they may be) on an equal basis. Women must be thought of as strong, intelligent, eager, capable human beings, not mere Kewpie dolls. They need the fulfillment that has long been denied them. And the strongest men will be the first to see this because they have nothing to fear from fair competition.

B. Appeal to fair-mindedness.

EXERCISES

A. Write a theme attacking Jean Heath's position, showing why there is not in fact any plot against women whatsoever. Be prepared to defend yourself.

B. Write a theme sympathetic with Jean Heath's position and amplify her concluding paragraph. Just how can women assert their rights when the educational system has trained them, as Heath suggests, to be housewives only? Heath's theme is a "call to action," but it lacks specific suggestions on how to put that indignation to work. Give some in your theme.

C. Attempt an exercise in "free association of ideas," or, as it is sometimes called, "automatic writing." Sit down at your desk and for thirty minutes write out every thought that wanders across your mind. Don't be inhibited if forbidden thoughts appear, though you may wish to destroy the results or edit them for class consumption. The idea is to move closer to the hidden resources of your subconscious.

D. Take a "trigger" word such as *water,* and see how many words you can associate with it, or write a paragraph of impressions keeping the thought of *water* at the center, as in this example:

> Water trickles, flows, spouts, gurgles, rushes, spills, falls, drops, rises, falls, churns, bubbles, swells, ripples, dribbles, leaks, eddies, swirls, heaves, spews, gushes, laps, squirts, roars, and babbles over mossy boulders and rocks in a mountain stream. Sodden leaves surround the streambed, dampened from spring rains and thaws when melting snows soaked the steep trails through the woods of spruce and pine and birch and maple and oak.

O damp, damp is my soul, when this liquefaction I behold.

You may wish to draw on this list of words for a similar exercise:

church	atmosphere	laborer	water
school	football	physician	heaven
garden	teacher	medicine	pizza
pool	drunkard	hospital	carpet
automobile	criminal	illness	sky
sanctity	anecdote	aircraft	terror
religion	antidote	jet	death

FORMULATION: OUTLINING, BEGINNING, AND ENDING

6.   How Do I Organize?

Watching Jean Heath compose a theme on women's liberation, we could see that the essential work in any writing is formulating a thesis statement and demonstrating its validity by proofs. The final design grows partly out of the subject and partly out of the writer's feelings about it.

Almost any statement we make ("This has been a good year") becomes a kind of proposition that, if need be, we will defend with such "proofs" as establishing the author's credibility ("I have behind me the experience of many years"), examples ("Last year I made a million dollars"), comparisons ("The year before, I lost my shirt"), logical relationships ("Because the plant prospered, my income grew"), and emotional appeals ("Moreover, what I did was good for my country"). We can amplify more by developing figures of speech and analogies ("A good year is like a ray of sunshine in the darkness") or even irony ("I despise years like this!").

Anyone who would say "this is a good year" has an indwelling optimism that will make his other assertions cheerful. His attitude toward the subject is well defined. Further developing this simple thesis, he may then either state a thesis and give proofs of it, or give proofs and then generalize about them. The former method is less sophisticated and is the one most beginners prefer, though they may work up to the greater challenges of the latter. Here are the basic rhetorical patterns at work (thesis in italics):

FROM GENERAL TO SPECIFIC

From my long experience, *I can say that last year was a great year.* Not only did I make a million dollars but I served my country as well. Compared to the year before, when I went bankrupt, I am in marvelous shape. Mainly because of the prospering of the family industry, my bank account flourished. No doubt, a good year is like a ray of sunshine.

FROM SPECIFIC TO GENERAL

If you had made a million dollars and served your country as well; if you had in all your long experience never seen such growth in the family industry; if you had in the previous year gone bankrupt and in this year seen nothing but sunshine, would you not agree that good fortune was yours? *It has indeed been a great year.*

6a.   How Do I Outline?

The subject decided upon, most people find outlining a helpful step in discovering the best way of handling a writing assignment. Not that everyone agrees about the value of outlining. Some good students have surreptitiously prepared outlines from work they have already completed. They work without an outline, composing several drafts, revising as they go along, until a satisfactory organization becomes visible. Even the most successful practitioners of this "lazy man's school" of writing would admit, however, to the sloppiness and wasted effort built into it. Others find, particularly in an essay examination, that even the sketchiest kinds of jottings help guide their thinking. More detailed outlines, however, save much filling in and backtracking, and make the work of writing relatively efficient. Moreover, outlining starts and reinforces the habit of instinctively building structure into themes and reports. The finished product may not resemble the original plan but it will be better for having first been thought through on paper. An enumeration, as we saw in the development of the paper, "Male Chauvinism Exposed," shows how a topic can be approached by eliminating alternatives and then refined by enumerating its important points. More ambitious projects may require a detailed topic or sentence outline, as shown below. Whatever form the outline takes, it reminds us of the need for order, before order slips away in a mist of words.

6b.   What Are Topic and Sentence Outlines?

Making topic and sentence outlines can be almost as much work as writing the paper, but for those who compose them they cut wasted effort in half. Topic outlines call for several phrases arranged in parallel form, and sub-divided with a system of Roman and Arabic numerals, and upper-case and lower-case letters; sentence outlines are similar, except they call for full sentences instead of phrases:

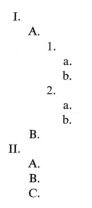

I.
   A.
      1.
         a.
         b.
      2.
         a.
         b.
   B.
II.
   A.
   B.
   C.

Study the following examples:

THE TOPIC OUTLINE

THESIS STATEMENT: The American prison system has neither reformed nor rehabilitated its prisoners.

   I. The past: prisons as places of punishment
      A. Older prisons as medieval dungeons
         1. Sing Sing in New York
         2. Lansing in Kansas
         3. Army Disciplinary Barracks at Fort Leavenworth
      B. Imprisonment as deterrent to crime
         1. Policies of iron discipline
            a. Hard beds
            b. Spare diet
         2. Hard labor
            a. Rock piles
            b. Chain gang
  II. Present theory: prison as place of rehabilitation
      A. Training programs
      B. Libraries
      C. Counseling

III. Present reality: prison as school for crime
    A. Shortage of training staff
    B. Poor libraries
    C. Indifferent counseling
    D. Film *A Clockwork Orange* as example
IV. The future: Multiple alternatives to handling criminals, only one of which would be the prison

THE SENTENCE OUTLINE

THESIS STATEMENT: The American prison system has failed either to reform or rehabilitate its prisoners [the author's own feelings are revealed by "failed." This *is* his point of view and it should saturate the whole paper].

I. In the past, prisons have been thought of as primarily places of punishment.
    A. The older state prisons in America still resemble medieval dungeons.
        1. A look at New York's Sing Sing from the outside chills the blood.
        2. Kansas' Lansing prison also has the flavor of Victorian grimness, a place where the damned roast in hell.
        3. The United States Army Disciplinary Barracks at Fort Leavenworth has a wall high and thick enough to intimidate even the toughest among us.
    B. Our grandfathers saw prisons as a place for the wicked to repent.
        1. Prisoners endured a policy of iron discipline.
            a. Hard beds made sleeping a misery.
            b. Wretched food reminded the sinner of his crime.
        2. Daily work calls summoned prisoners to hard labor.
            a. The rock pile remains a popular stereotype of those days.
            b. The southern chain gang suggests another image of the harsh prison.
II. In theory modern specialists see the prison as a place for rehabilitation.
    A. Training programs in woodworking, mechanics, and repair work allow prisoners opportunity to learn a trade.
    B. Prison libraries provide opportunities for self-education.
    C. Counseling staffs offer prisoners insight into themselves.
III. Modern practices are quite different from theories.
    A. Training programs are not funded.
    B. Libraries are inadequate and unused.
    C. Counseling staffs attract only the professionally marginal.
    D. Film *A Clockwork Orange* is an example.
IV. The future: history suggests that society may one day provide multiple alternatives for handling criminals, only one of which would be the prison.

6c.   What Are Illogical Subdivisions?

Each category and subcategory of the outline should have at least two subdivisions; that is to say, an outline that reads:

> B. Policies of iron discipline
>   1. Hard beds

is illogical. If 1 is the only subset under B, then logically it should be part of B itself:

> B. Policies of iron discipline: hard beds

The alternative is to invent a second subset by ransacking the mind for additional examples. Suppose you were professionally interested in making life miserable for others? What would accompany hard beds as a fierce deterrent to crime? How about a "wretched diet"? The outline now looks like this:

> B. Policies of iron discipline
>   1. Hard beds
>   2. Wretched diet

Violating the principle of subdivision can lead to this kind of difficulty:

STUDENT PARAGRAPH

To preserve iron discipline, nineteenth-century prison officials made life miserable for the inmates by several practices. Hard, uncomfortable beds guaranteed restless nights of tossing and turning on a plank, or sometimes even on a bare floor. Lack of a good night's rest will break the spirit of even the strongest human being. The hard bed may have been the cruelest torture ever devised.

The writer has promised to show how prison officials devised *several* practices to make life unpleasant. Actually she mentions only *one* method, hard beds.

In outline form the flaw in this passage becomes apparent:

> B. Prison officials maintained iron discipline
>   1. Inmates were subjected to hard beds
>   2. Inmates were subjected to ???
>   3. Inmates were subjected to ???

Equally illogical is the overlapping subdivision, when two subsets overlap:

> B. Prison as place of rehabilitation
>   1. Counseling
>   2. Prison psychiatry

The outline may develop into a paragraph like this one:

All modern prisons feature programs for counseling prisoners. The latest techniques in psychology, including group therapy, have been used in the most advanced programs. Some of the more progressive institutions also employ ministers trained in psychiatric work.

The student has really combined B.2 with B.1. It is less counseling *that is being discussed than* prison psychiatry.

The outline should have read:

B. Prison as a place of rehabilitation: prison psychiatry

A final word about outlining. As these examples suggest, outlining *after* as well as *before* you write the first draft can help you tell how effective your organization is.

EXERCISES

A. Outline one or two of these topics, first informally, next topically, and finally in sentence form. Be sure to choose a subject about which you know something. Your task is to inform someone.

1. The steps in organizing the high school senior play, for someone who must undertake this task at another school.

2. The procedure for putting a bill through the lower house of a legislature, for a women's club ordinarily dedicated to playing bridge.

3. The rushing ritual for sororities at your school to reassure a campus skeptic that snobbery is *not* the essence of the matter.

4. The rushing ritual for sororities at your school to reassure a campus skeptic that snobbery *is* the essence of the matter.

5. The daily routine at a summer camp, to convince a reluctant parent that he should send his child.

6. The practical values of learning to play the piano, to reassure a parent that a major in fine arts instead of engineering does not mean the end of the world.

7. The steps in constructing a wooden picnic table, for a coed who thinks *saw* is the past tense of *see*.

8. The rules for determining eligibility for office of campus politicians, for a foreign student who thinks that American campus politics are childish.

9. The subject matter covered by a home economics major, for a man who thinks cooking is the only thing studied.

10. The virtues of a political party, for a nonbeliever.

B. Arrange this information in the proper form for a topic outline using the scheme for headings and subheadings shown in 6b.

Sacco and Vanzetti were a shoe cobbler and a fish peddler. They were finally executed in 1927 for a payroll robbery and murder. The judge was Webster Thayer, a Dartmouth man and an athlete of some ability in his college days. Governor Fuller of Massachusetts was a successful salesman. At the time, there was great hysteria over the red menace, and Attorney General Palmer feared in 1921 that anarchists and communists were going to take over the government imminently. Sacco and Vanzetti were anarchists and confessed nonbelievers in God and in country. Many people nevertheless thought them innocent of murder. Vanzetti wrote many letters in prison that have become part of American literature. The Lowell committee, appointed by the governor, agreed to the executions. The gun found on Sacco matched the weapon that killed the detective, a piece of evidence never explained by the defense. Liberals and communists all over the world took up the cause of Sacco and Vanzetti. Edna St. Vincent Millay picketed the State House in Boston. Prof. Felix Frankfurter, later a justice of the United States Supreme Court, hotly defended the accused immigrants. To this day, the question of the guilt or innocence of the two obscure Italians still arouses passion. The funeral in the rain was attended by thousands, some of whom were beaten by the Boston police.

C. Rewrite the free-association exercise on page 19 to make it into a coherent statement on some part of the subject, on which you might take a position. For example, are you for or against the effect of the automobile on our ecology?

D. Describe at some length a work of art that has special appeal for you. You may need to go to an art gallery for this assignment.

E. Write a two- or three-page paper on one of these topics. Insofar as possible draw on your experience and observation, though, if you must, consult reference works for background materials only. As a way of preparing to think about audience, follow the instructions for directing the paper toward specific groups of people.

1. Explain to your parents why it will be necessary for them to provide you with a sports car in your senior year.

2. Explain to a solemn businessman how studying such "frivolous" subjects as literature and music may be important in general education.

3. Explain to a lifelong resident of a large city like New York how much he has missed by not living in a rural area.

4. Explain to a native of a rural area how much he has missed by not living in a large city like New York.

5. Write about a local student hangout, describing and classifying the kinds of people found there.

7.   How Do I Open?

Most people generate deep anxiety over the best way of beginning a paper. It may help to remember that papers can begin inductively (with a specific instance), or deductively (with a generality). The ancient rhetoricians spoke of the beginning part of speech or treatise as an *exordium,* which meant literally to "begin a web." Your job in beginning is to draw the reader into a web of facts and statements from which he will not willingly disconnect himself. Various strands of the web must (1) make the purpose of the paper plain, (2) arouse the reader's interest, and (3) suggest your approach to the problem. The subject and audience will determine the weight to be assigned to each consideration. Technical papers will be aimed less than journalistic articles at arousing the reader's interest and more at making the purpose of the paper plain and suggesting the writer's approach to the problem.

By analyzing proven formulas for beginning papers, you may perfect your own techniques, though you'll have to avoid mechanical and unimaginative adaptations of these methods. Reshape the devices suggested here to suit both you and the occasion.

7a.   Use a Specific Detail

For 22 years Rudolf Bing ruled over the Metropolitan Opera, and it still survives. Let that be said for him. Like another Austrian autocrat, Metternich, the Metropolitan's retired general manager will be known — *wants* to be known — chiefly as a defender of the old regime. . . . DONAL HENAHAN

Story about the opera manager begins with specific fact about his career, and then compares him to Metternich.

7b.   Use a Definition

Anthropology is, for many of its American practitioners and amateurs, a way of trying to get out of our particular culture, or at least a way of finding out whether "other ways of life" are possible and, if so, perhaps better than our own. PAUL RIESMAN

Writer has undertaken an impromptu definition of *anthropology* as a way of leading into his subject (see also page 55).

7c.   Use a Quotation

In writing about literature, an opening with a direct quotation from the work being discussed can serve two functions, attracting the reader's interest and suggesting the major theme of the paper, as in a student's analysis of Zeffirelli's film version of Shakespeare's *Taming of the Shrew:*

" 'Tis a wonder, by your leave, she will be tam'd so," remarks Lucentio as Shakespeare's *The Taming of the Shrew* comes to a close. His comment is directed toward Kate, played by Elizabeth Taylor in Franco Zeffirelli's film adaptation. And indeed it is a *wonder* that so aggressive a female could ever be tamed.

Student uses the line from the play to keynote a discussion about the paradox of so forceful a woman coming to so submissive an end.

Some papers will benefit from general quotations culled from a reference work listing proverbs, aphorisms, witticisms, and so forth.[1] The left-hand column lists general topics; the right-hand column, quotations for arousing reader interest.

TOPIC OF THEME	BEGINNING QUOTATION
Good manners	A gentleman is a person who never insults anyone unintentionally. ANON.
Death	Men fear death as little children fear to go into the dark. SIR FRANCIS BACON
Frustration	The greatest flaw in life is that it is always imperfect. SENECA

7d.   Mention a Recent Event

In the past few months, public health experts, working closely with teams of sanitary engineers, have uncovered an alarming incidence of yellow fever along the lower regions of the Central American coast.

This beginning, though quite specific, also signals a general topic: *public health procedures.*

7e.   Open with a Question

A piquant question sometimes can strike the right note for opening a paper, but always consider the danger of rubbing an audience the wrong way. As a rule of thumb, if you do elect to open with a question, stay away from further questions in that theme, or the paper may turn into rhetorical questions strung together.

---

[1] See John Bartlett, *Familiar Quotations,* 14th ed. (Boston: Little, Brown, 1968); *The Home Book of Quotations,* ed. Burton Stevenson (New York: Dodd, Mead, 1967); *The Macmillan Book of Proverbs, Maxims, and Famous Phrases,* ed. Burton Stevenson (New York: Macmillan, 1965); *Magill's Quotations in Context,* ed. F. N. Magill (New York: Harper and Row, 1969); *The New Dictionary of Thoughts,* ed. T. Edwards (New York: Standard Book, 1963); *The Penguin Dictionary of Modern Quotations,* ed. J. M. and M. J. Cohen (New York: Penguin, 1971); and *The Oxford Dictionary of Quotations,* 2nd ed. rev. (New York: Oxford Univ. Press, 1966).

Yes, but how would *you* go about it if you were given the job of writing a biography of Richard M. Nixon for the twelve and up group? It is, after all, Horatio Alger in the Age of the Tube. Small town grocer's son makes it through college. . . .
PRISCILLA L. BUCKLEY

This opening for a book review challenges the reader to confront the realities of writing such a book, and establishes the reviewer's attitude toward book and subject.

The opening question is effective only when you make it just long enough and just as specific as the subject requires. Compare these unsuccessful and successful openers:

POOR	ACCEPTABLE
Have you ever been to Tonganoxie?	What was life like in a medieval monastery?
What about the sorority girl?	Is there a special reason for viewing the conduct of today's young people with alarm?
Have you found God?	
How would you like to be H-bombed?	
What's wrong with today's young?	How can minority groups on a campus such as this achieve a share of equality?
Is the progressive, accelerating, ingenious person at fault? No, he is not.	What is a poem?
Do you know about Napoleon?	What are the differences between college and pro football?

7f.   Open with an Anecdote

The anecdotal beginning is more appropriate in the speech than the written paper, but occasionally it may have a place. Basically an "insinuation," the anecdote disarms the audience's hostility or indifference. Almost invariably the speaker says, "I am reminded of the story of . . . ," and then launches into a tale he has memorized for the occasion. One is reminded here of the story about the man who called on Winston Churchill and was told that he was busy upstairs in his study working on one of his impromptu speeches.

A short theme may have room for only a brief anecdotal comment:

While visiting in China in 1921 Bertrand Russell contracted bronchitis and word got around that he had died. The editors of one religious journal wrote that "Missionaries may be pardoned for breathing a sigh of relief at the news of Mr. Bertrand Russell's death." JAMES RACHELS

Anecdote is terse enough for a brief paper, and yet adds flavor and definition to the opening remarks.

For anecdotes dealing with general topics, use the library's reference room. Here are books in which you can find "impromptu" anecdotes:

Compleat Practical Joker. Ed. H. A. Smith. New York: Doubleday, 1953.

The Modern Handbook of Humor. Ed. Ralph L. Woods. New York: McGraw-Hill, 1967.

1000 Tips and Quips for Speakers and Toastmasters. Ed. H. V. Prochnow. Grand Rapids: Baker House, 1969.

2500 Anecdotes for All Occasions. Ed. Edmund Fuller. New York: Doubleday, 1961.

A Treasury of American Anecdotes. Ed. B. A. Botkin. New York: Random House, 1957.

A Treasury of Ribaldry. Ed. Louis Untermeyer. London: Elek, 1960.

When It's Laughter You're After. Ed. Stewart Harral. Norman: Univ. of Oklahoma Press, 1969.

7g.   Use a Journalistic Lead

Newspaper editors tell cub reporters to be sure to answer the questions *who? what? when? where?* and *how?* in the first (lead) sentence. The advice is worth remembering because it guards against wandering too far from the topic. Applying the newspaper formula gives an opening something like this:

Robert Flint, 19, of 116 Hubbard Street, a student at Municipal Junior College [*who*], died [*what*] last night about 8:00 P.M. [*when*] near the intersection of Vine and Route 40 [*where*] when his speeding sports car skidded and overturned on slick pavement [*how*].

With this formula, readers can skim the news quickly, and make-up editors can trim and cut the closing paragraphs without damaging the story's continuity.

7h.   Use a Newspaper Headline

Like the direct quotation, the newspaper headline can sometimes be useful as an opener for a theme, but watch out or it will turn into the *headline* discussed on page 172.

SUBJECT	HEADLINE
Cambodia	Bombing Halted in Cambodia
Pro football	Miami Dolphins Win 18th Game
Narcotics	Narcs Bust Six in Colchester Raid

7i.   Make a Brief Thesis Statement

A simple declarative sentence plunging into the middle of the subject is always effective.

Supersonic flight would upset the aircraft industry's economy.

Paper on the aircraft industry states a thesis at once and sets the stage for further commentary.

Searching for the origin of words can be fun.

The forbidding topic of etymology is made palatable

7j.   Combine Beginning Devices

You might put into an introduction a first sentence with a striking quotation, a second sentence offering a thesis, a third sentence furnishing background material, and a fourth sentence with an anecdote.

"All the world's a stage," says Jaques, the melancholy figure of Shakespeare's *As You Like It*. And he might have added, so is the Globe playhouse, the site of Shakespeare's dramatic triumphs, a little imitation of the world. A recent discovery of a forgotten book on Elizabethan memory devices reinforces the belief that Jaques was employing something more than a mere metaphor in his comparison between the world and stage. Quite possibly the gulls and gallants, culled from the pages of Tom Dekker's *The Gull's Hornbook*, a guidebook to London low life, found inside the Globe playhouse a deliberate replica of the larger world of man.

Quotation from Shakespeare arouses interest and also implies purpose of paper. Second sentence gives enough background information to bring the whole problem into focus and also offers a statement of purpose: to show the link between the theater of the playhouse and the theater of the world.
Third sentence adds further clarifying information. Fourth sentence begins to move toward the anecdotal as it cites the activity of underworld characters described in Dekker's 1609 book.

7k.   Vague Beginnings

Vague and rambling openings like those in the left-hand column guarantee failure. The best antidote to vagueness is a firm grasp on the subject of the paper so that giveaway words like "many kinds" and "several" are crowded out by solid information. In general, be concrete and specific. We run into the kinds of abstractions in the left-hand column all too often.

POOR

This topic offers many kinds of problems. The problems are difficult to solve, just as the problems of life are difficult to solve. Life can be hard, as the experience of everyone shows. The problems we face and how we solve them are the way in which the world sees us.

There are many factors to be considered when approaching the question we are called upon to answer here. No one knows what the answers are. In a way, it is all a matter of opinion.

REVISED

The problem of narcotics among students has been grossly exaggerated by journalists, because the addicts as a group are limited largely to the unstable and rejected. Few students choose the drug way as a solution to life's problems.

Given the choice between an early marriage and a professional career, any middle-class youth would probably choose the latter. There is no denying, however, that anyone would like to combine both.

7l. Obvious Outlining

It has been said that the immature artist follows obvious patterns of organization (assuming he strives for any organization at all), which the mature artist learns either to discard or disguise. An exalted example is Shakespeare, who in his early plays stressed geometrical pairings of situations and characters. The later plays may accomplish this same end, but in an unobtrusive way. Compare *The Comedy of Errors* with *Twelfth Night.* In a lesser way, this syndrome appears in college writing courses when the student, trying to keep away from the vagueness mentioned in 7k, errs in the opposite direction by making the beginning painfully obvious. A short paper should not begin with an outline in paragraph form, though longer and more formal papers, especially if they are technical, can stand this approach. If your talents allow no choice, however, it is far better to be a little obvious than to write the kind of vague and rambling beginning described in 7k.

POOR	REVISED
This paper is going to be about the parking problem at Midwest University. The way I see it, the parking problem breaks down into three major factors: (1) the lack of space to park; (2) the excessive number of cars; (3) the unwillingness of the faculty to park off campus. Now I am going to discuss factor one first, and then factor two, followed by factor three. Now let's first look at factor one.	The parking problem at Midwest University has reached alarming proportions. The campus is choked every day with insolent foreign sports cars belonging to the fraternity and sorority crowd. The whole mess grows out of a shortage of parking spaces, an excessive number of cars, and the reluctance of faculty to park miles from their offices. The key to the problem lies in increasing the number of parking spaces, a solution that needs to be thoroughly explored.

7m. Overreliance on the Title

You cannot substitute a title for a clear statement of subject in the opening sentence or paragraph. This difficulty can often be gotten around simply by not using "this" in an opening sentence as a subject by itself.

POOR	IMPROVED
This is a big problem. Just last night I was forced to park my car. . . .	Traffic is a major problem at Midwest University, where student affluence and increased enrollment have combined to produce more automobiles than parking spaces. [This version substitutes full information in place of *this*.]

7n.   Use Active Voice

Whenever you can, use an active in preference to a passive verb in an opening sentence. An active verb carries greater force and emphasis, more color. In technical and similar kinds of objective writing calling for precision and accuracy more than color, a passive verb may be a better choice. Searching for an exact, active verb, however, clarifies the writer's own meaning. In this example, "severed" may have a connotation not found in "broken off."

BEGINNING WITH PASSIVE	BEGINNING WITH ACTIVE
Shortly after World War II diplomatic relations with Red China were *broken off* by the United States.	Shortly after World War II, the United States *severed* diplomatic relations with Red China.

8.   How Do I End?

The paper's ending is important directly in proportion to the paper's length. A short essay of two or three hundred words does not need an elaborate termination but an essay of several thousand words may. Ideally the good ending will suggest itself, just as the right words to say to a hostess when leaving a dinner party will come to mind spontaneously. Just in case you dry up and good endings do not occur to you spontaneously, you can find stock endings. Most come from the ancient rhetorical tradition that spelled out in detail the precise steps to be taken in the peroration, or formal close, to a speech.

8a.   End with a Verification

Verifying what you have said previously is the most obvious way to end a paper. It is best reserved, however, for the long essay, where it may really be needed.

> And so the forces shaping the Tudor dynasty remained throughout the sixteenth century rooted deeply in religious, economic, and political issues. The establishment of a national church assured the triumph of English values over those of the Mediterranean; the increased tempo of trade brought new wealth to the middle classes who supported crown against landowners; and the increased power of the city merchants in turn assured a reservoir of sentiment friendly to the queen, herself the descendant of a commoner.

8b.   End with a Quotation

A quotation can be as useful at the end of a paper as at the beginning. A theme on Isaac Newton (1642–1727), the great astronomer-mathematician, might be ended with Pascal's profound utterance, "The silence of these empty spaces terrifies me." A good trick is to match opening and closing quotations and tie them to each other. In musical composition, this technique is called "restatement of the theme." If a paper on free speech begins with Voltaire's "I wholly disagree with what you say but I will defend to the death your right to say it," it might appropriately end with Justice Holmes's warning that facing "a clear and present danger," no one has the right "to shout fire in a crowded theater."

8c.   End with a Striking Statement

In the brief theme, a declarative sentence, set off by itself, can provide a strong conclusion. "And what remains of the concept of free speech in America is in the hands of Americans themselves." "The problem of seating priorities at Midwest U. basketball games still threatens faculty-student relationships." "There seems little question that the United States has learned of tariff problems only by trial and error, at great pain and loss to itself."

8d.   End with a Call for Action

Editorials and themes that *argue* for a line of action may be terminated with a "call for action," though you owe the reader a full explanation of all the circumstances leading up to the "call for action" before you invoke it.

Sometimes a declarative sentence will do the job: "And all that remains of free speech in America is in the hands of Americans themselves." "Seating priorities for Northwoods University hockey games will be resolved only when the student association becomes something more than a rubber stamp for the University administration."

8e.   End with a Warning

A warning hinting that the close is near can include such phrases as: *finally, in conclusion, the solution then, as we have seen, to sum up, to recapitulate, to restate the matter, last,* and *to review the matter again.* This strategy extends the thesis into a summarizing sentence, leaving the reader with a sense of finality, a feeling that the last word on the subject has been uttered. Here is an example:

> Finally, Socrates was always adroit at manipulating the question to bring out the weakest side of the opponent's argument. The way in which Crito is demolished at the close of the dialogue is the measure of Socrates' prowess as debater and thinker.

8f.   End with Answer to Question

The book review by Priscilla L. Buckley, which illustrates opening with a question (see 7e), terminates by answering the initial question, a neat device sometimes called "the hook."

The answer to: "But how would you write a biography of Richard Nixon for teenagers?" is: differently. As Frank Nixon might have said in his salty way: With more of a kick in the seat of the pants. More controversy. More truth. More fun.

By answering question raised at beginning of review, the author deftly closes the circle.

9. How Do I Write a Title?

Essays need titles, which are not always the same as topics. A title is *specific*, and a topic *general*. "Through the Wheat Belt with Lens and Notebook" is a title, but "A Foreigner's Analysis and Survey of Life in the American Middle West" is a topic. Of course, working too hard for an effective title may get you charged with "cuteness," which you must avoid whatever the cost. Scientific and technical authors will find this possibility irrelevant or distasteful. For the technical article in the medical journal, "Some Aspects of Essential Thrombocytopenic Purpura: Werlhof's Disease" will be adequate. No need to come up with something like "Did Dracula Suffer from Werlhof's Disease?" If you do believe, however, that the audience would appreciate a provocative title, these suggestions may be helpful.

The effective title tells what the paper is about and stimulates the reader's interest. One way of improving your titles is by analyzing those in popular magazines. Any representative list of fifty titles will show that writers and editors have built them around patterns of alliteration, quotation, paraphrase, and questions.

9a. Use a Phrase

With luck, the writer will discover a word or phrase somewhere in his own writing that embodies both the topic and thesis of the paper. Titles like "The Essence of Zen," "A New Look at Mother Goose," and "Victory Through Air Power" tell what the paper is about and hint at the author's approach to the subject.

9b. Use Alliteration

Alliterative language is catchy, but alliteration may sound excessively cute. The range varies from the Sunday supplement story announcing that "*C*ommunism *C*annot *C*onquer" to the women's magazine story on "*M*aturity in *M*iddle Life" to the technical journal on construction asking "*D*o *D*etergents *D*amage *D*rains?"

9c. Vary Familiar Phrases

One trick that can be helpful, though it must always be used with propriety and good taste, is the inversion of a familiar phrase or proverb. The genius who first remarked that "work is the curse of the drinking man" was master of this sort of thing. Some possibilities might be "Seeing Is NOT Believing," "I Feel Therefore I Am," "A Bridge in Cambodia Saves Nine," and "A Doctor a Day Keeps the Pocketbook Frayed."

9d.   Quote or Paraphrase a Familiar Phrase

The Bible and Shakespeare are the two greatest sources for apt quotations. Of great value also is *Bartlett's Familiar Quotations,* a collection of pithy utterances conveniently arranged by subject. A single speech by a Shakespearean character such as Macbeth (V.v.18) yields numerous possibilities for provocative titles: "Tomorrow and Tomorrow," "This Petty Pace," "From Day to Day," "The Last Syllable," "All Our Yesterdays," "Dusty Death," "Out, Brief Candle," "A Walking Shadow," and "An Idiot's Tale." Sections of scripture, particularly the so-called wisdom books (Ecclesiastes, Proverbs) that are full of proverbial utterances, offer similar resources.

9e.   Ask a Question

Questions make pointed titles. A paper on automotive maintenance is titled "Does Ten-Weight Oil Work?" and one on military tactics is called "Do Platoon Leaders Really Take Charge?"

EXERCISES

A. How could the following well-worn statements be turned inside out, inverted, to make clever titles? Would they make good openings for a theme?

Sample: The American way of life
Revised: The American way of death (title of a book by Jessica Mitford)

1. A stitch in time saves nine.   2. A penny saved is a penny earned.
3. The thinking man's filter.   4. Crime does not pay.   5. It's the truth that hurts.   6. A rolling stone gathers no moss.   7. The early bird catches the worm.   8. Birds of a feather flock together.   9. A watched pot never boils.   10. All the news that's fit to print.   11. Pride goeth before a fall.
12. A soft answer turneth away wrath.

B. Examine the opening and closing sentences of ten magazine articles in recent issues of *Harper's, Atlantic Monthly, Esquire, Saturday Review World, The New Yorker,* and *Ebony.*

C. Write effective opening statements, which include a thesis, on these subjects:

1. Prisoners of war in Vietnam.   2. Corrupt city police.   3. Women's liberation.   4. Threat to environment.   5. Jet hijackings.   6. Quota hiring systems.   7. European Common Market.   8. Cigarettes and cancer.

9. Smoking of marijuana. 10. The school dropout. 11. Street violence. 12. Law and Order. 13. Busing. 14. Wiretapping. 15. Amnesty for conscientious objectors. 16. The draft laws. 17. Public transportation. 18. Radio programming. 19. Television commercials. 20. The energy crisis.

D. For the fun of it, see how many books you can think of that have titles from well-known passages in scripture, proverb, or literature. What is the advantage to an author of using this device?

Let Him be kept from Paper, Pen, and Ink:
So may He cease to Write, and learn to Thinke.
MATTHEW PRIOR, "To a Person who wrote Ill, and spake
Worse against Me . . . On the Same Person," 1710

True ease in writing comes from art, not chance,
As those move easiest who have learned to dance.
ALEXANDER POPE, An Essay on Criticism, 1711

3   The Writer's Strategies:

Programs for Thought

10.   What Are the Types of Prose?

Four kinds of prose make up the elements of written expression: exposition, description, argument, and narration. Like all literary categories, they overlap.

Exposition is meant to inform, to explain thoughts to the reader without distorting or manipulating facts. It is objective, without ulterior motive. If it occasionally persuades people, it does so by the fact and logic it presents, not by stuntsmanship with words. It embraces such topics as "Juvenile Crime in Boston," "New York State's Harsh Drug Law," or "Growth in Attendance at Professional Football Games."

Description represents to the imagination a scene, person, sensation, or emotion. Papers describing the campus, a best friend, a stroll through the woods, or a sense of dread fit into this category. Description is closely allied with exposition, for it's hard to be informative without giving helpful descriptions.

Argument, the third type of discourse, does not stop with informing the reader but also converts him. Efforts to convert people can be overt or covert, explicit or implicit, logical or illogical, intelligent or stupid, high-minded or low-minded. At one end of the scale, an argument that is overt, explicit, logical, intelligent, and high-minded is designed to convince scientists of some truth about the atom. At the opposite end, an argument that is covert, implicit, illogical, stupid, and low-minded is used to persuade people to smoke cigarettes. But describing argument adequately is complicated by the many way stations between the extremes.

The fourth kind of discourse, *narration,* almost always combines description with dialogue to capture the flavor of an event, or series of events, in which human beings, or their surrogates, play an important role. In journalism, narration usually takes a simple chronological form as in descriptions of the sinking of the *Titanic,* or the final hours of Hitler. In fiction, it may be rearranged to fit an intricate plot design, as in Laurence Sterne's *Tristram Shandy,* or James Joyce's *Finnegan's Wake.* The peril of using narration for factual events is that truth readily yields to imagination.

It helps to know the difference between a noun and a verb, and it is just as useful to recognize the various strands of discourse that are brought together in a prose passage. It's helpful to sense when you have passed the borderline from straightforward exposition to sermonizing, from being nonjudgmental to being judgmental. When you're unaware of such a change you've lost control of the rhetorical situation. In academic writing, exposition usually dominates, the other modes being used mainly for their alternative and supplementary possibilities. Here are some examples of the four types of discourse:

EXPOSITION

I now revert to man's higher faculties. Like the body, the brain was divided into a triple hierarchy. The lowest contained the five senses. The middle contained first the common sense, which received and summarised the reports of the five senses, second the fancy, and third the memory. This middle area supplied the materials for the highest to work on. The highest contained the supreme human faculty the reason, by which man is separated from the beasts and allied to God and the angels, with its two parts, the understanding (or wit) and the will. It is on these two highest human faculties, understanding and will, that Elizabethan ethics are based. E. M. W. TILLYARD

The tone is objective and impersonal as the author *explains* a forgotten way of looking at the world. Answers the question, *How?*

DESCRIPTION

The mistletoe plays an important part at Christmas. Besides all the ivy and holly with which looking glasses and pictures are framed, branches of mistletoe are suspended from the ceiling. This part of the decorating is superintended by the young girls of the family, who have their reasons for making sure that the mistletoe is conveniently placed.

MAX O'RELL

The writer stresses physical details such as color and shape, but uses elements other than purely descriptive ones. Answers the question, *What?*

ARGUMENT

Little books are occasionally published in which we are told that it is a sin to lose a minute. From the intellectual point of view this doctrine is simply stupid. What the Philistines call wasted time is often rich in the most varied experience to the intelligent. If all that we have learned in idle moments could be suddenly expelled from our minds by some chemical process, it is probable that they would be worth very little afterwards. What, after such a process, would have remained to Shakespeare, Scott, Cervantes, Thackeray, Dickens, Hogarth, Goldsmith, Molière? P. G. HAMERTON

Tone is somewhat judicial. Definite conclusions are drawn from the assembled facts. Answers the question, *Why?*

NARRATION

She thought she would stay and watch him light his lamp, when she was startled by a sharp and angry exclamation from Nan, and turned just in time to see her snatch her darling kitten from the table. Gerty sprang forward to the rescue, jumped into a chair, and caught Nan by the arm; but she firmly pushed her back with one hand, while with the other she threw the kitten half across the room. Gerty heard a sudden splash and a piercing cry. Nan had flung the poor creature into a large vessel of steaming-hot water, which stood ready for some household purpose. The little animal struggled and writhed an instant, then died in torture.

MARIA S. CUMMINS

Main effort is to capture human experience, in this instance a rather harrowing one. Attempts to answer questions, *How? What? Why?*

Now that the kingdom of prose is carved up into four parts, I hasten to reiterate that an activity so complex as writing does not lend itself to simple categorization. Explanation, or exposition, often combines two or more kinds of development:

COMBINATION OF MODES

Mass tastes, if prime-time TV is any evidence, are admittedly not very lofty. And many of the highly successful special-interest magazines are extremely frivolous. ("We should have put out a magazine for one-eyed, geriatric bird watchers," one *Life* writer was heard to remark.) Yet scores of excellent magazines that contribute much to "civilized life" regularly earn at least adequate profits, some mainly from advertisers anxious to reach their elite audience and others, including many scholarly journals, mainly from readers unable to obtain that particular editorial focus or point of view anywhere else. Many other high-quality journals have survived for years through private subsidies, indicating that at least someone, if not advertisers or readers, is willing to ensure their existence. The merit of any publication that dies, therefore, is open to serious question. CHRIS WELLES

Thesis is low level of mass taste. Direct quotation is narrative device to support thesis statement. Midpoint of paragraph passes into argument, as author gives opposite point of view. Passage combines narration, description, exposition, and argument.

EXERCISE

A. Writing about the same event in each of the modes is excellent practice for getting control over prose. In this episode, a police raid at a house on Elm Street has been handled as exposition, description, argument, and narration. Try the same thing with the other topics suggested, making adjustments in meaning as seldom as you can.

Sample Topic: A Police Raid on Elm Street

EXPOSITION

The annals of crime will henceforth include also the county attorney's raid on the night of July 11, 1965, on the house on Elm Street. Stringent measures, including the dispatch of three carloads of detectives and patrolmen, were required to apprehend the renegade Jones. Despite every precaution on the part of the police and a genuine effort to conform to acceptable procedures for making an arrest, some violence occurred. A weapon manned by unnamed assailants caused considerable injury to

several members of the raiding party. Jones himself was brought to justice
at Old Rowley, before the presiding circuit judge, by noon of the next day.

DESCRIPTION

The house on Elm Street was a seedy looking derelict of a building, its
windows cracked and its rooftop packed with pigeon lofts. Across the
dirty brick, someone had inscribed the words "Anarjisme Forever" which
was some corrupted spelling of "anarchism." The dirty, airless room that
Jones lived in looked out on an airshaft decorated with drying laundry.

ARGUMENT

The recent raid on the house on Elm Street shows once again the folly
of tying the hands of the police with judicial restraints. When the dangerous anarchist Jones was cornered in his lair, the police with perfect logic
should have shot him down like a dog. Instead, when the criminal called
out for an attorney and shouted from the rooftop about his rights under
the fifth amendment, the law enforcement authorities became temporarily
confused and were ripe targets for the bullets of the assassin, perhaps a
hippie, on the nearby rooftop. When will the people rise up in their wrath
and demand that the hands of the police be unfettered to seize and grasp
the unrepentant flouter of law?

NARRATION

When the car pulled up in front of the house on Elm Street, I saw the
man we wanted framed in the yellow light of the second story window.
"Jones," I yelled, "come on out, we've got you."
"Come and get me," he shouted.
Windows flew up all over the neighborhood. As I got out of the car
door and went up the concrete steps to the front door, I could hear the
wail of the sirens from the approaching squad cars, and I felt the first
slight shocks from the bullets cracking the cement behind me.

Topics for Development in the Four Modes:

1. A football game.   2. Two people in love.   3. The day after the party.
4. The fraternity weekend.   5. A student political campaign.   6. A jet
flight.   7. Life in a dormitory.   8. A spring weekend.   9. The summer
camp.   10. A day in the city.   11. An automobile accident.   12. A shop-
lifter apprehended.   13. A teacher strike.

11.   What Are the Elements of Description?

Writing a description of a place, person, or event is one of the least painful ways of starting a course in composition. As handmaiden to exposition, description joins it in countless numbers of rhetorical combinations, though it
appears in pure form only in a set-piece describing the countryside in a nine-

teenth-century novel, or in a handbook on yachting describing the rigging of a Marconi-rigged sloop. Writing a description sharpens our attention and our observation, attributes every writer needs. A description can be objective, as in the first example, or it can be a subtle call for action, a disguised argument really, as in the second.

Thousands of millions of nerve cells *are woven* into the texture of the human brain, and each can communicate with near or distant neighbors. Judson Herrick, the University of Chicago neurologist, has calculated that if only a million of these nerve cells *were joined* two by two in every possible way, the number of combinations would total $10^{2,783,000}$. This is a figure so tremendous that if it were written out and set up in the type you are reading, it would more than fill two volumes of this size. And we may be sure that the brain has many times a million nerve cells, each capable of groupings of far more than two cells per hookup. . . .

It is the forebrain that attains the crowning organization and integration of the nervous system — the cerebral cortex. Beginning as an insignificant segment of the embryonic brain, this gray mantle eventually grows so large that it must fold in on itself in wrinkles to accommodate its expanding surface to the walls of the skull. When fully grown, the cerebral cortex completely covers the brain structures from which it developed. It overshadows and dominates them, taking control of many of their functions. From every nerve cell, or neurone, fibers pass to other neurones, both of the cortex and of the other brain parts. Millions of lines of communication connect one region of gray matter with another, and these in turn with distant organs. By such means the brain is in communication with the lungs, the heart and other organs; with the specialized cells which serve as the receptors of touch, taste, smell, vision, hearing and other sensations; and with the muscles which produce action.

GEORGE W. GRAY

Writer shows he can take infinite pains with details. He accumulates data, transmits them, makes visual impression on reader's mind, but refrains from judgment.

Notice how passive verbs occur in objective writing.

Here on this knoll, 19.6 feet higher than a parking lot 230 feet away, at 12:22 P.M. on May 4, 1970, twenty-six Ohio National Guardsmen from the 145th Infantry and 107th Armored Cavalry Regiments fired fifty-nine shots at a group of student demonstrators and, in thirteen seconds of gunfire, killed four and wounded nine.

> Compared to the paragraph above, this one selects details to impose an emotional effect. Contrast between students and guardsmen implies confrontation between power and helplessness. Last paragraph implies judgment against *system*.

The shooting took place exactly five days before the first Kent State University Campus Day in the Age of Aquarius was to have been held. A victory bell, used to signal gridiron prowess, tolled as the shots rang out. The sky was blue. The temperature was seventy degrees. There was a gusty wind. The rifles were M-1s of World War II vintage with a range of more than half a mile. Most of the victims were dressed in bell-bottoms and flowered Apache shirts, and most had Rolling Stone haircuts. Some carried books. The guardsmen wore battle helmets, gas masks, fatigues, and combat boots. The two sides looked, to each other, like the inhabitants of different worlds.

JOE ESZTERHAS and MICHAEL D. ROBERTS

EXERCISES

A. Write a 100-word objective description.

B. Write a subjective description designed to arouse the reader's positive or negative feelings toward the subject, using topics suggested by your instructor.

C. Write a description of a person or a television program you like; then revise the description and write it from the point of view of someone who dislikes that person or program. This exercise demonstrates how subjectively most of us see the world around us, and how much our picture of the world is colored by ourselves rather than by external reality.

12. What Is Analysis?

Analysis is relating the parts to a whole, which it does by comparing, contrasting, enumerating, defining, dividing, and sorting. Vital to explanation, analysis is needed in any expository prose explaining something. Analytical reasoning can be separated into three categories: (1) analysis by classification; (2) structural analysis (sometimes called "division" or "partition"); (3) operational analysis (sometimes called "process"). All three modes of thought operate contiguously; that is, they border closely on one another. Airplanes can be classified according to their size or shape or the name of the manufacturer, analyzed structurally by dividing an airplane into its component parts, and analyzed operationally by describing the steps involved from take-off to landing.

12a. How Do I Classify?

Analysis by classification always begins with a plural whole: airplane*s*, or automobile*s*, or student*s*. To complete the classification, the investigator must find a common denominator for sorting the raw data. A common denominator for classifying airplanes might be the manufacturer, so that the aircraft can be classified as Martins, Boeings, Douglases, Beechcrafts, Cessnas, or Fokkers. The question is "What kinds of things are these?" To-classify human beings, the investigator might decide on body types as the common denominator, arranging people according to whether they are skinny, muscular, or obese. They can also be classified according to their tastes. Russell Lynes named three classes of people: highbrow, lowbrow, or middlebrow, depending on such cultural habits as the magazines they read. Grouping classmates into such categories as "straights" and "freaks" is classification. In classification the parts must remain identical in species to the whole: Martin airplanes remain airplanes, and not something else. You will find that in other modes of analysis this criterion vanishes.

In his *Holy and Profane State* (1642), Thomas Fuller, an Anglican clergyman, discussed teachers and pupils. His common denominator for pupils was their degree of aptitude and industry.

> He studieth his scholars' natures as carefully as they their books, and ranks their dispositions into several forms. And though it may seem difficult for him in a great school to descend to all particulars, yet experienced schoolmasters may quickly make a grammar of boys' natures, and reduce them all, saving some few exceptions, to these general rules:
> 1. Those that are ingenious and industrious. The conjunction of two such planets in a youth presages much good unto him. To such a lad a frown may be a whipping, and a whipping a death; yea, where their master whips them once, shame whips them all the week after. Such natures he useth with all gentleness.
> 2. Those that are ingenious and idle. These think, with the hare in the fable, that running with snails (so they count the rest of their schoolfellows) they shall come soon enough to the post, though sleeping a good while before their starting. Oh, a good rod would finely take them napping.
> 3. Those that are dull and diligent. Wines, the stronger they be, the more lees they have when they are new. Many boys are muddy-headed till they be

clarified with age, and such afterwards prove the best. Bristol diamonds [rock crystals] are both bright and squared and pointed by nature, and yet are soft and worthless; whereas orient ones in India are rough and rugged naturally. Hard, rugged, and dull natures of youth acquit themselves afterwards the jewels of the country, and therefore their dullness at first is to be borne with, if they be diligent. That schoolmaster deserves to be beaten himself who beats nature in a boy for a fault. And I question whether all the whipping in the world can make their parts, which are naturally sluggish, rise one minute before the hour nature hath appointed.

4. Those that are invincibly dull and negligent also. Correction may reform the latter, not amend the former. All the whetting in the world can never set a razor's edge on that which hath no steel in it. Such boys be consigneth over to other professions. Shipwrights and boatmakers will choose those crooked pieces of timber which other carpenters refuse. Those may make excellent merchants and mechanics who will not serve for scholars.

12b.   Further Aids to Classification

Illogical shifts in the common denominator are easy to fall into. Once you have set the basis for classification, or common denominator, stick to it. College courses are classified into humanities, social sciences, and physical sciences according to the principle of their relationship to man and the universe. But a classification like humanities, social sciences, physical sciences, and chemistry is illogical. Chemistry is only a subdivision of the physical sciences and does not merit separate status. Equally faulty would be a classification putting humanities, physical sciences, social sciences, and modern dance together. The principle in this scheme has veered away from man's relationship to his universe toward a subspecies of skill in physical education. (There is nothing wrong with modern dance, but it is irrelevant in this scheme of classification.)

Make certain the thing you are analyzing is a whole, not a part. Don't say you are going to analyze a poem by William Wordsworth, perhaps "Westminster Bridge," and then become so absorbed in the imagery of the sonnet that you forget all about the rest of the poem.

EXERCISES

A. Analysis involves sorting much like that used by a stamp collector who arranges his collection into categories such as European, Asian, and American stamps, and further subdivides the major categories into nations. His basis for classification is, of course, geographical and political. A book lover arranges his books on the library shelves in categories based on subject: fiction, poetry, and biography. The stacks of a library have the books arranged in all kinds of classifications and subclassifications.

After studying the example below, examine the three lists of terms that follow. Discover a logical principle for sorting the terms into categories and arrange them according to that principle. Use your dictionary as a guide, if a term is unfamiliar to you, and also use the blank classification charts.

Sample: physics, bacteriology, chemistry, American, physical sciences, anthropology, European, romance, philology, knowledge, cosmology, ethics, Slavic, linguistics, political science, botany, entomology, sociology, humanities, life sciences, Germanic, social sciences, cosmogony, astronomy, sciences, astrophysics, history, Renaissance, metaphysics, physical anthropology, zoology, physiology, Greek, epistemology, philosophy, cultural anthropology

KNOWLEDGE

SCIENCES			HUMANITIES		
Physical	*Life*	*Social*	*Philology*	*History*	*Philosophy*
Physics	Zoology	Political	Romance	American	Ethics
Chemistry	Botany	Sociology	Germanic	European	Epistemology
Astronomy	Entomology	Anthropology	Slavic	Renaissance	Cosmology
Astrophysics	Physiology	Physical	Greek		Metaphysics
Cosmogony	Bacteriology	Cultural			
		Linguistics			

See if you can fill in these charts:

1. Musical Comedy, Deerslayer, Trees, Our Town, Literature, Moby Dick, King and I, The Waste Land, A Farewell to Arms, Oklahoma, Mending Wall, Adam Bede, Antigone, Plays, The Scarlet Letter, Poetry, Excelsior, Novels, My Fair Lady, Drama, Barbara Frietchie, Huckleberry Finn, J. B., Death of a Salesman

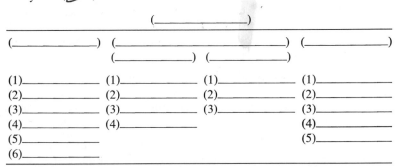

(_____)			
(_____)	(_____)	(_____)	(_____)
	(_____)	(_____)	
(1)_____	(1)_____	(1)_____	(1)_____
(2)_____	(2)_____	(2)_____	(2)_____
(3)_____	(3)_____	(3)_____	(3)_____
(4)_____	(4)_____		(4)_____
(5)_____			(5)_____
(6)_____			

2. Brahms, Puccini, Schumann, Verdi, Composers, Gershwin, German, Wagner, Italian, Bach, American, Bernstein, Foster, Beethoven, Porter, Mendelssohn

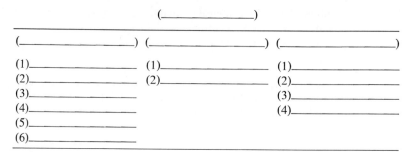

3. Poland, China, Japan, World Geography, Brazil, Peru, Ohio, Europe, France, Burma, North and South America, Sweden, Oklahoma, Vietnam, Denmark, Philippines, Colombia, Italy, United States, Asia, Norway, Costa Rica, Kansas, Canada

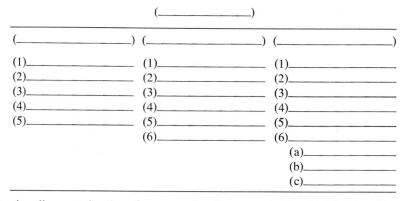

B. A college catalog is a fine example of an exercise in classification. Examine your catalog to see under what principles the courses have been arranged.

C. The common denominator for sorting is imposed by the writer on the materials, and is not an absolute. The principle will vary depending on the investigator's needs. What common denominator, or sorting device could be used for classifying these?

1. Teachers of English.   2. Blind dates.   3. Football players.   4. Philosophers.   5. Engineers.   6. Scientists.   7. Coeds.   8. Deans.   9. Medical men.   10. Campus buildings.   11. Students at a university.   12. Postage stamps.   13. Rocks.   14. Plants.

D. The common denominator for sorting will depend on the needs and purposes of the investigator. What principle for sorting the student body at your institution might be used by each of these?

1. The dean of students.   2. The dean of women.   3. The bursar or treasurer.   4. The admissions office.   5. The football coach.   6. The dormitory manager.   7. The parking committee.   8. The student health

center. 9. The student chaplains. 10. The sororities' rushing chair-person.

Expand one of these subjects into a 500-word paper, using classification.

E. Write essays using classification, based on these general topics (assume the audience is your parents). In each essay, state the common denominator clearly in a footnote on the opening page, not in the essay itself.

1. The kinds of dogs that make lovable household pets. 2. The kinds of politicians that dominate the national scene. 3. The kinds of advice given you by teachers and parents. 4. The kinds of students in this class. 5. The kinds of courses provided in your college or university. 6. The kinds of parties popular in your social set. 7. The kinds of men (or women) you like best.

12c. How Do I Divide (Structural Analysis)?

As classification begins with plural entities (such as airplanes) and sorts them into a pattern, structural analysis (often called "division" or "partition") begins with a singular entity and breaks it down (anatomizes it) into its components. For a structural analysis you enumerate the parts, and give a sequenced commentary on the major elements of a problem. Charles Reich neatly divided three general types of consciousness in America:

> To show how this has worked out in America, and to show the true meaning of the new generation, we have attempted to classify three general types of consciousness. These three types predominate in America today. One was formed in the nineteenth century, the second in the first half of this century, the third is just emerging. Consciousness I is the traditional outlook of the American farmer, small businessman, and worker who is trying to get ahead. Consciousness II represents the values of an organizational society. Consciousness III is the new generation. The three categories are, of course, highly impressionistic and arbitrary; they make no pretense to be scientific. And, since each type of consciousness is a construct, we would not expect any real individual to exhibit in symmetrical perfection all the characteristics of one type of consciousness.

Structural analysis doesn't have to be quite so skeletal, however. In this analysis of the American educational system's alleged defects, Hannah Arendt has clothed the bare bones of the enumeration with a running commentary:

These ruinous measures can be schematically traced back to three basic assumptions, all of which are only too familiar. The *first* is that there exist a child's world and a society formed among children that are autonomous and must insofar as possible be left to them to govern. Adults are only there to help with this government. The authority	Introduction I. Statement of assumptions II. Identification of first assumption

that tells the individual child what to do and what not to do rests with the child group itself — and this produces, among other consequences, a situation in which the adult stands helpless before the individual child and out of contact with him. He can only tell him to do what he likes and then prevent the worst from happening. The real and normal relations between children and adults, arising from the fact that people of all ages are always simultaneously together in the world, are thus broken off. And so it is of the essence of this first basic assumption that it takes into account only the group and not the individual child. . . .

    A. Consequences of assumption

    B. Further consequences

    C. Summary of effects

The *second* basic assumption which has come into question in the present crisis has to do with teaching. Under the influence of modern psychology and the tenets of pragmatism, pedagogy has developed a science of teaching in general in such a way as to be wholly emancipated from the actual material to be taught. A teacher, so it was thought, is a man who can simply teach anything; his training is in teaching, not in the mastery of any particular subject. This attitude, as we shall presently see, is naturally very closely connected with a basic assumption about learning. Moreover, it has resulted in recent decades in a most serious neglect of the training of teachers in their own subjects. . . .

III. Identification of second assumption

    A. Consequences of assumption

    B. Further consequences

But this pernicious role that pedagogy and the teachers' colleges are playing in the present crisis was only possible because of a modern theory about learning. This was, quite simply, the logical application of the *third* basic assumption in our context, an assumption which the modern world has held for centuries and which found its systematic conceptual expression in pragmatism. This basic assumption is that you can know and understand only what you have done yourself, and its application to education is as primitive as it is obvious: to substitute, insofar as possible, doing for learning.

IV. Identification of third assumption

EXERCISES

A. Sometimes it helps to think of classification as an upward movement and
    partition as a downward movement. In classifying, you try to assign a
    smaller part to a larger whole, but in partition you want to divide a
    larger part into smaller units. Look at the structure of the Episcopal
    church. The clergymen can be classified according to their relationship to
    the bishop of the diocese. The church has curates who assist rectors of
    parishes, mission priests (who depend on the bishop for financial support),
    and chaplains who carry out special jobs for the bishop. All these belong
    to the larger whole, the clergy of the diocese. Partitioning, though, means
    thinking in the opposite direction, beginning with the diocese and sys-
    tematically breaking it down into its components: bishop, bishop co-
    adjutor, archdeacon, canon, priest, curate, mission priest, deacon, lay
    reader, warden, vestryman, and so forth.

    Apply the same technique to these organizations: (1) the United States
    Army, (2) a federal agency such as the Office of Management and Budget,
    (3) your university, (4) a city government, (5) a large corporation like
    General Motors or IBM. In 500 words explain the organization of the
    agency or business to either an angry taxpayer or a suspicious stock-
    holder, the former enraged about high taxes and the latter upset over
    low dividends.

B. Write a description of one of these subjects, stressing the structural rela-
    tionship of the parts. Assume your audience has never particularly noticed
    the thing being described. For a model check back to the excerpt from
    George Gray's "The Great Ravelled Knot" (see page 43).

    1. The human eye.   2. A celestial telescope.   3. A sewage treatment
    plant.   4. A violin.   5. A scanning electron microscope.   6. An apart-
    ment.   7. A subsonic jet aircraft.   8. A piano.   9. An apartment build-
    ing.   10. A Marconi-rigged sailboat.

12d.   How Do I Describe a Process (Operational Analysis)?

American industries employ thousands of technical writers whose job
is to write manuals on how to do everything from repairing a television set to
changing an automobile tire. Essentially process papers, the most rudimentary
form of these instructions is the mechanical directions in a cookbook for baking
a cake. Because they are organized by a sequence of events instead of being
developed from a controlling idea, they are not the kinds of papers ("themes")
that are written in a composition course. That makes them less challenging to
compose, in some ways. The hobby magazine article, explaining the art of performing a household improvement, offers a greater challenge to the writer. Designed to delight as well as to instruct, this article outlines the steps for sealing
wallboard.

HOW TO SEAL WALLBOARD

The amateur carpenter, having placed the studs against the basement walls and having nailed 4-by-7 foot sections of wallboard to the studs, may think that now his job is virtually completed. After all, what remains but the mere plastering of the cracks between the sections of wallboard, the decoration of the ceiling, and the painting of the entire ensemble? Of course, there will be also the small detail of placing molding around the floors and ceilings, but that too should be a simple matter.

How sadly mistaken the poor beginner is. His work, if only he knew it, has just begun. He is in the position of a writer who has only completed a first draft and still must undertake the painful work of revision, of polishing, typing, and proofreading.

The first step is to assemble (1) an electric sander, (2) a trowel, (3) a plasterer's mortarboard, (4) a sack of dry plaster, (5) tape, and (6) a large mixing pot. The directions accompanying the sack of plaster should provide sufficient information to allow for proper mixing of the concoction. When it has achieved the consistency of a thin paste, the plaster is ready for application. The beginner should not be afraid to smear the plaster on the seams, wholeheartedly and vigorously (this is no time for effeteness or displays of delicacy). Quickly, before the plaster begins to set, the tape should be run from floor to ceiling along the wallboard seam and completely mashed down with the backside of the trowel or some other flat instrument, until the plaster oozes through the holes on the tape. Before the plaster has had a chance to set, the operator should immediately slap a second coat of plaster across the back of the tape. When this operation has been carried out on all 18 or 20 seams in the room, a morning's work will have been completed, and the amateur craftsman should take time out for refreshment, perhaps a cool draught of beer.

I. Introduction

A. Process identified

B. Process described

II. Assembly of equipment

III. Operational analysis

A. Step one

B. Step two

C. Step three

Once the plaster has set, the carpenter (who is now a "drywall" man and should perhaps apply for admission to another union) is ready to begin sanding. As a preliminary step, it might be a good idea (though somewhat impracticable) to move furniture, clothing, bric-a-brac, objets d'art, and wife and children right out into the street. The amount of dust generated by the sanding of plaster can achieve alarming proportions. Moreover, it has a knack for infiltrating into closets, into furniture, into food, into nurseries, and into lungs. For that reason, try to seal off the basement, and by all means wear some kind of mask or goggles. (I found it useful to wear my little boy's skin-diving mask.)

D. Step four

1. Further explanation

2. Further explanation

Another type of process paper, the how-it-is-done variety, a staple of magazines everywhere, relies mainly on curiosity about how interesting and remote tasks are carried out by specialists. Here is Bernard Fall's account of the fall of Dienbienphu in Vietnam, an event far from the experience of the average American:

On May 7, 1954, the end of the battle for the jungle fortress of Dienbienphu marked the end of French military influence in Asia, just as the sieges of Port Arthur, Corregidor and Singapore had, to a certain extent, broken the spell of Russian, American and British hegemony in Asia. The Asians, after centuries of subjugation, had beaten the white man at his own game. And today, 10 years after Dienbienphu, Vietcong guerrillas in South Vietnam again challenge the West's ability to withstand a potent combination of political and military pressure in a totally alien environment.

On that day in May, 1954, it had become apparent by 10 A.M. that Dienbienphu's position was hopeless. French artillery and mortars had been progressively silenced by murderously accurate Communist Vietminh artillery fire; and the monsoon rains had slowed down supply drops to a trickle and transformed the French trenches and dugouts into bottomless quagmires. The surviving officers and men, many of whom had lived for 54 days on a steady diet of instant coffee and cigarettes, were in a catatonic state of exhaustion.

As their commander, Brig. Gen. Christian de la Croix de Castries, reported the situation over the radio-telephone to General René Cogny, his theater commander 220 miles away in Hanoi in a high-pitched but curiously impersonal voice, the end obviously had come for the fortress. De Castries ticked off a long list of 800-man battalions which had been reduced to companies of 80 men and of companies that were reduced to the size of weak platoons. All he could hope for was to hold out until nightfall in order to give the surviving members of his command a chance to break out into the jungle under the cover of darkness, while he himself would stay with the more than 5,000 severely wounded (out of a total of 15,094 men inside the valley) and face the enemy.

By 3 P.M., however, it had become obvious that the fortress would not last until nightfall. Communist forces, in human-wave attacks, were swarming over the last remaining defenses. De Castries polled the surviving unit commanders within reach, and the consensus was that a breakout would only lead to a senseless piecemeal massacre in the jungle. The decision was made then to fight on to the end, as long as the ammunition lasted, and let individual units be overrun after destruction of their heavy weapons. That course of action was approved by the senior commander in Hanoi at about 5 P.M., but with the proviso that "Isabelle," the southernmost strongpoint closest to the jungle, and to friendly forces in Laos, should be given a chance to make a break for it.

Cogny's last conversation with de Castries dealt with the dramatic problem of what to do with the wounded piled up under incredible conditions in the various strongpoints and in the fortress's central hospital — originally built to contain 42 wounded. There had been suggestions that an orderly surrender should be arranged in order to save the wounded the added anguish of falling into enemy hands as isolated individuals. But Cogny was adamant on that point:

"*Mon vieux,* of course you have to finish the whole thing now. But what you have done until now surely is magnificent. Don't spoil it by hoisting the white flag. You are going to be submerged [by the enemy], but no surrender, no white flag."

"All right, *mon général,* I only wanted to preserve the wounded."

"Yes, I know. Well, do as best you can, leaving it to your [static: subordinate units?] to act for themselves. What you have done is too magnificent to do such a thing. You understand, *mon vieux.*"

There was a silence. Then de Castries said his final words:

"*Bien, mon général.*"

"Well, good-by, *mon vieux,*" said Cogny. "I'll see you soon."

EXERCISES

A. Write a process paper on one of these subjects, directing the topic toward an audience of persons likely to spend more time in watching television than in reading, perhaps average housewives and blue-collar workers. You will have to make your meaning very clear by using appropriate examples and illustrations and avoiding jargon and technical terms.

1. How to appreciate abstract expressionist paintings. 2. How to appreciate atonal music. 3. How to plan a wedding. 4. How to control teenage children. 5. How to figure interest rates on a car loan. 6. How to sing folk music. 7. How to enjoy life in a large city on $30 a day. 8. How to play chess. 9. How to detect phoniness in television commercials. 10. How to make home brew. 11. How to organize a union.

B. If you were to write papers on some of these topics, what mode of analysis would you have to use? Classification? Structural analysis? Operational analysis?

1. A gasoline engine at rest. 2. A gasoline engine in motion. 3. A museum of engines. 4. A building. 5. A group of buildings. 6. The flow of traffic through the lobby of a building. 7. A chemical plant shut down. 8. A chemical plant operating. 9. Sixty assorted chemicals. 10. A commentary on ten poems. 11. A commentary on one poem. 12. An analysis of the transitional devices in a poem.

C. Drawing on your general knowledge of life and science and modern industry, write a 500-word how-it-is-done essay on one of these topics for a person who expects never to have a similar experience:

1. How the sorority (or fraternity) discovered and pledged me. 2. The events I found the most crucial in becoming a successful student of _____. 3. How the Federal Reserve Bank discounts paper money. 4. How coal is extracted from the ground. 5. How the American colonies broke away from England because of the taxation issue. 6. How to shop for food bargains. 7. The strategy behind television commercials. 8. How the police ensure that speeders will be caught. 9. Duties of our town's mayor. 10. How the rivers of America can be kept unpolluted or navigable. 11. How the American people elect, or impeach, a president. 12. How an amateur athlete is recruited to play college sports.

13. What Are Formal, Extended, and Impromptu Definitions?

An immense amount of the effort that writing demands goes into defining words. We had better then look into the formal thinking that goes into definition, even though in practice it intertwines with other forms of development. The dictionary is the obvious place to search for the definition of a word (see 25b). Dictionary definitions may be quoted word for word when the writer wants to show exactness and precision. Normally, however, the dictionary definition will be modified through an impromptu, selective treatment. Which of these definitions would be the more attractive to read in an informal essay?

The Funk and Wagnalls *Standard College Dictionary* defines Virtue as "n. 1. The quality of moral righteousness or excellence; rectitude. 2. The practice of moral duties and abstinence from immorality and vice; a life devoted to *virtue*. 3. Sexual purity; chastity, especially in women. 4. A particular type of moral excellence, especially one of

"Virtue," as any dictionary will suggest, is a word having to do with all kinds of moral excellence, ranging from a desire for righteousness and rectitude to a devotion to chastity and valor. It is, as the Funk and Wagnalls *Standard College Dictionary* suggests, "the quality of moral righteousness or excellence."

those considered to be of special
importance in philosophical or religious doctrine." Also the dictionary says virtue is "5. Any admirable
quality or trait, or 6. an inherent or
essential quality, or power."

When you are asked for extraordinary precision and exactness, a formal
definition may be appropriate. An effective definition approximates in a small
way the best features of a well-stated thematic sentence. That is, it both shapes
and limits a topic and thereby shapes and focuses a paper. Formal definitions
contain a *term,* a *genus,* and a *differentiator.* The logic is simple: the word to be
defined (*term*) must be fitted into the next higher class of things to which it belongs (*genus*) and then a distinction (*differentiator*) must be made between term
and genus. The formal definition of *foolscap* will read: Foolscap is a printing
paper measuring about 13 by 16 inches. Schematically, formal definitions look
like this:

TERM	GENUS	DIFFERENTIATOR
foolscap	printing paper	measuring 13 by 16 inches
mukluk	boot	of sealskin or reindeer skin
virtue	moral quality	characterized by righteousness, excellence, and rectitude

If these definitions of nouns are sound, we should be able to turn them around,
to reverse them completely. "Foolscap is printing paper measuring 13 by 16
inches" should be the same as "Printing paper measuring 13 by 16 inches is
foolscap." "A mukluk is a boot of sealskin or reindeer skin" should equal "Reindeer skin or sealskin boots are mukluks." If the definition is accurate, we should
be able to use either the term, or the genus plus differentiator, interchangeably.
"The troops in the Aleutians wore mukluks." "The troops in the Aleutians wore
boots made of sealskin or reindeer skin." "The original versions of foolscap had
a sketch of a jester in the watermark." "The original versions of printing paper
measuring 13 by 16 inches had a sketch of a jester in the watermark."

13a.   What Is Extended Definition?

Writing an extended definition demands many analytic and rhetorical
skills, including these supportive resources: (1) giving examples (exemplification),
(2) illustrating, (3) describing, (4) furnishing synonyms (comparison), (5) furnishing antonyms (contrast), (6) giving a dictionary definition, (7) improving an
informal definition, (8) composing a formal definition, (9) classifying, and (10)
analyzing. Here is an extended definition of the word *hot*:

"Hot," as anyone who has ever sat on a   Writer surveys synonyms.
red-hot stove knows, can mean "scorching"

[synonym], or even "burning" and "fiery." In other situations it can mean "ardent" or "sultry" but the circumstances for those meanings are rather special, treating of moments when hotness can be a pleasant rather than an unpleasant experience. Those unable to grasp the meaning of "hot" by sitting on glowing stoves can perhaps benefit from squatting on a cake of ice, for "cold" [antonym] has the opposite meaning. If the ice treatment fails, further ventures in heat might include eating pepper sandwiches sprinkled with mustard while lying out on the Kansas prairie at high noon in July [examples]. Still more enlightenment can come by holding one hand in hot water and another in warm water, for "warm" lies somewhere between "hot" and "cold" [comparison]. Most people will find the sensation of warmth as comforting as the sensation of "hot" is disconcerting [contrast]. Indeed the dictionary defines "hot" as having or giving off great heat; "having a high temperature; very warm" [dictionary definition]. It also points out that a slangy sense of "hot" is "lustful" or "sexy." These rather circular ways of defining the word suggest that our own definition might not be too irrelevant. "Hot is an adjective signifying temperature in excess" [impromptu definition] is not too far removed from the formal definition that a physics text might offer: "The quality of hotness, or heat, is a form of energy directly associated with and proportional to the random molecular motions of a body or substance as caused by combustion, friction, chemical action, radiation, etc., and convertible into other forms of energy" [formal definition].

He looks at antonyms next

Scrutiny of paragraph shows it is amplified (see 17a) mostly by *defining* terms. Writer offers examples, comparison, contrast, and so forth.

13b.   What Are the Fallacies in Definition?

Legend says that in World War I, officer candidates were screened from potential infantry privates by just one question: "What is a spoon?" If the draftee replied, "A spoon is what you eat with," off went the poor devil to infantry basic training camp; but if the young man said, "A spoon is an eating utensil for conveying liquid foods from a cup or bowl to the mouth," off he went to officer candidate school. The happy OCS candidate, having been to college and having taken freshman rhetoric, used in his definition a term (spoon), genus (an eating utensil), and differentiator (for conveying liquid). He did not commit the error of substituting a pronoun for a term in a definition. A spoon is not a *what*; it is some kind of an object. In such definitions as "Graduation is *when* you get your diploma" and "Home is *where* they love you" the same difficulty occurs. A graduation is not a *when* and a home is not a *where*. "A spoon is what you eat with" may be more colorful and dashing than the pompous "A spoon is an eating utensil," but academic writing favors accuracy over color.

Do not define a word by repeating words identical to the word in the term. Everyone has been put off by this circular kind of definition: "A pusillanimous person is a person having the quality of pusillanimity." Something like this would be better received: "A pusillanimous person is an anxiety-ridden human being lacking either determination or courage, or both."

Whenever possible, phrase the genus and differentiator in words more familiar than the term. To define *anger* as "a display of nonadaptive behavior" might be meaningful to a psychologist but is merely frustrating to the average person.

A definition with too broad a genus is likely to be too inclusive. If *submarine* is defined as a "ship for military purposes," the definition would also include all other varieties of naval vessels, from minesweepers to aircraft carriers, and would not include submarines used for nonmilitary purposes. The genus must be narrowed to "a submersible ship."

The opposite of a too-inclusive definition is the kind of definition that is too narrow to handle all possibilities, such as "The theater is a playhouse in New York for producing dramatic literature." This definition has at least two major flaws. There are playhouses in the United States outside of New York, and the theater is not limited to producing dramatic literature but includes musical comedies as well. Defining too exclusively is a weakness everyone shares. We do it unconsciously in making such assumptions as "A decent and reliable person is a member of my own special group" or "A real American is a man who scorns any kind of foreign influence."

The too-inclusive definition may also turn out to be a question-begging statement, translated from the logicians' *petitio principii* (see 24a). In begging the question one dresses an unproved or untested assumption in the guise of a fact. The masquerade often is so subtle and elusive it escapes detection. Defining a "decent and reliable person" as a "member of my own social group" begs the question because the standard for becoming "a decent and reliable person" is not made clear.

Finally, a metaphor and a definition are not the same. If someone says, "Bread is the staff of life" or "My love is a red, red rose," he may be praised for his old-fashioned florid style but not for composing a workable definition.

EXERCISES

A. Definition includes the use of (1) synonyms, (2) antonyms, (3) exemplification, (4) comparison, (5) classification, (6) structural analysis (partition of things or objects), and (7) operations analysis (partition of events). How can they be applied to a practical problem in definition? Using your dictionary, look up a synonym, antonym (if applicable), example, and comparison for two of these terms:

slow	Satan	wet	sharp
evil	tornado	serious	feeble
spirit	sea	witty	clear

Here is how your solutions to the problem should look:

TERM	SYNONYM	ANTONYM	EXAMPLE (WORD IN CONTEXT)	COMPARISON
small	diminutive	large	tiny child; wee infant; small boy	miniature, minute, trivial

B. Write out formal definitions for two of these terms:

honor	ethics	beauty	justice
duty	idealism	friendship	equity
obedience	truth	good	reason

Make certain that each definition contains a term, genus, and differentiator, and label them like this:

TERM	GENUS	DIFFERENTIATOR

Love / is that state, or quality, of mind and spirit / which allows human beings to develop strong emotional attachments for a person, family, town, state, nation, or God.

C. Read and discuss this definition of the "feminine mystique" by Betty Friedan. How effective is it as definition? Does the author make her conception clear to the reader?

And so the feminine mystique began to spread through the land, grafted onto old prejudices and comfortable conventions which so easily give the past a stranglehold on the future. Behind the new mystique were concepts and theories deceptive in their sophistication and their assumption of accepted truth. These theories were supposedly so complex that they were inaccessible to all but a few initiates, and therefore irrefutable. It will be necessary to break through this wall of mystery and look more closely at these complex concepts, these accepted truths, to understand fully what has happened to American women.

The feminine mystique says that the highest value and the only commitment for women is the fulfillment of their own femininity. It says that the great mistake of Western culture, through most of its history, has been the undervaluation of this femininity. It says this femininity is so mysterious and intuitive and close to the creation and origin of life that manmade science may never be able to understand it. But however special and different, it is in no way inferior to the nature of man; it may even in certain respects be superior. The mistake, says the mystique, the root of women's troubles in the past is that women envied men, women tried to be like men, instead of accepting their own nature, which can find fulfillment only in sexual passivity, male domination, and nurturing maternal love.

But the new image this mystique gives to American women is the old image: "Occupation: housewife." The new mystique makes the housewife-mothers, who never had a chance to be anything else, the model for all women; it presupposes that history has reached a final and glorious end in the here and now, as far as women are concerned.

D. Study these excerpts as impromptu definitions and be prepared to discuss the writer's methods for making his intention clear.

1. What a piece of work is a man! How noble in reason! how infinite in faculty! in form, in moving, how express and admirable! in action how like an angel! in apprehension how like a god! the beauty of the world! the paragon of animals! And yet, to me, what is this quintessence of dust? WILLIAM SHAKESPEARE, *Hamlet* II.ii.316

2. Therefore I will have our Courtier a perfect horseman for every saddle. And beside the skill in horses and whatever else belongs to a horseman, let him be zealous to exceed all other men in the extent to which he is willing to explore all subjects, so that he may be marked among men for his excellence of mind and spirit. Like Alcibiades, this Courtier shall surpass all men in his own profession. And because it is the special gift of Italians to ride well, to manage horses with reason, especially rough horses, to run at the ring and to tilt, he shall be in this among the best Italians. At tournament, in keeping a passage, in fighting at barriers, he shall be good among the best Frenchmen. At running at the bull, casting of spears and darts, he shall be excellent among the Spaniards. But principally, let him accomplish these tasks with a certain good judgment and easy grace, with nonchalance even, if he will deserve that general favor which is so much desired by all men. In addition there are other activities, which though they do not depend entirely on skill in arms, contain much in them worthy of manly activity. Of these the chief is hunting, for it has a certain likeness with war, and is therefore truly a pastime for great men who live at the court. The courtier should also excel in the art of swimming, leaping, running, casting the stone, and playing tennis. And at all times he should display a genial humor, being affable and witty with all ranks of men whether high or low. In everything that he does or says, let him do it with grace. BALDASSARE CASTIGLIONE

Polonius: *Your noble son is mad;*
Mad call I it, for, to define true madness,
What is 't but to be nothing else but mad?
But let that go.
Queen: *More matter with less art.*
SHAKESPEARE, Hamlet II.ii.101, 1601

4 The Writer's Tactics:

Paragraphing

FOCUS AND FLOW

14. What Is a Paragraph?

The paragraph, a cluster of sentences dealing with a related thought, was devised to adapt the manuscript page to the technological limitations of printing. Medieval scribes signaled a break in thought by writing a paragraph symbol (¶) in the margin of the manuscript page. From this custom, apparently, the word *paragraph* was derived, because it means "to write" (*graphos*) "beside" (*para*) or, "write in the margin." Printers later abandoned the old paragraph sign, using indentation as a way of beginning a new subdivision. Although originally designed only as a way of breaking up the solid mass of print, paragraph indentation has grown into the convention that paragraphs form some kind of logical unit in the larger body of essay, letter, or treatise. They are creatures of the printed page, not speech; hardly anyone spontaneously talks in paragraphs. And just as several sentences relating to one idea make up a paragraph, so a cluster of related paragraphs often forms a larger subdivision in the entire paper. The requirement, or convention, that a paragraph signal a thought cluster of some significance makes one-sentence paragraphs taboo, except when the writer has a special task for them, such as making a transition between major units of thought, emphasizing a point, or recording dialogue.

15.   How Are Paragraphs Designed?

A good writer will build a paragraph just as you would a composition, stating the topic, amplifying it, and terminating it. The important difference in the paragraph is that you usually design its ending to encourage the reader to hang onto the theme, not let go as if the story were over. No matter what your paragraph is about or of which type it is, you are always working toward the same goals — smooth continuity and confident self-expression. These come only when you learn to control (1) *focus* — staying on the subject with no meandering; (2) *flow* — inventing smooth and inconspicuous transitions to tie sentences together; and (3) *amplification* — developing the thought in the paragraph convincingly. These three qualities (also called unity, coherence, and development) are easy to remember if you think of them as integrating and controlling the flow of energy you put into writing just as transmission lines carry the energy of electricity.

Two common types of paragraphs will help you keep your energy flowing — *analytic* and *synthetic*. You build an analytic paragraph by analyzing your subject, breaking down the whole into parts. Starting with a general assertion you follow with support for the statement by amplifying it, surrounding it with illustrations (examples), and at last you *terminate* it, at the same time preparing the reader for the next paragraph. In this analytic paragraph the author states her thesis and then proves it.

[1] The fiddler crab is not the only creature of tidal marsh and estuary to be threatened by pesticides; others of more obvious importance to man are endangered. [2] The famous blue crab of the Chesapeake Bay and other Atlantic Coast areas is an example. [a] These crabs are so highly susceptible to insecticides that every spraying of creeks, ditches, and ponds in tidal marshes kills most of the crabs living there. Not only do the local crabs die, but others moving into a sprayed area from the sea succumb to the	1. Topic sentence states the threat to fiddler, and other species.
	2. Support for thesis is derived by citing example of
	a. areas in which crab is threatened

lingering poison. [b] And sometimes poisoning may be indirect, as in the marshes near Indian River, where scavenger crabs attacked the dying fishes, but soon themselves succumbed to the poison. Less is known about the hazard to the lobster. However, it belongs to the same group of arthropods as the blue crab, has essentially the same physiology, and would presumably suffer the same effects. [3] This would be true also of the stone crab and other crustaceans which have direct economic importance as human food.

RACHEL CARSON

> b. other varieties of sea life: *scavenger, lobster,* and *stone crab.*
>
> 3. Termination hints at even greater threats to sea life, for later discussion.

The *synthetic* paragraph makes you *synthesize,* cementing the parts of an idea together one by one until they fuse into one whole thought. You don't usually state the thesis; you lead up to it.

[1] His picture was, until recently, everywhere: on television, on posters that stared out at one in airports and railroad stations, on leaflets, matchbooks and magazines. He was an inspired creation of Madison Avenue — a fictional character with whom millions could subconsciously identify, [2] Young and clean-cut, he carried an attaché case, glanced at his watch, and looked like an ordinary businessman scurrying to his next appointment. He had, however, an enormous protuberance on his back. For sticking out from between his shoulder blades was a great, butterfly-shaped key of the type used to wind up mechanical toys. [3] The text that accompanied his picture urged keyed-up executives to "unwind" — to slow down — at the Sheraton Hotels. [4] This wound-up man-on-the-go was, and still is, a potent symbol of the people of the future, millions of whom feel just as driven and hurried as if they, too, had a huge key in the back.

ALVIN TOFFLER

> 1. Opening sentences describe a man without revealing identity.
>
> 2. Further describes appearance and mannerism, a detailed picture.
>
> 3. Author reveals that the man is in an advertisement.
>
> 4. The last, and topic, sentence, reveals he is a driven man of the future, which is what this paragraph and the chapter that follows are about.

Both these modes of paragraph development, which either defend a thesis or lead up to one, are deep in the fabric of all writing. Because the first method is easier to master, you should perfect it before experimenting with the second.

15a.   How Does the Topic Sentence Work?

The topic sentence acts as the focal point of the paragraph; from it all energy radiates — or else all energy returns to it. It tells what the paragraph is about and it also defines the writer's attitude toward the subject. As decision-maker, it regulates the flow of thought into words, infects all other sentences in the paragraph, and generates supporting statements. When the paragraph logically grows out of the topic sentence, it is said to be *focused,* or to have *unity.* Except where the topic sentence is "understood," or implied, its location depends on whether the paragraph is analytic or synthetic. Usually topic sentences appear early in the analytic paragraph and farther along in the synthetic, though their placement has no fixed laws. In this paragraph from *Car and Driver,* a popular magazine for automobile enthusiasts, the first and last sentences of the paragraph both provide focus for the major point:

[1] Devout worshippers of the Lotus name-plate thrive at the very fringes of automotive enthusiasm. [2] But like most radicals, their small number can be quickly identified. You find them devastating imaginary lap records down the rural venues regarded as imposing . . . even treacherous . . . by the more conservative. [3] Their Elysium is much like the skier's — the down side of a mountain with an endless serious of lefts and rights joined by brief linear chutes to maintain speed. Each twist unique in its curvature and camber, each a challenge to be executed at the limit of man and machine. [4] They are addicted to the thrills of cornering and a car such as the Lotus Elan Sprint is their "works" — the utensil that provides their high.	1. Opening sentence is generally about Lotus fans. 2. Fans' characteristics defined; practice on back roads. 3. Additional proof is an analogy: downhill skiers. 4. Last sentence specifies topic: the Lotus Elan Sprint, a sports car.

The classic paragraph organization puts the topic sentence at the beginning, as in this student's paragraph:

Without any question, Flanders was one of the great blunders in military history. The chief enemy ceased to be the Germans and became the mud. Troops moving up into the lines sank into the gooiest, gloppiest mess imaginable. Horses, wagons, guns, supplies — everything became stuck in the goo. Even the duckboards constructed to keep the men out of the mud were swallowed up. The shellholes and trenches filled with water after	The topic is *Flanders* but an important theme is *blunders.* The second sentence limits the *blunders* to the question of mud. Subsequent sentences show how the *mud* affected the British Tommy. Derogatory *brass hats,* pulls reader back to theme of *blunders.*

each rain until Flanders was nothing more than a flooded swamp. The worst part of it was that none of the brass hats knew anything at all about what the troops were being subjected to. None ever visited the front lines.

The beginner is better off following the tried-and-true method of placing the topic sentence at the opening of the paragraph. Later on, there will be time for trying other ways. As always in rhetoric, you decide where to put the topic sentence after studying the best ways of attracting the reader's interest. How can you best stimulate the reader to read on? Experienced writers may even construct a paragraph with an *understood* topic sentence in which no sentence can be said to be the focal point; all the sentences imply an unstated controlling thought. Other paragraphs may even have two or more topic sentences, at the beginning and end of the unit. Almost any combination is possible, as long as the paragraph has a focal point somewhere.

EXERCISE

A. In these paragraphs, decide where the topic sentence is and how the paragraph is structured (from whole to part or from part to whole). Be prepared to defend your choice. As in most problems requiring you to use your judgment instead of merely counting, you may find that no answer is altogether right.

1. Yet enough remains to explain why the legend grew up above the name, why the name attached itself, in many instances, to the bravest work of other men. The *Concert in the Pitti Palace,* in which a monk, with cowl and tonsure, touches the keys of a harpsichord, while a clerk, placed behind him, grasps the handle of the viol, and a third, with cap and plume, seems to wait upon the true interval for beginning to sing, is undoubtedly Giorgione's. The outline of the lifted finger, the trace of the plume, the very threads of the fine line, which fasten themselves on the memory, in the moment before they are lost altogether in that calm unearthly glow, the skill which has caught the waves of wandering sound, and fixed them for ever on the lips and hands — these are indeed the master's own; and the criticism which, while dismissing so much hitherto believed to be Giorgione's, has established the claims of this one picture, has left it among the most precious things in the world of art.

WALTER PATER

2. No play of Shakespeare's is better than *Henry IV*. Certain subsequent ones may show him more settled in the maturity which he here attains at almost a single bound, but nothing that he wrote is more crowded with life or happier in its imitation of human talk. The pen that moves across these pages is perfectly free of itself. The host of persons assembled for

our pleasure can say anything for their author he wants to say. The poetry of Hotspur and the prose of Falstaff have never been surpassed in their respective categories; the History as a dramatic form ripens here to a point past which no further growth is possible; and in Falstaff alone there is sufficient evidence of Shakespeare's mastery in the art of understanding style, and through style of creating men. MARK VAN DOREN

3. Nantucket! Take out your map and look at it. See what a real corner of the world it occupies; how it stands there, away off shore, more lonely than the Eddystone lighthouse. Look at it — a mere hillock, an elbow of sand; all beach, without a background. There is more sand there than you would use in twenty years as a substitute for blotting paper. Some game-some wights will tell you that they have to plant weeds there, they don't grow naturally; that they import Canada thistles; that they have to send beyond seas for a spile to stop a leak in an oil cask; that pieces of wood in Nantucket are carried about like bits of the true cross in Rome; that people there plant toadstools before their houses, to get under the shade in summer time; that one blade of grass makes an oasis, three blades in a day's walk a prairie; that they wear quicksand shoes, something like Lap-lander snowshoes; that they are so shut up, belted about, every way in-closed, surrounded, and made an utter island of by the ocean, that to their very chairs and tables small clams will sometimes be found adhering, as to the backs of sea turtles. But these extravaganzas only show that Nan-tucket is no Illinois. HERMAN MELVILLE

15b.   The Writer's Attitude: How Do Topic Plus Theme Equal Focus?

The strong topic sentence will tell what the paragraph is about (its topic) and will also imply the writer's attitude toward, or position on, the topic. Out of this grows a controlling theme. In the sentence "Life on a large university campus confuses me almost as much as watching a three-ring circus," the topic is *life on large university campus* but the writer's attitude toward the university is implied by the verb *confuses* and by the comparison to a *three-ring circus*. By asserting the connection with *confusion* and a *circus-like* atmosphere, he has at once committed himself to an attitude in amplifying the paragraph. That de-cision will color everything said thereafter. How different the paragraph would be if it began: "Life on a university campus depresses me by its resemblance to a mouldering cemetery," or ". . . excites me by its similarity to a great metrop-olis," or ". . . stifles me because it is an oversized museum." All these statements imply an attitude that will show in everything that is later written on the topic. And these attitudes are all quite different from seeing the university as a three-ring circus, even though the topic, *university*, remains the same. This kind of statement about position almost guarantees that you and your paragraph will be forced to focus on the topic. A paragraph from Thomas Hardy's novel *The Return of the Native* shows this technique:

The vagary of Timothy Fairway was *infectious*. The turf-cutter *seized* old Olly Dowden, and, somewhat more gently, *poussetted* with her likewise. The young men were not slow to imitate the example of their elders, and *seized* the maids; Grandfer Cantle and his stick *jigged* in the form of a three-legged object among the rest; and in half a minute all that could be seen on Rainbarrow was a *whirling* of dark shapes amid a *boiling confusion* of sparks, which *leapt* around the dancers as high as their waists. The chief noises were women's shrill *cries,* men's *laughter,* Susan's stays and pattens [wooden shoes], Olly Dowden's "heu-heu-heu!" and the *strumming of the wind* upon the furze-bushes, which formed a kind of tune to the demoniac measure they trod. Christian alone stood aloof, uneasily rocking himself as he murmured, "They ought not to do it — how the vlankers do fly! 'tis tempting the Wicked one, 'tis."

The theme word is *infectious*. The antic dance of Timothy and Susan spreads through the group like an infection. The surface subject is dancing but the *whirling, leaping,* and *strumming of the wind* on a firelit heath suggests the diabolic, a kind of witches' sabbath. Is that why Christian (his name is significant) stands alone, aloof and uneasy, silently rebuking the others?

Other paragraphs in expository prose will show the same principles of thematic elaboration found in the work of a narrative artist like Hardy:

But magic notwithstanding, land booms always *burst*. There have been few American cities that have not had on their outskirts ambitious "developments" that have *not come off at all,* or have come off only after a long period of holding on. Sometimes the *holding on* was no great strain. It may be assumed that the *losses* incurred during the period when only handsome street lamps and magnificent pavements marked most of the development of the old Rockefeller farm in Shaker Heights on the outskirts of Cleveland were no *great strain* on the Rockefeller fortune. But for less well-financed speculations, the period of holding on might be *fatal*. The first speculator has so often taken *the rap*. How few American railroads, how few New York hotels, or even more splendid structures in Texas, have not *gone through the wringer!* How profitable has been the job

The topic is *land booms,* but the theme is held together by the word *burst*. The vocabulary of economic collapse is everywhere: *not come off at all, great strain, fatal, gone through the wringer, receivership,* and *hold the bag.*

of *receiver!* Indeed, there have been times
when the innocent investors have been forced
to wonder whether "receiver" — meaning
the recipient of *stolen goods* — was not
merely a special case of "receiver" meaning
the officer appointed by a complaisant court
to take over and administer the bankrupt
assets of great and small concerns alike. It
would be unkind to say on what American
railroad this incident occurred, but when I
complimented a friend of mine on the improved service on his local railroad, he replied, with no conscious irony: "Oh, service
has been swell since it went into *receivership;*
the management can afford to spend money
now that it hasn't got to worry about the
stockholders." This was a commuter's view,
not a stockholder's, but there has always
been among Americans, including the luck-
less investors themselves, a philosophical acceptance of the fact that somebody must
hold the bag for the great economic improve-
ments of modern America. DENIS BROGAN

Brogan moves into dis-
cussing *receivership* as a
by-product of *land booms*.

EXERCISES

A. Examine paragraphs from recent issues of *Atlantic, Saturday Review
World, Harper's,* and *Esquire* to see how effectively the topic-attitude
principle works out when popular writers structure paragraphs.

B. Distinguish between topic and theme in each of these sentences. How
firmly does the verb establish the writer's attitude toward the topic?

1. Mrs. Anthony Trollope surprised everyone with her formidable talents.
2. More than anything else, the noisiness of the stock exchange shocked
the small boy.   3. Germany badly misjudged the character of the English
"shopkeeper" during World War II.   4. Charles Dickens' visit to America
convinced him that life there was surprisingly pleasant and friendly.
5. Plato's life of Socrates may reveal more about Plato than Socrates.
6. The bombing of Hanoi outraged the sensibilities of moralistic Americans.   7. The rioting prisoners at Attica converted a prison revolt into a
political revolution.   8. Pro football on television has nudged out religion as the opiate of the masses.   9. Few natural sights can equal the
power and size of Niagara Falls.   10. After recess, the trial judge horrified the jury with the brutal details of the defendant's crime.

C. In these paragraphs, pick out the theme word in the topic sentence and the words and phrases in each sentence amplifying and developing the theme:

1. In 1937, except for the dwindling White House flotilla, the Yangtze Patrol was the most comfortable assignment in the Navy. The treaty right to patrol Chinese rivers and territorial waters had been won by the United States, France, Britain, and Russia after they had jointly subdued the terrorist mandarin Yeh in 1858. The duties of the Yangtze Patrol were simple: to watch over the safety and protect the rights and property of American businessmen and missionaries in China. The Patrol had done the job with diligence — and, at times, with cost. It was, however, a job that had its rewards. The quarters, with few exceptions, were light, airy, and unusually comfortable — with bunks for all hands instead of hammocks. Beards were allowed (no other U.S. Navy ships or stations tolerated anything bushier than a pencil-line mustache). Gunboat cooks took great pride in the tables they set: the menus were varied and even exotic, for food prices ashore — graft included — were so universally low that even the most zealous supply officer finally had to wink at the padded cost figures; there was hardly any point in trying to shake up the whole Oriental system for the sake of the Navy's Bureau of Supplies and Accounts. DARBY PERRY

2. Actually, however, Mrs. Trollope's objections to American speech — even though she probably did not realize it herself — ran deeper than objection to mere accent or cadence. It was the whole tone of the Americans' speech that annoyed her. She was annoyed because the very tone of address — a kind of familiarity and flippancy now found only among taxi drivers in New York City — grew squarely out of the common man's faith in the American credo that "all men are created free and equal." As she saw it such a belief was merely another example of the folly of liberalism, which perverted "freedom and equality" into a license for insolence and familiarity. This attitude of the Americans she saw reflected in the presumptuousness of servant girls who said "I be come to help you." Who, one might ask, could possibly be of any help to a Mrs. Frances Trollope?

D. Develop long paragraphs or brief themes from these topic sentences. Be sure to distinguish between topic and attitude and make the attitude in the opening statement permeate your entire paper. If necessary, trim and adjust the sentences to conform to your own feelings about the subject.

1. A Saturday afternoon in the football stadium offers a colorful panorama.   2. Few university museums can be so tastefully arranged as that at Clarendon Tech.   3. Automotive traffic in European cities jostles the nerves of pedestrians with its noise and unruliness.   4. Dropping formal requirements for graduation upsets students as much as it soothes them.   5. Consumers may choose from many options in ordering the engine for

a new automobile.   6. Irresponsible talk of corruption in the police department has hampered law enforcement in this community.   7. Many high school seniors reject as irrelevant the idea of a university education. 8. The modern jet aircraft surpasses all forms of transportation in man's history for speed and comfort.   9. Most television programs insult the public's intelligence with their repetitiveness and unoriginality.   10. The idea that "it is more blessed to give than to receive" contradicts the harsh reality of human nature.

16.   How Does the Paragraph Flow?

The paragraph hangs together, makes sense, and achieves coherence and continuity when you provide a logical and pleasing flow of thought from sentence to sentence, and from paragraph to paragraph. Just as focus governs the quantity and quality of thought in the paragraph, so flow ensures its orderly and smooth movement throughout all parts. When a paragraph flows satisfactorily, the reader has a sense of being taken somewhere, of being led from a little to a greater understanding of the subject. You can make your paragraphs flow by putting to work parallelism in thought, parallelism in syntax, transitional words and phrases, pronouns, and combinations of these devices.

16a.   Flow: Parallelism in Thought

Parallelism means giving equal coverage to equal ideas (see 19a). Ideas of the same general importance are entitled to treatment of approximately the same length and in approximately the same sequence:

[1] A boys' gang is too well organized to be classed as a crowd, but, nevertheless, it often behaves like one. [2] When, following the impulse of the moment, [a] it upsets the peddler's cart, [b] attacks the hangout of an enemy gang, [c] or smashes the windows of an unpopular storekeeper, one would guess that a miniature mob was in action. [3] The following qualities of gang life give it these appearances: [a] its behavior is often impulsive, unpredictable; [b] the gang is uninhibited by the usual social conventions; [c] it often expresses its antipathies in aggressive behavior; [d] and, of most significance, the gang is sometimes the inciting nucleus for widespread crowd and mob activity.

SUTHERLAND, WOODWARD, and MAXWELL

Thought is divided into equivalent parts. Each unit of thought is of about the same logical importance and receives about the same amount of treatment.
1. The gang as crowd
2. Mob behavior
   a. Upsets carts
   b. Attacks hangouts
   c. Smashes windows
3. Qualities of a mob
   a. Impulsive
   b. Uninhibited
   c. Aggressive
   d. Inciting

16b.   Flow: Parallelism in Syntax

Deliberately repeating identical patterns of syntax (arrangements of words) will hold a paragraph together too. Always distinguish deliberate repetition from careless repetition; the former is calculated, the latter sloppy.

[1] *There is much discussion* about how to give our schools a more serious intellectual tone, about the relative emphasis on athletics, popularity, and social life on the one hand and on scholarly application on the other. [2] *There is an effort* afoot throughout the nation to redress what has clearly been an imbalance. [3] Admiration for and interest in scholarship is likely to increase faster than expected. [4] *There are* even some amusing sidelights in which the old symbols are being poured into new bottles — as in certain high schools where the coveted athlete's "letter" is being given as well to students who make distinguished grade averages. [5] But *there is* another problem, more remote in time, that may eventually prove more serious and for which planning can now be effectively undertaken. JEROME BRUNER

Sentences 1,2,4, and 5 begin with the *there is [are]* pattern.

Why the variation from the *There is* pattern in sentence 3?

16c.   Flow: Transitional Words and Phrases

One way of getting prose to flow is to fall back on stock transitional words and phrases. But beware — they are often overused. Their conciseness makes them easy to drop into the sentence; it also makes them *very* visible to your reader. We can categorize them by the job they are meant to do:

1. Give additional information: *and, also, likewise, again, similarly, finally, furthermore, next, in addition.*

2. Signal a conclusion: *accordingly, in conclusion, thus, therefore, as a result, in brief, in short, to sum up.*

3. Introduce examples or illustrative matter: *as is well known, as has been said, for example, to illustrate, that is, in fact, in other words.*

4. Announce contrast: *but, instead, nor, on the other hand, conversely, in spite of, yet, and yet, still, however, nevertheless, notwithstanding.*

Notice how transitional words and phrases are used in this excerpt from a political science textbook:

The Party [Russian Communist Party] does place great emphasis upon self-criticism or, as it is called, "Bolshevik self-criticism." *According to this practice* the party is supposed to search for and point out its own weaknesses. To the foreigner, *however,* such criticism inevitably seems artificial. There is never any criticism of Stalin or his close associates or of the current policy of the Party, only of the way in which it is being executed. Stalin or one of the other leaders of the Party may criticize a policy — *but* this is already the equivalent of an announcement that the policy is being changed. *In addition,* leaders of the Party often attack certain practices of subordinate officials, and once the signal has been given and the appropriate prey designated, ordinary Party members join in the denunciation. This is a useful device for keeping subordinates in order and breaking up any local combinations which might challenge the central Party authorities. *But* the Party's leaders and the Party line are sacrosanct. G. M. CARTER, J. C. RANNEY, and J. H. HERZ

You can see how transitional devices work by entirely removing them. Compare these two paragraphs. The transitional devices are gone from the one on the right:

As has often been said, an inability to admit error is a grave defect of character, often more indicative of weakness than of strength. *For that reason* the very young, the beginners in professional life, find it far more difficult to confess their mistakes publicly than do the old hands. The young teacher, *for example,* can rarely bring himself to admit a mistake committed before an entire class. He may feel that the public admission of error will undermine his position with the students. Experienced teachers, *on the other hand,* readily and cheerfully acknowledge mistakes without fear that the students will think the less of them. *Thus* by a kind of paradox the very people who most need to admit error are the ones least prepared to do so.	An inability to admit error is a grave defect of character, often more indicative of weakness than of strength. The very young, the beginners in professional life, find it far more difficult to confess their mistakes publicly than do the old hands. The young teacher can rarely bring himself to admit a mistake committed before an entire class. He may feel that public admission of error will undermine his position with the students. Experienced teachers can readily and cheerfully acknowledge mistakes without fear that the students will think less of them. The very people who most need to admit error are the ones least prepared to do so.

16d.   Flow: Pronouns

Pronouns can also hold thoughts together. But you must be sure to make the subject that each pronoun refers to clear and unambiguous.

Coming into Richmond, Indiana, Barton knew better than to run the risk of stopping again. Roadside rests, drive-in parking lots, truck stops, all seemed out of the question. For the hundredth time *he* pushed his numbed mind through possible alternatives, alternatives arranged in his head like some gargantuan laundry list. *He* could pull in behind a garage, pay the attendant a dollar, and sleep in the parked car. The idea was attractive, but suppose the attendant grew suspicious about the reluctance of the sleeping passenger to visit the men's room? *He* could look for a lonely road, turn off, and park somewhere in a wood. But suppose *he* were to oversleep in the morning? What then? A farmer would discover *him* in the early dawn light. *He* began to realize all over again how much more difficult inconspicuousness was in the country than in the city. Sleeping along the highway was also unthinkable. The turnpike scare had taught *him* that (*he* could still feel the heat of the cop's flashlight in his eyes). What about a motel? The idea seemed absurd on the face of it, but as *he* weighed the merits and demerits of the scheme it seemed less foolish. After all, *he* thought, motels generally give you the key and let you drive over to your room alone.

16e.   Flow: Combining the Methods

Usually a paragraph will be put together with two or more of these methods to get it to flow. A passage by George Orwell shows how the design can be unified by an intricate network of cross-references:

And yet the gentleness of English civilisation is mixed up with *barbarities and anachronisms*. Our criminal law is as *out of date* as the *muskets in the Tower*. Over against the Nazi Storm Trooper you have got to set that typically English figure, the *hanging* judge, some gouty old *bully* with his mind rooted in the nineteenth century, handing out savage sentences. In England until recently people were still *hanged* by the neck and *flogged* with the *cat o'nine tails*. Both of these punishments are *obscene* as well as *cruel,* but there has never been any genuinely popular outcry against them. People accept *them* (and Dartmoor and Borstal) almost as they accept the weather. *They* are part of "the law," which is assumed to be unalterable.

Theme words that control the paragraph are *barbarities* and *anachronisms; out of date* picks up idea of *anachronisms; hanging* and *bully* refer back to *barbarities; hanged* and *flogged* continue *barbarities* theme. Pronoun *them* refers back to *punishments*. Pronoun *they* relates close of paragraph to opening sentence, tying things together neatly.

EXERCISES

A. Look for transitional devices in the opening paragraphs of your history, sociology, or economics textbook. Do they fit a pattern described here, or do they combine these methods in various ways?

B. Discuss the devices used to get focus and flow in this paragraph. How often does the writer repeat key words and phrases to amplify the controlling idea? Where does he use transitional words and phrases and pronouns?

It is almost as safe to assume that an artist of any dignity is against his country, i.e., against the environment in which God hath placed him, as it is to assume that his country is against the artist. The special quality which makes an artist of him might almost be defined, indeed, as an extraordinary capacity for irritation, a pathological sensitiveness to environmental pricks and stings. He differs from the rest of us mainly because he reacts sharply and in an uncommon manner to phenomena which leave the rest of us unmoved, or, at most, merely annoy us vaguely. He is, in brief, a more delicate fellow than we are, and hence less fitted to prosper and enjoy himself under the conditions of life which he and we must face alike. Therefore, he takes to artistic endeavor, which is at once a criticism of life and an attempt to escape from life. H. L. MENCKEN

C. One way of testing paragraph coherence is to scramble the order of the sentences and then ask someone who has not seen the original version to put them back in their original sequence. Rearrange these into their original order:

1. (A) Newton's contemporaries came to believe that not only were the secrets of nature discoverable by human reason but that nature herself must be reasonable. (B) According to Newton, the universe was a kind of well-oiled machine which operated according to well-defined laws of mathematical probability. (C) They therefore placed great stress on reason in the realm of art as well as in nature. (D) The result was a poetry and music dominated by wit rather than emotion, an architecture characterized by harmony rather than discord, and a social outlook increasingly marked by humanitarianism rather than indifference to the sufferings of the poor. (E) In the eighteenth century the lives of men were heavily influenced by Isaac Newton's theory about the nature of the universe.

2. (A) Like poetry and music, modern painting is also maddeningly obscure, mostly because the painter is more interested in capturing essential than superficial truth about what he sees around him. (B) Most modern art reflects the disorder the artist finds in the world he lives in. (C) Similarly modern music is harsh and dissonant because the composer in an industrial age hears only factory whistles and jet engines, not the bucolic peace of the countryside Beethoven and Mozart heard. (D) A fragmentary poem like T. S. Eliot's *The Waste Land* is really a shattered epic, shattered because Eliot would have looked ridiculous writing an epic modeled on the cool certainty of the *Iliad* or the *Aeneid*. (E) Consequently the question that comes to mind is how far art can go when it ceases to embody a coherent form. (F) After all, art demands the imposition by the painter, composer, or poet of form on formlessness, of order on disorder, of cosmos on chaos.

D. Challenge your technical powers by writing paragraphs from these topic sentences in which you underline (1) all transitional words and phrases; (2) the theme word in the topic sentence; and (3) the word or phrases amplifying the theme word in each sentence. Of course, in consultation with your instructor, you may wish to modify the sentences or the assignment.

1. Since the 1970 riots, American campuses have reflected a growing student apathy. 2. Many young people today prefer careers as nature freaks to pursuing conventional professions. 3. Most of my classmates think and talk alike. 4. Nonconformists often invent new forms of conformity. 5. The myth of rural virtue annoys many city dwellers. 6. The automobile has almost singlehandedly wrecked America's ecology. 7. Women have been brainwashed by society into accepting the myth of their inferiority to men. 8. Ethnic consciousness has undermined the melting pot idea in America in the past decade. 9. Man's highest goal is to know himself. 10. Man's highest goal is to serve others. 11. The grading system destroys a student's ability to learn. 12. Violence in films and television threatens the sanity of the population. 13. Professional football displays the streak of sadism in the American psyche. 14. Football coaches discriminate against women by not allowing them equal opportunity to play. 15. There are times when a lie is justified.

AMPLIFICATION

17. How Do I Amplify a Paragraph?

Amplifying the topic sentence, and its implied attitude, involves the writer in all the major rhetorical strategies. What are the best means for getting his point across? Not to be confused with inflation (repetitiously padding a paper with meaningless statements), amplification results organically from raising questions about the topic of the paragraph. By putting yourself in the reader's position and by anticipating the reader's questions, you as writer decide what to include in the paragraph. Have you given examples? Have you defined words? Have you compared the topic with a related idea? Have you tried to explain causes? Effects? Have you divided the subject? Enumerated it? Classified it? Arranged it systematically in some kind of logical order? The question the paragraph answers will generate a pattern for the paragraph. A description of a ferry crossing the river is *temporal* and *spatial,* and the search for the causes of World War II is *causal.* A description of a dishwasher is *spatial,* and an analysis of a word's meaning is *definitive.* Paragraphs that are heavily descriptive rely mainly on words and analytical paragraphs depend on logic. These methods of amplification are arranged in order of the movement from word to thought:

1. Details and particulars
2. Illustration
3. Spatial order
4. Chronological order
5. Comparison and contrast
6. Analogy
7. Giving reasons
8. Logic, or order of importance
9. Cause and effect
10. Eliminating alternatives
11. Clarification and restatement
12. Combined methods

Think of these twelve methods as an alphabet for paragraphing, not as separate and absolute methods. The average paragraph combines two or more of them into a whole design. Probably the most common method of development is the twelfth, *combined methods* (see 171). And it goes without saying that most enter into constructing all types of expository prose as well as the paragraph.

17a.   Amplification: Details and Particulars

Supplying specific details to answer the questions "What?" or "How?" is the most obvious way of amplifying a paragraph. Most people are not satisfied with generalities. They want information in detail. Here George Orwell puts details to work:

How complete or truthful a picture has Kipling left us of the long-service, mercenary army of the late nineteenth century? One must say of this, as of what Kipling wrote about nineteenth-century Anglo-India, that it is not only the best but almost the only literary picture we have. He has put on record an immense amount of stuff that one could otherwise only gather from verbal tradition. . . . from the body of Kipling's early work there does seem to emerge a vivid and not seriously misleading picture of the *old pre-machine-gun army — the swelte ng barracks in Gibraltar* or *Lucknow,* the *red coats,* the *pipeclayed belts* and the *pillbox hats,* the *beer,* the *fights,* the *floggings, hangings* and *crucifixions,* the *bugle-calls,* the smell of *oats* . . . the *bellowing* sergeants with *foot-long moustaches,* the *bloody skirmishes,* invaria-

Rhetorical question is effective as lead sentence.

Subject (topic).

Harvest of details to support the main thesis. Paragraph is primarily analytic, not descriptive.

Close accumulation of details, gradually building up to a major assault on the reader's sight (*bloody skirmishes*), hearing (*bugle-calls*), touch (*floggings*), smell (*oats*), and even possibly taste (*beer*).

bly mismanaged, the *crowded* troopships, the *cholera-stricken* camps, the "native" concubines, the ultimate death in the *workhouse*. It is a crude, vulgar picture, in which a patriotic music-hall term seems to have got mixed up with one of Zola's gorier passages, but from it future generations will be able to gather some idea of what a long-term volunteer army was like.

Summarizing statement.

EXERCISE

A. Using details and particulars as the major mode of development, write paragraphs of at least 150 words on two of these topics, going from the general to the particular in one paragraph and from the particular to the general in the second paragraph. Pretend the audience for your paper is a student from another country.

1. A dorm room. 2. The campus bookstore. 3. Drag races. 4. A popular film. 5. The population explosion. 6. Air pollution. 7. Religion on campus. 8. Pop bands. 9. Pro football. 10. The drug peril.

17b. Amplification: Illustration

The difference between amplification by details and by illustration is merely quantitative. Details are small parts of a whole, and illustrations are larger examples of the whole. Details add up to description; illustration to a kind of mini-narration. A man's character is suggested by the details of his dress (hat, shoes, tie, socks), but something about his character can also be inferred from one or two illustrations of his behavior (how he asks for his coffee in a cafe, how he addresses his female office help).

The student paragraph about Socrates on the left is developed by details: the right-hand paragraph uses illustration:

AMPLIFICATION BY DETAILS

Socrates was a stoic saint. What made him a saint, or what his sainthood made him, was a man of great calm, even in the midst of appalling trouble. As a younger man in battle, he had shown powers of physical strength and courage beyond that of most men. The dialogues of Plato also testify to his abilities as a *talker, party-goer,* and *imbiber* (he *wined* and *dined* long after every-

AMPLIFICATION BY ILLUSTRATION

Socrates was the stoic saint. Few readers of Plato's dialogues will easily forget the conversation between Socrates and his friend Crito, who came with the news that the ship from Delos was shortly to arrive in the harbor. Crito, as always earnest and well meaning, had with the help of friends worked out a complete scheme for spiriting Socrates out of Athens to safety in exile. Any or-one else had collapsed). His finest hour came before the jury of *501* fellow *Athenians* who condemned him to die by *drinking* the *hemlock* cup in *399* B.C. Socrates, who never lost his nerve, delivered in the great amphitheater of the courtroom a speech so memorable that it still stands as a major document in Western culture. Undismayed by threats of *imprisonment, exile, flogging,* and even *death by poison,* he entered into the record of time his plea that "*the unexamined life is not worth living.*" Later, when he died, after *pacing* around the small room of his *detention,* his last thoughts were not of himself but of others: *Crito, Xanthippe, Cimmias,* and even the *jailer.*

dinary man, faced with the prospect of imminent death, would have yielded to temptation and would have taken advantage of the offer. Not Socrates. Showing the temper of the saint, he spurned the chance to escape as a cowardly and contemptible gesture. Thus he deliberately chose death, and in so doing marched into the pages of history.

The paragraph developed by details carries a higher percentage of specific words (italicized). It also relies mostly on the accumulated details, whereas the other paragraph counts mostly on telling one incident to make the same point: Socrates was a saint.

EXERCISE

A. Expand one or two of these topics into brief paragraphs of at least 150 words, using illustration as your major mode of development. Envision as audience someone who doesn't sympathize with your point of view and is suspicious of you.

1. The case for (or against) busing.   2. The perils of hard drugs.   3. The need for reform in American medical care.   4. Some first-rate investments in the stock market.   5. The film craze among students.   6. Advantages of a career army.   7. Shoplifting — a national disease.   8. The high cost of dying.   9. The suburban shopping center — threat to the cities.   10. Student input in faculty promotion and tenure — relevant or irrelevant?

17c.   Amplification: Spatial Order

Time and space are as fundamental in organizing prose as they were in building the universe. A description of objects will result in an ordering of space, and a description of a process will bring about an order in time. The subject that you develop spatially must have height, depth, or length, and must be fairly static. (Time should stand still during the description.) Description that you develop temporally must have passing time in it and must be kinetic, in a state of movement. If you were asked to describe New York's Adirondack Park you would write a spatially organized paragraph (for further discussion of chronology, see 17d).

If we consider its location in the most densely populated quadrant of the country, the very existence of the Adirondack Park is surprising, enough so that the measurements of quantity and size needed to describe it seem almost a form of ostentation. It contains 6 million acres — 3.5 million in private ownership, 2.5 million owned by the State of New York. It is an area about the size of Vermont, and almost a million acres more than the combined area of Yellowstone, Yosemite, Grand Canyon, Glacier and Olympic National Parks. It embraces all or part of 12 counties, two of which are larger than small states. It has more than 40 peaks above 4,000 feet, among them Mt. Marcy (5,344 ft.), the highest in New York. It has hundreds of lakes; the park is quilted with them from Champlain to Cranberry, from Chateaugay to Sacandaga. It contains and protects the headwaters of five major water basins, including the Mohawk, the St. Lawrence and the Hudson; and within its boundaries flow more than 10,000 miles of rivers and streams.

It is a landscape of infinite variety. It has millions of acres of forests, thousands of acres of wetlands. It has high waterfalls, deep gorges, rolling countryside, alpine summits. It houses both endangered and abundant species of plants and wildlife. It has names that linger in the ear, names like Noonmark, Boreas Pond, Tahawus, Lake Tear-of-the-Clouds. Its images linger in the mind. It is, in short, a natural pageant of unusual richness, a feast for the eye and spirit in a time of unusual need. COURTNEY JONES

EXERCISE

A. Expand some of these general ideas into paragraphs of no fewer than 100 words, developing them by spatial methods. Tell your audience, unfamiliar with your subject, what it looks like.

1. A sports car. 2. A baseball diamond. 3. A stadium. 4. An airport. 5. A modern house. 6. A jet airplane. 7. A stamp collection. 8. A sailboat. 9. A skyscraper. 10. A local park.

17d. Amplification: Chronological Order

Almost any time you describe an event you turn out a *chronological* or *sequential* arrangement of facts. A 1937 description of the return of the survivors from the United States Navy gunboat *Panay* answers the question, "In what order did the events occur?" The answer becomes not so much an amplification, as an expanded outline:

When the *Oahu* was first sighted, a curious murmur of suppressed excitement was felt the whole length of the 10,000 ton cruiser, whose decks were crowded with officers, sailors, marines, and a few civilians. It was not a manifestation of relief or enthusiasm when the *Oahu* made fast alongside the *Augusta*. Instead, those aboard the flagship stood in oppressed silence when they saw the survivors on the *Oahu* decks, whose faces in most cases were drawn and lined, many suffering obviously from shell shock; others had their arms in slings, while others wore conspicuous bandages.

A few hands were raised in salutes and greetings, and a few almost-hushed salutations were exchanged across the narrowing waters as the ships drew together while daylight faded rapidly. A hastily improvised gangway, of unplaned and unpainted lumber, was shoved from *Augusta's* deck onto *Oahu's* top deck, and a few of *Augusta's* officers boarded the rescue ship. Then came a long wait, after which *Augusta* sailors carried empty stretchers aboard the *Oahu,* while blue-uniformed marines guarded the gangway and a majority of *Augusta's* officers stood silent, waiting, in a semicircle. Admiral Harry E. Yarnell, Commander-in-Chief of the United States Asiatic Fleet, sat grim-faced in his quarters awaiting oral reports of surviving officers on the *Panay,* many of whom were grievously wounded. HALLET ABEND

EXERCISE

A. Expand some of these general ideas into paragraphs, developing them by chronological methods. Think of the paragraphs as parts of a letter to a friend still in high school.

1. How I get from bed to breakfast.   2. How I get from breakfast to class.   3. How I move from English class to my next class.   4. How I walk from the English building to the library.   5. How I wander through the union building.   6. How I go through an art gallery.   7. How I drive to school.   8. How I avoid my creditors.   9. How I evade bores. 10. How I prepare for an examination: the fantasy and the reality.

17e.   Amplification: Comparison and Contrast

Essentially methods of analysis, comparison, and contrast require that you detect likenesses and discover differences. You need deftness to manage the design of both the sentence and the paragraph to keep the comparison's two sides coordinated and symmetrical. Usually similar things, ideas, and people are compared; opposing things, ideas, and people are contrasted. Thus, two fictional heroes may be compared, but hero and villain must be contrasted. We can call the two methods most often used for comparing and contrasting the *divergent* and the *convergent*. The divergent, or apartness, method calls for comparing A with B by first telling everything about A and then telling everything about B. Ideally some kind of parallelism should appear in the order of presentation, so that the discussion of B follows the same order as that of A. On the other hand, some divergent paragraphs in comparison achieve success without much logical order. With the convergent method, the writer will not compare A to B as a whole but will instead compare logically related parts of A and B, presenting them in the least confusing way.

Consider the possibilities for an opening paragraph in an essay comparing and contrasting Sinclair Lewis' *Babbitt* and Edith Wharton's *The Age of Innocence*. If you choose the divergent method to expand your essay, your outline will be like the left one. Use the convergent method, and all that had been primary now is subsidiary. The structural scheme is reversed, as the outline on the right shows.

DIVERGENT METHOD	CONVERGENT METHOD
I. Sinclair Lewis' *Babbitt*	I. Analysis of Themes
A. Theme	A. *Babbitt*
B. Characters	B. *The Age of Innocence*
C. Situations	II. Analysis of Characters
II. Edith Wharton's *The Age of Innocence*	A. *Babbitt*
A. Theme	B. *The Age of Innocence*
B. Characters	III. Analysis of Situations
C. Situations	A. *Babbitt*
	B. *The Age of Innocence*

Sinclair Lewis' *Babbitt* and Edith Wharton's *The Age of Innocence* show similarities in treatment of theme, characters, and situations. Lewis' *Babbitt,* which is set against a backdrop of the midwestern city of Zenith, becomes a kind of mock-epic as the contrast emerges between the pettiness of the characters and the physical size of the bustling city. Torn between his obligation to self and family, the cartoon-like George Babbitt fumbles his way to a half-recognition of what he really is, though Sinclair Lewis remains true enough to the comic spirit not to allow his buffoon a complete anagnorisis. The round of dinner parties, of social gatherings, of shady business transactions is a mirror of American life during that period after World War I when the nation was coming of age. By comparison, Miss Wharton's *The*

At first glance no two novels of manners could seem more alien to each other than Sinclair Lewis' *Babbitt* and Edith Wharton's *The Age of Innocence.* What could be further removed from the Fifth Avenue of Newland Archer than the Zenith of George Babbitt? Babbitt sticks in the popular mind as the archetypal Midwestern booster, while Newland Archer — for those who know about him — remains the epitome of Eastern effeteness. The chasm between their wives — Myra Babbitt and May Welland — seems equally immense: the Babbitt living room and the Beaufort ballroom exist in divided and distinguished worlds. Moreover Lewis' novel is a frontal assault, while Edith Wharton's is an infiltration in depth: the one smashes, while the other probes. Taken together the two works illustrate the difference between the

Age of Innocence grows out of the quiet elegance of lower Fifth Avenue in the last part of the nineteenth century, when ladies and gentlemen still rode in coaches and broughams toward the park. Newland Archer is no grubby opportunist like Babbitt but a fixture in New York professional and social life, yet he shares Babbitt's indecisiveness about the duty of a man to himself and to his family. And Miss Wharton's novel reveals much about the lives of upper-crust New Yorkers of the Gilded Age, whose round of balls and parties and dinners shares curious parallels to those of Zenith's Myra Babbitt and George McKelvey.

"redskin" and the "paleface" in American fiction. Or from another perspective, they might be thought to represent two Americas: that of an East tinged with European awareness and that of a Midwest blessed by native innocence.

When do you choose the convergent and when the divergent method? That depends on whether you are more interested in the whole or in the parts of the subjects you are comparing. A comparison between the important mayors of two large cities may work quite well with the divergent method if you are interested mostly in the men's personalities; if you are looking mainly at their techniques or their performance, then the convergent method might be wiser.

EXERCISES

A. Write paragraphs of no fewer than 100 words comparing two or more of these pairs for someone who has said there is no difference between them:

1. Hotel and motel. 2. Oscillate and vibrate. 3. Fat and grease. 4. Rogue and villain. 5. Artist and artisan. 6. Deck and floor. 7. Jet and fanjet. 8. Uninviting and disgusting. 9. American football and English football. 10. Baseball and cricket. 11. Atmosphere and stratosphere. 12. Earth and moon. 13. Robbery and burglary. 14. Destroy and annul.

B. Write paragraphs of 100 words or more contrasting two or more of these pairs for an audience in the mood to be entertained:

1. Rest and motion. 2. Virtue and vice. 3. Limpid and hazy. 4. Joy and sorrow. 5. Talkative and mute. 6. Winter and summer. 7. Work and play. 8. Cowardice and courage. 9. Honorable and shameful. 10. Anxiety and calmness.

C. Write paragraphs of 150 words or more using either the convergent or divergent method of comparison. Select from among these pairs:

1. Adult westerns and children's westerns. 2. Safety in air and automobile travel. 3. A drafted army and a volunteer army. 4. Service in the army and in the navy. 5. Commercial and educational television. 6. Two similar cities. 7. Life in the inner city and in the suburbs. 8. Campus (and adult) attitudes toward religion. 9. Pass-fail grades and letter grades.

17f.   Amplification: Analogy

We use analogy, a teaching device, in response to the question, "Can you put this into words that I can understand?" It differs from mere comparison and contrast by getting at the underlying similarities between objects and ideas. Analogies contain some logical hazards (see 24n), but if properly managed rhetoric finds uses for them. Edward Bellamy's analogy between society and a stagecoach opens his *Looking Backward,* a nineteenth-century utopian novel:

By the way of attempting to give the reader some general impression of the way people lived together in those days, and especially of the relations of the rich and poor to one another, perhaps I cannot do better than to compare society as it then was to a prodigious coach which the masses of humanity were harnessed to and dragged toilsomely along a very hilly and soily road. The driver was hungry, and permitted no lagging, though the pace was necessarily very slow. Despite the difficulty of drawing the coach at all along so hard a road, the top was covered with passengers who never got down, even at the steepest ascents. The seats on top were very breezy and comfortable. Well up out of the dust, their occupants could enjoy the scenery at their leisure, or critically discuss the merits of the straining team. Naturally such places were in great demand and the competition for them was very keen, everyone seeking as the first end in life to secure a seat on the coach for himself and to leave it to his child after him. By the rule of the coach a man could leave his seat to whom he wished, but on the other hand there were many accidents by which it might at any time be wholly lost. For all that they were so easy, the seats were very insecure, and at every sudden jolt of the coach persons were slipping out of them and falling to the ground, where they were instantly compelled to take hold of the rope and help to drag the coach on which they had before ridden so pleasantly. It was naturally regarded as a terrible misfortune to lose one's seat, and the apprehension that this might happen to them or their friends was a constant cloud upon the happiness of those who rode.

But did they think only of themselves? you ask. Was not their very luxury rendered intolerable to them by comparison with the lot of their brothers and sisters in the harness, and the knowledge that their own weight added to their toil? Had they no compassion for fellow beings from whom fortune only distinguished them? Oh, yes: commiseration was frequently expressed by those who rode for those who had to pull the coach, especially when the vehicle came to a bad place in the road, as it was constantly doing, or to a particularly steep hill. At such times, the desperate straining of the team, their agonized leaping and plunging under the pitiless lashing of hunger, the many who fainted at the rope and were trampled in the mire, made a very distressing spectacle, which often called forth highly creditable displays of feeling on the top of the coach. At such times the passengers would call down encouragingly to the toilers of the rope, exhorting them to patience, and holding out hopes of possible compensation in another world for the harshness of their lot, while others contributed to buy salves and liniments for the crippled and injured. It was agreed that it was a great pity that the coach should be so hard to pull, and there was a sense of general relief when the specially bad piece of road was gotten over. This relief was not, indeed, wholly on account of the team, for there was always some danger at these bad places of a general overturn in which all would lose their seats.

It must in truth be admitted that the main effect of the spectacle of the misery of the toilers at the rope was to enhance the passengers' sense of the value of their seats upon the coach, and to cause them to hold onto them more desperately than before. If the passengers could only have felt assured that neither they nor their friends would ever fall from the top, it is probable that, beyond contributing to the funds for liniments and bandages, they would have troubled themselves extremely little about those who dragged the coach.

I am well aware that this will appear to the men and women of the twentieth century an incredible inhumanity.

EXERCISE

A. Write analogies of 100 words or more, tying these ideas together:

1. Atom and universe. 2. Football and war. 3. Team and business organization. 4. Family quarrel and tornado. 5. Course of true love and passage of a ship. 6. Search for truth and voyage around the world. 7. Conquering the self and slaying a mythical dragon. 8. Arrival into adult world and initiation rites of a fraternity. 9. Life's difficulties and climbing a mountain.

17g.   Amplification: Giving Reasons

The reasons we give to support our opinions make up much of our discourse. Employing both rhetoric and logic, paragraphs that give reasons or "proofs" answer the question, "Why do you think so?" One way to determine if a paragraph has been amplified by reasons is to apply the "because" test. If it begins "The University of Prairie is the greatest university in the Middle West," the controlling theme is greatness. What are some reasons why Prairie is a great university? Or, the University of Prairie is great because — why? The paragraph then becomes a list of causes for the university's greatness. And it then resembles the kind of paragraph in which we deliberately relate causes to effects (see 17i).

The University of Prairie is the greatest university in the Middle West because:

1. Its physical facilities are outstanding: dormitories, a student union, a theater, an art museum, and a natural history museum.

2. On its faculty are men and women outstanding in their chosen fields of scholarship: history, economics, literature, chemistry, or psychology.

3. Its curriculum is wide and diverse and is suited to the needs of all kinds of people, whether they are planning a career in law, medicine, business, scholarship, or engineering.

4. Its library has nearly one million volumes and important collections of rare books and manuscripts.

5. It upholds the search for truth in nature and beauty in art as the most worthwhile pursuit known to mankind.

6. It has an athletic program to hold the interest of most students and alumni.

When the inventory is done the author can rework a crude list into a well-made paragraph or even expand it to theme size:

[1] One of the great universities in the Middle West is the University of Prairie, located in Boondock, near the eastern border of the state. [2] The traveler approaching from the west first glimpses the red-topped roofs of the impressive physical plant that soar several hundred feet above the rolling plains below. [3] A complex of new dormitories, a luxuriously equipped student union building, a modern theater that has attracted favorable comment from theater authorities all over the world, a small but impeccably arranged art gallery, and an outstanding museum of natural history — all catch the eye of the visitor. [4] Less apparent, but perhaps even more important to the reputation of the university, are the outstanding men and women in many fields of scholarly endeavor who make up the school's faculty. [5] Nearly every department boasts one or two, and in most cases several, scholars or scientists of national and inter-

1. Overstated claim of *greatest* toned down to *one of the great.*

2. The *traveler* introduces a narrative touch.

3. Campus buildings now in logical sequence. Imaginary visitor used again.

4. An appropriate transition before introducing *faculty* in sentence 5.

5. *Faculty* described.

national reputation. [6] A glance at the
university catalogue shows that students benefit from the wide-ranging array of courses,
which permit training in everything from
Greek to business administration. [7] Particularly outstanding is the university library, now holding nearly one million volumes and many special collections of rare
and valuable books and manuscripts. [8] A
few years ago a British scholar working in
the Prairie library with the local staff discovered a leaf from an Old English manuscript in the binding of a seventeenth-century
book. [9] That such a discovery should be
made where a century ago stood little more
than a wilderness would astound the early
settlers of the state. [10] The university also
offers the kind of athletic program considered appropriate in its conference, but primarily its claim to present or future greatness must rest — along with all other universities — on its degree of commitment to
the life of the mind and spirit.

6. Specific examples:
   courses offered.

7. Stresses library
   holdings.

8. Precise and vivid
   illustration.

9. Expands point made
   in 8.

10. Ends with a summary.

EXERCISE

A. Find five reasons to support one of these topic sentences; rearrange the
   reasons in order of ascending importance; add transitional phrases and
   words; and polish and touch up the list to make it into a respectable paragraph (use the preceding illustration as a model):

   1. Attempts at drug control have failed because _____. 2. Young
   people have rejected the idea of compulsory military service because
   _____. 3. Coeducation has dominated American higher education
   because _____. 4. _____ stands out among television programs
   because _____. 5. Law enforcement should be a more prestigious
   occupation than it is because _____.

17h.   Amplification: Logic, or Order of Importance

   More a matter of logic than content, the reasons advanced for an opinion
should be presented according to some scale of ascending or descending importance. Usually the weightiest reason is reserved for last, though the opposite
approach may sometimes be appropriate. An arbitrary triadic scheme, such as
that Sir Francis Bacon applied in his *Essays* (1625), helps to schematize and
ensure logical progression. See the following example but remember that this
manner of presentation is not hard to overdo:

[1] Studies serve [a] for delight, [b] for ornament, and [c] for ability. [2] Their chief use for [a¹] delight is in privateness and retiring; [b¹] for ornament, is in discourse; and [c¹] for ability, is in the judgement and disposition of business. [3] For expert men can execute, and perhaps judge of particulars, one by one; but [a] the general counsels, and [b] the plots and [c] marshalling of affairs come best from those that are learned. [4] [a²] To spend too much time in studies is sloth; [b²] to use them too much for ornament is affectation; [c²] to make judgement wholly by their rules is the humour of a scholar.

Topic statement asserts tripartite problem in a, b, and c. Next sentence picks up the three parts and elaborates on them in the same sequence: a¹, b¹, c¹.

Sentence 3 continues the three-part arrangement, showing how learning helps develop leadership.

Sentence 4 restates and elaborates the assertion in sentence 1 by going back to the pitfalls for studies implied in sentence 1, in the same a², b², c² sequence.

A student writer works a modern variation on the Baconian method in arguing one-sidedly but energetically for a change in graduation requirements:

The requirements for the undergraduate degree are wrapped up in the clothing of a mummy. Who today needs the kind of education that was considered proper for a nineteenth-century clergyman or classics teacher? Irrelevance, fatuousness, and uselessness characterize much of what goes on in the modern classroom. It is fatuous to expect the average student to master mathematics when he will not even be asked to balance his own checkbook in later life. It is irrelevant to require students to study courses that they have no aptitude for whatsoever. "One man's meat is another man's poison" is an old adage that the educators have apparently never heard of. And it is all useless simply because it does not work. How many young people receiving their diplomas can be said to be educated in any meaningful sense of the word?

Triadic arrangement; *irrelevance, fatuousness,* and *uselessness.*

Most powerful of the three reasons is reserved for the last.

EXERCISE

A. Write paragraphs of 100 words or more each on two or more of these topics. Arrange the material in order of importance proceeding from the more to the less important, or from the less to the more important.

1. Under American industrial capitalism all ambitious citizens prosper. 2. Welfare clients should be forced to take on menial jobs.   3. Farmers and businessmen who accept subsidies from the federal government have lost the right to complain about welfare clients.   4. Fraternity membership remains immensely valuable, despite all the arguments against it from disgruntled outsiders.   5. Federal social security places an unfair burden on young people.   6. Despite complaints, minority groups in America fare better than those in other lands, such as the Soviet Union. 7. The conservatives are right in demanding that the schools return to an emphasis on fundamentals.   8. The evolution of the rocket industry has been very exciting.   9. Voyages to the moon should be given a low priority in the national budget.   10. Childless persons should not be taxed to pay for the schools.

17i.   Amplification: Cause and Effect

"What caused it?" is a fundamental question. Theories of cause and effect cut across logic, grammar, and rhetoric. In grammar, cause and effect generate the result clause in the kind of sentence that reads:

CAUSE	EFFECT
His temper was so savage	that the class felt uncomfortable.

In rhetoric, as in grammar, the cause and effect paragraph can grow from a statement about either a cause or an effect. Observation of phenomena precedes construction of the paragraph: "The campus is jammed with cars" (effect); what is the cause? "The professor is a learned man" (effect); what is the cause? "The grades of the fraternity are slipping" (effect); what is the cause? "The noise at night in the dormitory is intolerable" (cause); what are the effects? This paragraph by Charles Reich is organized around this pattern:

EFFECT *Loss of self.* Of all of the forms of impoverishment that can be seen or felt in America, loss of self, or death in life, is surely the most devastating. It is, even more than the draft and the Vietnam War, the source of discontent and rage in the new generation. Beginning with school, if not before, an individual is systematically stripped of his imagination, his creativity, his heritage, his dreams, and his personal uniqueness, in order to style him into a productive unit for a mass, technological society. Instinct, feeling, and spontaneity are repressed by overwhelming forces. As the individual is CAUSE drawn into the meritocracy, his working life is split from his home life, and both suffer from a lack of wholeness. Eventually, people virtually become their professions, roles, or occupations, and are thenceforth strangers to themselves. Blacks long ago felt their deprivation of identity and potential for life. But white "soul" and blues are just beginning. Only a segment of youth is articulately aware that they too suffer an enforced loss of self — they too are losing the lives that could be theirs.

EXERCISE

A. Write paragraphs in cause and effect of 100 words or more each, based on these statements:

1. Hiroshima was devastated on that irrevocable day in August 1946 when the Americans dropped the A-bomb.

2. At the end, the patient becomes a mere vegetable, subject to hallucination, commonly called d.t.'s, and to an unslakable thirst for strong drink.

3. Even by the end of World War II the popularity of Adolf Hitler with the German people remained almost the same as it had been in 1933.

4. The Watergate scandal threw American society into confusion.

5. The United States Supreme Court has taken a firmer stand against pornography.

17j.   Amplification: Eliminating Alternatives

The paragraph can be amplified by elimination, which John Stuart Mill (1806–1873) described as "the method of residues." Often useful in argument (see Chapter 7), this method negatively substantiates a thesis by pointing out that the alternatives are impossible. These paragraphs by Senator J. W. Fulbright and by a student use this technique:

[1] The uncritical acceptance of a simple equation between security and armaments can only lead us into an accelerating arms race, mounting international tensions, and diminishing security. [2] It is quite possible for us to possess overwhelming military superiority and still be confronted with the erosion of our power and influence in the world — [a] if our alliance system is allowed to weaken, [b] if confidence in our resolution is called into question, if our judgment is too often doubted, [c] if our political and economic policies are ineffective, [d] or if by ill-considered unilateral measures we provoke our adversaries into hostile countermeasures. We must therefore avoid giving undue weight to the political views of highly specialized technical experts whose experience and knowledge have only very limited relevance to the complexities of international relations. [3] War, said Clemenceau, is too serious a business to be left to the generals. [4] It is

1. Thesis attacks idea of equation between national security and armaments.

2. In turn, author offers other reasons in parallel series for national security:

   a. weakening of alliances.
   b. questioning of resolution.
   c. ineffective economic policies.
   d. provocation of adversaries.

3. Warns against heeding *expert* advice.

also too serious a business to be left to the nuclear physicists or, indeed, to anyone except an elected political leadership whose experience and competence are not in specific technical fields but in understanding the generality of the nation's problems, their effects upon each other, and the relative importance of one as against another.

4. By elimination, the best alternative is to heed the advice of *elected political leadership* who are generalists.

[1] The statement by T. S. Eliot that the influence of Milton has been pernicious seems all the more remarkable when one considers the place of *Paradise Lost* as the most important long poem of its era. [2] Even so popular a poet as Abraham Cowley could not stir up any real interest with his readable but fragmentary *Davideis,* a biblical poem based on Old Testament legend. [3] The industrious William D'Avenant, heavily influenced by the French romances of Mme. de Scudéry and John Barclay, poured his talents into *Gondibert,* a chivalric romance that died almost at birth, little being left of it now but the celebrated preface by Thomas Hobbes. [4] Only the most forlorn graduate students, starved for materials, will read productions as involuted and gnarled as William Chamberlayne's *Pharonnida,* a neo-Spenserian poem as cavalier in bias as *Paradise Lost* is puritan. [5] In much the same category with Chamberlayne's effort was John Chalkhill's *Thealma and Clearchus: A Pastoral History in Smooth and Easy Verse,* which, though written about 1600, went unpublished until 1683. [6] The inventory of minor poetry could be continued to include the work of Francis Kynaston, of Shakerley Marmion, and perhaps Nathaniel Whiting, but the verdict would remain unchanged. [7] Viewed in the setting of the late seventeenth century, *Paradise Lost* stands out from its contemporaries like some beacon at sea.

1. Thesis states *Paradise Lost* is most important long poem of its time.

2. Cowley eliminated from consideration.

3. D'Avenant is also discarded.

4. Chamberlayne eliminated.

5. Chalkhill eliminated.

6. Kynaston, Marmion, and Whiting are also discarded.

7. *Paradise Lost* remains.

EXERCISE

A. Write paragraphs on one or more of these topics, developing them according to the principle of eliminating alternatives:

1. _____ is the greatest quarterback in the National Football League.
2. Without any question our living group has the (poorest) (best) record on campus for the ability to organize successful social gatherings.   3. The _____ automobile is the best kind of value for its price.   4. The university campus is a girl's best shopping ground for a husband.   5. The philosophy of _____ best fits the needs of a young American student.

17k.   Amplification: Clarification and Restatement

Another way to expand, or fill out, a paragraph is to restate, or perhaps refute, what you have already said. The technique is perilous — in the hands of a bungler it can look like mere padding, and even professional writers can't always keep it from looking like a pretentious pose — nevertheless it can be useful. Probably the supreme master was the American novelist, Henry James. Here is a successful example by a recent writer:

It is men with minds and outlooks formed by such conditions who in postwar America have come to occupy positions of great decision. It cannot be said — as we shall presently make clear — that they have necessarily sought these new positions; much of their increased stature has come to them by virtue of a default on the part of civilian political men. But perhaps it can be said, as C. S. Forester has remarked in a similar connection, that men without lively imagination are needed to execute policies without imagination devised by an elite without imagination. But it must also be said that to Tolstoy's conception of the general at war — as confidence builder pretending by his manner that he knows what the confusion of battle is all about — we must add the image of the general as the administrator of the men and machines which now make up the greatly enlarged means of violence. C. WRIGHT MILLS	I. Military now have authority and power A. They have not sought it. B. Their lack of imagination has fitted them for the role. II. Officer class has moved from confidence building to administration.

17l.   Amplification: Combining the Methods

As you know, you probably won't run into any of the methods of amplifying paragraphs described here in a pure state, any more than oxygen atoms occur independent of other elements in the periodic table. The typical paragraph or composition uses several methods in combination:

And the very similarities of suburbia are pitfalls. When everyone lives in an identical house, the most important item of their estate is washed out as a factor, and the marginal purchases become the key ones. How to choose, then? Would an automatic dishwasher be right at this stage of the game — or would it seem like putting on the dog? On this knotty problem of whether an item is a luxury or a necessity, aggregate national statistics are no guide. Some purchases, such as a car, can be accurately described as a necessity; others, such as a swimming pool, a luxury. But in between these two categories is a great shadow area in which national averages can be illusory. Even in a single neighborhood, what in one block would be an item eminently acceptable might in another be regarded as flagrant showing-off. WILLIAM H. WHYTE, JR.

Takes up question of suburban conformity. Second sentence states problem. Rhetorical question introduces a kind of interior monologue suggesting a voice other than that of the author. Monologue encourages comparisons to illustrate the problem. Specific examples and details.

Comparison between neighborhoods also brings up an implied cause and effect relationship; the behavior of people in suburbs is caused by the social structure.

Foreign visitors are fascinated by the "charm of Italy." Italian life is gay, effervescent, intoxicating. The *dolce vita* looks now more *dolce* than it ever was. Very few travelers see the ugliness underneath, the humiliation, the suffering. The illusion Italy creates is a relief. The Italian way of life down the centuries attracted people who wanted to take a holiday from their national virtues. In the heart of every man there is one small corner which is Italian, that part which loves frivolous and entertaining art, admires larger-than-life solitary heroes, and dreams of an impossible liberation from the strictures of a tidy life. LUIGI BARZINI

Paragraph is built of contrasts and illustrations. First three sentences stress the appearance of Italian life. The fourth sentence introduces the contrast by moving from gay illusion to ugly reality, and makes the key assertion. Next three sentences advance reasons for failure of travelers to see reality. Last sentence gives parallel statements illustrating three ways in which every man is an Italian.

EXERCISE

The ways of amplifying paragraphs described in this chapter give you a checklist to help you find the best options for developing any position. In practice, they make up an alphabet for building paragraphs that you can weave into the fabric of different kinds of paragraphs.

A. These topic sentences can be amplified by using combined methods. Write paragraphs of 100 words or more and use at least two methods, labeling them clearly in the margin. Remember, the methods of amplifying are: (1) details and particulars; (2) illustration; (3) spatial order; (4) chronological order; (5) comparison and contrast; (6) analogy; (7) giving reasons; (8) order of importance; (9) cause and effect (10) eliminating alternatives (11) clarifying and restating; and (12) combined methods.

1. Poor motivation for learning afflicts too high a percentage of high school students.   2. Inability to conform to group values handicaps many unsuccessful persons.   3. Women have traditionally subordinated their own careers to those of their husbands.   4. Some women find liberation in not being forced to work outside the home.   5. The vote for eighteen-year-olds has not really changed American politics at all.   6. Hatred of the umpire reveals deep-seated rebelliousness among baseball fans.   7. Social life among American youth depends entirely on the automobile. 8. Students have recently shown a remarkable interest in the study of death and dying.   9. My favorite singer is _____.   10. The mother-of-the-year should henceforth be a woman who has produced fewer than three children.

17m.   A Related Problem: How Long Is a Paragraph?

A paragraph must be lengthy enough to exhaust the challenge set in the topic sentence. You will have to use intuition and experience to know how long that should be — each paragraph has its own best length. But a good rule of thumb is to put in four to seven sentences varied in length and complexity. Except in formal academic writing and in serious journals, such as *Hudson Review* or *Science,* the long paragraph has just about vanished. Modern journalism, mass audiences, the quickened tempo of life, have discouraged the leisurely meanderings of nineteenth-century essays. A 500-word theme may have four or six paragraphs averaging 80–100 words, though your choice should be anything but mechanical. Generally, increased specialization and seriousness bring on longer paragraphs.

17n.   A Related Problem: When Will a One-Sentence Paragraph Work?

Once you've mastered paragraph construction, you may wish to consider when a one-sentence paragraph is appropriate. As a terminal or initial utterance, a connector, or a punctuator, it can be useful for:

A. DIALOGUE

They sat at the table at the small cafe.

"I need you," she said.

"You've always needed me," he said.

"I never wanted you," she said.

"But that was when the bad part came," he said.

The one-sentence paragraph is used as a punctuator, a device for separating the utterances of characters.

B. EMPHASIS AT A KEY POINT: BEGINNINGS

Harry Williams will not soon forget the nightmare that began for him with a knock on the door that spring evening in 1958.

Before the knock on the door, however, and long before that spring, certain events had occurred which made what was to happen in 1958 inevitable. Few people, let alone Harry Williams, would have paid any attention, for example, to the strange cargo being unloaded from a Japanese freighter, the *Kakikikazu Maru,* at a San Francisco wharf early in 1955. Outwardly the cargo looked like crates of textiles perhaps, or even containers of books. But what those cartons contained was something quite different, something that would in a few months' time enter into Williams' life in a totally strange and unexpected way. While Williams knew nothing about the cargo on the San Francisco wharf, he did know about the telephone call in April 1955, the telephone call which had at first seemed merely the work of a prankster or perhaps some addled teen-ager. "Do you want to see your wife on an embalmer's slab?" the voice had muttered.

The student uses a single sentence for an emphatic beginning and to prepare the way for an atmosphere of suspense.

C. EMPHASIS AT KEY POINT: ENDINGS

Already as the hordes of oppressed were moving out of the cities toward the mountains and the plains, the forces of the emperor were marching toward both Sylvania and Eruptania, important principalities within the Alpine complex. They carried with them as talisman of the cultural *zeitgeist* the raised sword and the gleaming shield covered with the crosses of the Christian God.

No factor in the history of the Holy Roman Empire was more significant or vital than this conquest of Illyria by the Visigoths.

One sentence at close gives a strong period.

The sentence that links the substantial parts of a longer essay is also serviceable. Usually, however, it is too ponderous for a student essay, which is designed to have its parts tied together by the logic of thought and arrangement rather than by such explicit devices as these:

And now we can turn our attention at last to the question of the Waffen SS in the Nazi regime.

Having completed a survey of the Spinozian doctrine of substance and essence, it now seems appropriate to consider the implications of Spinozian belief to western thought in the period immediately prior to what Alfred North Whitehead has called the "century of revolution."

As is well known, the role of the housewife in all societies is crucial to cultural stability, a point to which we can now direct the full attention of this essay.

EXERCISES

A. Here are some sample paragraphs for analysis. As you read them, pick out (1) the topic sentence; (2) the theme word in the topic sentence; (3) the words or phrases amplifying or developing the theme word; (4) key transitional devices, whether words or phrases; and (5) modes of amplification. How many modes dominate the paragraph's structure?

1. It was one of the consequences, and sometimes one of the penalties, of Longfellow's universal fame that, during all these years and to the end of his life, the Craigie House was the resort of an endless succession of visitors, both distinguished and obscure, both fellow countrymen and callers from abroad. Hardly an English man of letters, traveling in America, failed to pay his respects to this most beloved of American writers, and often they were entertained at meals. Dickens, on his first trip to this country, had been given "a bright little breakfast" — the brightness of which seems not to have been dimmed by the presence of "the Unitarian pope," Andrews Norton — and the two young writers struck up a lifelong friendship. Such men as Trollope, Charles Kingsley, Wilkie Collins, and Monckton Milnes arrived on Brattle Street as a matter of course. When Dom Pedro II, Emperor of Brazil, was traveling in this country, not officially but privately — like a modern Haroun Al Raschid, said Longfellow — he expressed his desire to dine with the poet, and rather imperially named the persons — Emerson, Lowell, and Holmes — whom he wished also to have invited. Perhaps the most unlikely visitor, from our point of view, was the Russian anarchist Mikhail Bakúnin, who had escaped from Siberia a few months earlier and, having made his way eastward across the Pacific, en route to Europe, had reached the northern United States, and came to call at the Craigie House. He stayed so long, Ernest Longfellow tells us, that he had to be invited to lunch; "Yiss," he answered, "and I will dine with you too" — as he did. He may have proved a somewhat fatiguing guest — his vehemence was notorious — but Longfellow seems to have been charmed by him, and describes him in his journal as "a giant of a man, with a most ardent, seething temperament." NEWTON ARVIN

2. Both Aldous and Maria loved picnics; the thought of one made them happy as little children. I recall one particular outing with *dramatis personae* so fantastic that they might have come out of *Alice in Wonderland*. There were several Theosophists from India, the most prominent being Krishnamurti. The Indian ladies were dressed in saris which were elegant enough, but the rest of us wore the most casual old sports outfits. Aldous might have been the giant from some circus sideshow; Maria and I could have served as dwarves, but with our tacky clothes the circus would have been pretty second-rate. Nobody would ever have recognized the glamour of Greta Garbo and Paulette Goddard in that tatterdemalion group. To protect themselves from fans who might crop up out of nowhere, Greta was disguised in a pair of men's trousers and a battered hat with a floppy brim that almost covered her face; Paulette wore a native Mexican outfit with colored yarn braided into her hair. Bertrand Russell, visiting Hollywood at the time, Charlie Chaplin, and Christopher Isherwood all looked like naughty pixies out on a spree. Matthew Huxley was the only one of the group who was a mere normally disheveled teen-ager. ANITA LOOS

B. The highly informal, slangy tone of this Tom Wolfe paragraph, reflecting the cultural revolution of the Sixties, did not keep him from using a traditional structure for the paragraph. What methods of amplification does Wolfe use?

The truth is that unless you have flown in combat, you can never be truly accepted into the Brotherhood, no matter what else you may do. There were plenty of pilots in their thirties who, to the consternation of their moms, dads, wives, bosses, Buddy & Sis — they just couldn't freaking believe it — who confounded all by volunteering to go active and fly in Korea. In godforsaken *Korea!* But it was simple enough. Half of them were flyers who had trained during World War II but never seen combat, and this was their last crack at it — at the ascension, at the Right Stuff. This may be hard to believe, but there are astronauts — including some of us who have been to the moon — who have it gnawing at our hearts that we are not truly accepted into the Brotherhood of The Right Stuff because we have never stood that particular trial, which is combat. And there are others of us who have felt worse than that, who have felt the breath of the hairy bear, namely, Guilt, because we spent five or six years training to go to the moon — while good buddies of ours have been flying in Vietnam.

The style is the man himself.
GEORGES BUFFON, Discourse, 1753

While others fish with craft for great opinion,
I with great truth catch mere simplicity;
Whilst some with cunning gild their copper crowns,
With truth and plainness I do wear mine bare.
Fear not my truth; the moral of my wit
Is plain, and true; there's all the reach of it.
SHAKESPEARE, Troilus and Cressida.
IV.iv.102–107, 1601

5   The Writer's Devices:

Style as Function

18.   What Is Style?

Style is the signature a writer puts on words. Mechanically speaking, it results from choosing the right words and putting them in the right order, though precisely how a man of genius does this is one of the universe's ultimate mysteries. Style is manner or form — *how* the subject is written about. Message is the other part of written discourse — *what* is written about, the content. The "how" and the "what" of writing cannot really be separated, because meaning grows out of interaction between form and content. Poets have invented a thousand ways to talk about love, each unique. There is John Donne's "only our love hath no decay / this no tomorrow hath nor yesterday"; Shakespeare's "Let me not to the marriage of true minds admit impediments"; and e. e. cummings' "nobody, not even the rain, has such small hands." Content, love, remains the same, but the form derives from that special imprint of personality, that literary signature, which is the private stamp of each poet. All of this simply reaffirms the wisdom of the aphorism by Georges Buffon: "the style is the man himself."

Yet even the celebrated Buffon did not utter the last word. A creature of both function and artifice, style grows from interaction between "the man himself" and "the subject itself." A writer attempts to control the subject with his style. But the subject sometimes controls the controller, when the functional importance of the subject he is writing about is stronger than the artifice he wields in controlling it. This functional side of prose is our subject now; artifice can wait a chapter. Whether function or artifice is the commanding purpose behind a piece of writing, the writer's responsibility is finding exactly the style or manner that comfortably brings author, subject, and audience together. The business of informing (giving information) calls for an author of unquestioned expertise, not charm; the business of persuasion, an author sensitive to complex human motivations; and the business of convincing, a man of logic. A manual for operating oil burners shuns figurative language and irony, as much as a personal essay disdains technological jargon. Prose is as much a function of purpose as personality, which means you must ask yourself these questions about functional writing: Why am I writing this piece? For whom? Do they know more about it than I do? About as much? Much less?

18a.   What Are Some Options in Style?

Writing style is hard to analyze and teach because of the many kinds of styles that writers can choose among and the sometimes extreme variations they allow themselves within those styles. These extremes do sometimes make it possible for us to recognize the styles. Writers can run their prose all the way from formal to informal, objective to subjective, uncommitted to committed, abstract and technical and dry to concrete, personal, colloquial, even chatty. Each style has attributes (or flaws) that we can describe and apply to our own purposes in writing prose.

The printed English of high-level journalism is the closest thing we have in America for measuring the norm of prose styles. It is in some ways an equivalent to the "classical" language of countries in the Near and Far East with a variety of regional dialects. In prerevolutionary China, for example, Mandarin was the dialect of the educated, no matter what the provincial dialect they had spoken as children. In this country, the language of the college term paper becomes the identifying badge of the educated, regardless of geographical or ethnic origins.

The extreme kind of formal, impersonal writing can be done almost without "person," relying on passives and indirect discourse, with an occasional third-person pronoun ("one does") when the author can no longer avoid showing signs of human influence.

The most impersonal writing lurks in technical manuals, legal contracts, and learned articles written by experts for their peers, persons more interested in matter than manner. For rhetoric, the means of persuasion in such writing may be said to reside in the author's credibility. It is enough to know that he knows what he is talking about; no embellishments are required. Thus a dry-as-dust prospectus from a brokerage company is designed for customers already knowledgeable about investments:

> In addition, as incentive compensation the Fund presently pays an additional annual fee, based upon the average market value of the Fund's net assets, if the investment performance of the Fund for its fiscal year exceeds that of the Standard & Poor's Index of 500 Stocks. This fee amounts to $\frac{1}{16}$ of 1% if the excess amounts to 1.5 percentage points, $\frac{1}{8}$ of 1% for an excess of 3 percentage points, $\frac{3}{16}$ of 1% for an excess of 4.5 percentage points, or $\frac{1}{4}$ of 1% for an excess of 6 percentage points or more. On the other hand, the basic management fee is reduced if the Fund's investment performance for the year is lower than that of the Index to the extent of $\frac{1}{16}$ of 1% for a difference of 1.5 percentage points, $\frac{1}{8}$ of 1% for a difference of 3 percentage points, $\frac{3}{16}$ of 1% for a difference of 4.5 percentage points, or $\frac{1}{4}$ of 1% for a difference of 6 percentage points or more. The total of the basic fee and the additional fee, if any, shall not exceed 1%. *The basic management fee of $\frac{3}{4}$ of 1% per annum is in excess of that paid by many funds.* Because of incentive compensation, the present fee can increase by as much as $\frac{1}{4}$ of 1% per annum; on the other hand, the fee can also decrease by as much as $\frac{1}{4}$ of 1% per annum to $\frac{1}{2}$ of 1% per annum.
>
> DREYFUS LEVERAGE FUND PROSPECTUS, January 21, 1972

A fairly specialized book addressed to scholars, and their students, lets its author indulge in a somewhat less stringently formal, objective style. Here the subject, poetry, makes it unfitting that the author stamp out all stylistic felicities and personal turns of phrase:

> Such anti-traditional distortions must have been made for the most part by men who were closer to being rhapsodes than to being *aoidoi*, who were professional reciters of a fixed repertoire of famous poetry rather than minstrels able to improvise their own versions. . . . There will inevitably be disagreement over particular instances, but I submit that the principle is correct: that anti-traditional language usually implies post-traditional composition. The composers of the *Iliad* and the *Odyssey* came near the end of the active and creative oral tradition in Greece — indeed they probably unconsciously hastened its decline by producing poems great enough in quality and magnitude to provide a livelihood for the mere

Diction is somewhat technical, sentences lengthy, syntax complex, and tone impersonal. *Stresses exactness,* not ornament.

declaimer. Such a criterion is admittedly a poor substitute for absolute dates in the development of language, since it lacks precision and depends on a number of assumptions which are unprovable even if they seem highly probable. Until new linguistic evidence appears which provides fixed points for the development of Greek between 1000 and 650, our criterion seems to be the best there is. G. S. KIRK

When an expert has to explain a difficult subject, like Einstein's Theory of Relativity, to a general audience (partly or mostly nonmathematicians), he must make himself understood by drawing word pictures with an analogy:

In accordance with his usual mode of creative thought Einstein set the stage with an imaginary situation. The details have doubtless been envisaged by many another dreamer in restless slumber or in moments of insomniac fancy. He pictured an immensely high building and inside it an elevator that had slipped from its cables and is falling freely. Within the elevator a group of physicists, undisturbed by any suspicion that their ride might end in disaster, are performing experiments. They take objects from their pockets, a fountain pen, a coin, a bunch of keys, and release them from their grasp. Nothing happens. The pen, the coin, the keys appear to the men in the elevator to remain poised in mid-air — because all of them are falling, along with the elevator and the men, at precisely the same rate in accordance with Newton's Law of Gravitation. Since the men in the elevator are unaware of their predicament, however, they may explain these peculiar happenings by a different assumption. They may believe they have been magically transported outside the gravitational field of the earth and are in fact poised somewhere in empty space. And they have good grounds for such a belief. If one of them jumps from the floor he floats smoothly toward the ceiling with a velocity just proportional to the

> He relates reader to Einstein by suggesting common bond in a dream.

> Analogy with *falling elevator* gives vivid, understandable picture of gravity's effect.

vigor of his jump. If he pushes his pen or his keys in any direction, they continue to move uniformly in that direction until they hit the wall of the car. Everything apparently obeys Newton's Law of Inertia, and continues in its state of rest or of uniform motion in a straight line. The elevator has somehow become an inertial system, and there is no way for the men inside it to tell whether they are falling in a gravitational field or are simply floating in empty space, free from all external forces. LINCOLN BARNETT

The sort of informal prose typical of American journalism lies midway between the extremes. The author may veer away from the objective third person, "he" and "one," and experiment with the pronoun "you," or even "I," "me," "we," trying for a balance between liberty and restraint. The informal writer may look for a compromise between the exactness of formal prose and the breeziness in ordinary speech. He wants to attract his reader. He works at enlisting interest and sympathy. He offers anecdotes, illustrations, examples, and striking figures of speech. He makes thought come alive in words. He treats even profound subjects agreeably and entertainingly, for he sees no need to confuse the serious with the solemn. He accepts wit and humor as allies of the rhetorician. Max Eastman writes analytically but entertainingly on comic theory:

What deters me from taking up jocular analysis as a profession is not the difficulty inherent in the job, but the fact that when the job is well done, nobody gets any fun out of it. The correct explanation of a joke not only does not sound funny, but it does not sound like a correct explanation. It consists of imagining ourselves totally humorless and most anxiously and minutely concerned with the matter in question, and in realizing that under those queer and uninteresting circumstances a disagreeable feeling would arise exactly where in our mirthful receptivity we experience a comic emotion. That is not funny, and except for the pure love of understanding, it is not fun. You can no more find humor in the proper dissection of a joke than you can fly into a rage over the physiology of anger, or get drunk on a formula for synthetic gin.

plain Talk (choice of words)

Unpretentious diction in sentences of moderate length is combined with coordinated grammatical elements to achieve readability.

Syntax — organization

Another style gives the writer a way of presenting potentially boring information — how a candy factory operates — in a warm, witty, and agreeable way. The author is as eager to delight as to instruct:

Hershey, Pa. Even if you have never tried to identify with a chocolate bar before, you come out of the Hershey Chocolate tour here in this little town in central Pennsylvania feeling so thoroughly kissed, conched, vibrated, coded, debubbled, cooled, dated, wrapped, sorted and labeled that you may right away begin introducing yourself as Mr. Goodbar. At the height of the season, in summer, some 16,000 chocolate fanatics pile into the Hershey chocolate plant on East Chocolate Avenue in downtown Hershey every day for a jostling 40 minutes of the purest surrealistic sweetness.

Second person you establishes warm bond.

String of verbs brings atmosphere of factory to life.

By 8:15 in the morning, tourists are already jamming the lobby, with its posterlike paintings of famous chocolate moments — Columbus picking up some cacao beans from the Indians, Cortez tippling hot cocoa with Montezuma — and then they're off at a jog behind an energetic young girl tour guide in a butterscotch dress and a Hershey-Kiss hat. (That's not all: the streetlights outside are fashioned to resemble Hershey Kisses, some brown — unwrapped — and some silver.)
ROY BONGARTZ

Description of murals a little satirical.

Still another style (or anti-style) grew out of the underground subculture of the Sixties and the "new journalism" of writers like Norman Mailer and Tom Wolfe. This type of prose really isn't new at all. Satirists have practiced such bitter, railing mockery down through the centuries. This incarnation of it was fertilized by *anomie,* a sense of rootlessness, disorganization, lack of purpose in society. It seems, but it is not true, that this kind of writing has obliterated all the hoary old barriers against "unprintable" words. Many far-out newspapers expunge scatological vocabulary from their objective news, though they may let it by in their subjective feature stories. Even in the obscurest regions of experimentation, ancient notions of decorum still prevail. Some of this school's habits are now worn threadbare from repetition, but at its best, in the hands of a Tom Wolfe, it conveys tremendous vitality. Although its influence on modern prose has been dramatic, it is not recommended for beginners. Badly executed, it can be a disaster.

For months Kesey has been trying to work out . . . the fantasy . . . of the Dome. This was going to be a great geodesic dome on top of a cylindrical shaft. It would look like a great mushroom. Many levels. People would climb a stairway up the cylinder — *buy a ticket?* — *we-e-e-elllll* — and the dome would have a great foam-rubber floor they could lie down on. Sunk down in the foam rubber, below floor level, would be movie projectors, video-tape projectors, light projectors. All over the place, up in the dome, everywhere, would be speakers, microphones, tape machines, live, replay, variable lag. People could take LSD or speed or smoke grass and lie back and experience what they would, enclosed and submerged in a planet of lights and sounds such as the universe never knew. Lights, movies, video tapes, video tapes of themselves, flashing and swirling over the dome from the beams of searchlights rising from the floor from between their bodies. The sounds roiling around in the globe like a typhoon. Movies and tapes of the past, tapes and video tapes, broadcasts and pictures of the present, tapes and humanoid sounds of the future — but all brought together *now* — here and now — *Kairos* — into the dilated cerebral cortex. . . .

Ellipses, dashes, parenthetical dialogue bring about collapse of conventional syntax.

Concentration of details stresses the sensory over the intellectual experience.

Not just a bunch of dang, pesky kids, the hirsute new breed of journalists has contributed the "Whole Earth Catalog" style. Somehow the talk that used to be called "slang" has become the very fabric of their prose. In many ways a private language, an argot for an in-group, accepted by youthful audiences but not enthusiastically endorsed by middle-aged readers, the movement may be another step in liberating American from British language. Purged of the underground's love for taboo words (still repugnant to most people), when this style blends the traditional with the innovative it forges a powerful new sales instrument, as this passage from a *Stereo Warehouse* blurb suggests:

Since you're reading this rap, you may be in the market for an inexpensive music system. Either by budget or by choice, you've decided to spend somewhere around $200 — and you're naturally concerned with getting your money's worth. Fearing that an audio

Word like *rap*, and use of second person *you* establish intimate bond between author and youthful audience.

specialty outlet (like us) won't be able to offer
you anything for the money you have to
spend, you may first visit the friendly salesman at your local discount appliance store.
. . . Following him past the air conditioners,
the all-in-one-home-entertainment-centers,
and freezers, you come to the corner devoted
to stereo equipment. "Here's a nice one," he
wheezes, pointing to a few nameless boxes.
"Marked down from $400 to $199.99 — just
this week. Buy it, you'll like it."

Remark about *friendly salesmen* lets reader know that
the writer is also a man
of the world who cannot
easily be taken in by music
men.
Last quotation from television commercial further
brings author and reader
together in context of pop
culture.

What about dialect? Is it ever appropriate to introduce an ethnic group's
private language into written expression? Belonging almost altogether to the
spoken, not the written, tradition, dialects rarely work in expository prose. But
dialect in narrative prose and in poetry requires a highly trained ear. No one
was better at it than Mark Twain, whose portrait of Huck's old man is a classic:

And looky here — you drop that school,
you hear? I'll learn people to bring up a boy
to put on airs over his own father and let on
to be better'n what *he* is. You lemme catch
you fooling around that school again, you
hear? Your mother couldn't read, and she
couldn't write, nuther, before she died. None
of the family couldn't before *they* died. I
can't; and here you're a-swelling yourself up
like this. I ain't the man to stand it — you
hear? Say, lemme hear you read.

The gross illiteracy cannot
conceal the native energy
and peasant cunning.

One last type of prose style is the kind of writing which rarely finds
its way into print but which may occur in classroom writing. It is close to illiteracy.
Its grandest features are meager vocabulary, poor spelling, inexact diction,
ignorance of the standards of usage, and inability to capitalize and punctuate.
It is some consolation to know that these spectres occasionally haunt even professional writers, whose battles to exorcise them are endless.

EXERCISE

A. At which level of discourse is each of these passages? Give your reasons.

1. "Mr. Fikey at home?" "No, he ain't." "Expected home soon?" "Why,
no, not soon." "Ah! Is his brother here?" "*I'm* his brother." "Oh! well,
this is an ill-conwenience, this is. I wrote him a letter yesterday, saying I'd
got a little turn-out to dispose of, and I've took the trouble to bring the
turn-out down a' purpose, and now he ain't in the way." CHARLES DICKENS

2. The remaining years of Leonardo's life are more or less years of wandering. From his brilliant life at court he had saved nothing, and he returned to Florence a poor man. Perhaps necessity kept his spirit excited: the next four years are one prolonged rapture of ecstasy of invention. He painted now the pictures of the Louvre, his most authentic works, which came there straight from the cabinet of Francis the First, at Fontainebleau. One picture of his, the Saint Anne — not the Saint Anne of the Louvre, but a simple cartoon, now in London — revived for a moment a sort of appreciation more common in an earlier time, when good pictures had still seemed miraculous. WALTER PATER

3. The entertainment on airlines has suddenly become a big and a very competitive business. Ever since TWA started showing films on their planes, every airline has tried to get in the act.

Some airlines are offering the choice of films, television, hi-fi, symphonic music, pop music, jazz, or children's stories.

One airline we flew with even showed television pictures of the take-off and landing, which didn't thrill the lady sitting next to me. . . .

"It gives us a chance to see the pilot make a good landing," I explained to her.

"And what are we supposed to do if we don't think he's making a good landing?"

It was something to think about. ART BUCHWALD

18b. What Is Tone?

Tone, a by-product of the writer's attitude toward either his subject or his audience, is set by the distance between the author and his materials. If he feels his subject has superior status, the tone will be admiring; if he feels intimate with his subject, the tone will be familiar; and if he feels superior, the tone will be condescending or even scornful. The gradations between these tones are limitless, however. These four versions of the life of Joan of Arc vary from veneration to condescension.

The first writer venerates Joan and looks up to her:

Joan, weeping, knelt and began to pray. For whom? Herself? Oh, no — for the King of France. Her voice rose sweet and clear, and penetrated all hearts with its passionate pathos. She never thought of his treacheries to her, she never thought of his desertion of her, she never remembered that it was because he was an ingrate that she was here to die a miserable death; she remembered only that he was her King, that she was his loyal and loving subject, and that his enemies had

Words, such as *sweet, loyal, loving, humble, pity,* give elevated picture of Joan. Strong contrast between heartless king and saintly Joan.

undermined his cause with evil reports and
false charges, and he not by to defend himself. And so, in the very presence of death,
she forgot her own troubles to implore all
in her hearing to be just to him; to believe
that he was good and noble and sincere, and
not in any way to blame for any acts of hers,
neither advising them nor urging them, but
being wholly clear and free of all responsi-
bility for them. Then, closing, she begged in   Ends with appeal to pity.
humble and touching words that all here
present would pray for her and would par-
don her, both her enemies and such as might
look friendly upon her and feel pity for her
in their hearts. MARK TWAIN

The second writer sees Joan as a human being, much like any other:

What then is the modern view of Joan's   Phrase, *modern view,* sug-
voices and visions and messages from God?   gests Joan is being reduced
The nineteenth century said that they were   to life size.
delusions, but that as she was a pretty girl,
and had been abominably ill-treated and
finally done to death by a superstitious rabble
of medieval priests hounded on by a corrupt
political bishop, it must be assumed that she
was the innocent dupe of these delusions.   *Delusions* drops topic from
The twentieth century finds this explanation   supernatural to natural.
too vapidly commonplace, and demands
something more mystic. I think the twentieth   Writer sounds judicious and
century is right, because an explanation   is amicable but analytical.
which amounts to Joan being mentally de-
fective instead of, as she obviously was,
mentally excessive, will not wash.
GEORGE BERNARD SHAW

The next writer, an objective historian, tries to be neutral:

It is very hard to exclude the personal
story when dealing with Jeanne d'Arc; but
this is a sketch of French history, not a study
of even its most important and interesting
characters. In bald, matter-of-fact language,   He states desire to be fac-
what happened was this: (1) Jeanne d'Arc   tual. Factual words empha-
was born a peasant girl in 1409 in the Village   size neutral attitude. Passive
of Domremy, on the borders of Champagne.   verbs (*was born*) often go
The region was one of the few eastern dis-   with objective, scientific
                                                  prose.

tricts still held by Charles. As she grew up as a pious village maid she began to have elaborate visions of a France redeemed from the yoke of the English, and the Virgin kept telling her, "Jeanne, go and deliver the King of France, and restore him to his kingdom." Psychologists may determine of what these visions, her "voices," consisted. There is no doubt she honestly believed that she had them. (2) In 1429, when Orléans was at its last gasp, she appeared at the court of the Dauphin at the castle of Chinon, near Tours. She convinced even the skeptical court and the prince that hers was a divine commission.

WILLIAM S. DAVIS

The last writer, a student, sees the saint as inferior to other persons:

Of all the hoaxes perpetrated on mankind none has received more publicity than the execution and marytrdom of Saint Joan of Arc, a witless peasant girl whose claim to fame rests on the accident of her having been a political liability to the British. Had not the circumstances of her death been so savage, the possibility of turning her career from a tragedy into a comedy would be overwhelming. This delusion of Joan was after all not merely hers but a shared insanity with all the pitiful creatures of her time, who mistook hallucinations for divinity and masochism for sainthood.

Bitter words like *hoaxes* and *witless* give harsh tone. Undertone of mockery throughout.

EXERCISES

A. These passages illustrate different levels in the writer's attitude toward his materials, ranging from admiration to scorn. Decide what tone the writer has adopted, and point out the words and phrases that reveal the attitude toward his subject. Is the writer looking up to his subject, feeling comfortable with it, looking down at it, or trying to be scientific and objective? A borderline tone is also quite natural and should be expected.

1. There was none of Churchill's eloquent defiance in this speech. There was certainly no trace of Hitler's hysterical bombast. And there was no doubt in the minds of the American people of Roosevelt's confidence. I do not think there was another occasion in his life when he was so completely representative of the whole people. If, as Hopkins wrote, Roosevelt

felt a sense of relief that the Japanese had chosen this method of settling the issue of war or peace, so with remarkably few exceptions did the people themselves. ROBERT E. SHERWOOD

2. That thinking is closely tied up with inner speech is suggested by attempts to analyze thought processes. Try to analyze your everyday thinking and you will find that words are everywhere evident. It usually appears that, in thinking, you are talking to yourself. Children often do their thinking out loud for everyone to hear it — until they learn that it is customary, and often worthwhile, to keep one's thoughts to oneself. The deaf and dumb, who have previously learned the sign language, have been observed to move their fingers while thinking, much as they move them while talking, only to an abbreviated degree. NORMAN L. MUNN

3. This perpetual fear, always accompanying mankind in the ignorance of causes, as it were in the dark, must needs have for object something. And therefore when there is nothing to be seen, there is nothing to accuse, either of their good, or evil fortune, but some *power,* or agent *invisible:* in which sense perhaps it was, that some of the old poets said, that the gods were at first created by human fear: which spoken of the gods, that is to say, of the many gods of the Gentiles, is very true. But the acknowledging of one God, eternal, infinite, and omnipotent, may more easily be derived, from the desire men have to know the causes of natural bodies, and their several virtues, and operations; than from the fear of what was to befall them in time to come. THOMAS HOBBES

4. Now and again Father entertained us at dinner — when no guests were present — by relating the contents of books he was reading, such as *Gulliver's Travels, The Arabian Nights,* or sea stories. More than once I wondered how Father could think, talk, and eat all at once in so vehement a manner. This capacity, added to his restless pacing the floor between courses at table, gave the meal a lively character. CLARA CLEMENS

B. Write a few sentences on one of these topics, shifting from respect, to familiarity, to scorn, and finally to a neutral tone of scientific objectivity.

1. A major foreign power.   2. A rival school.   3. A friend back home. 4. A subject studied in school.   5. Any political figure of national prominence.   6. Your college or university.   7. College athletics.   8. The average student.   9. American foreign policy.   10. A film star.   11. A favorite television program.   12. A game.   13. A party you recently attended.   14. An acquaintance.   15. Television programming.   16. Popular music.   17. Snowmobiles.

18c.   What Is Irony?

Most people think of irony as sarcasm, though in fact sarcasm is only a minor, and not very attractive, subspecies of irony. Essentially irony is a contrast between what is meant and what is being said, or between appearance and reality, word and deed, or expectancy and actuality. Irony may take the form of subtle wit, in which form it can be defined as "that sharp instrument which is blunted on dull wits." Irony has been the stock-in-trade of *The New Yorker* and *Mad* magazines, publications that appeal to urbane sensibilities of different age groups. Six forms of irony are recognizable.

In Socratic irony the speaker pretends to know much less than he really does to gain the confidence of his audience. The word comes from the pose of Socrates in Plato's dialogues. He found it useful to pretend to know nothing as a way of drawing out his pupils and disciples and even enemies.

In dramatic irony the audience knows more about what is going on in the book or on the stage than do some of the actors. Hence the joy among small boys in the audience when the hairy arm pops out from behind the paneled walls to snake closer and closer to the throat of the actor oblivious to the horror behind him. At another level is the audience's awareness that Sophocles' King Oedipus will discover that the criminal is himself.

Overstatement is deliberate exaggeration, hyperbole used for comic effect. The Texas tall story is made of the playful boasting that characterizes overstatement. The millionaire who had his automobile windshield ground to his oculist's prescription and the Dallas department store that sells "his" and "hers" airplanes have entered American folklore. This kind of effect, difficult to manage in writing, must be handled very delicately.

Understatement is playing down of events deliberately. The opposite of overstatement, it has been thought of as typical of the British. The calm of the British naval officer who, as a sixteen-inch shell whizzes an inch in front of his nose, turns to his executive officer and remarks, "Bit of a near thing, what?" is understatement.

Irony of situation finds the least deserving student in the class receiving an A, or the man who hoards for retirement in Florida dying on the day he retires. Life is full of such bitter moments contrasting what we expect and what happens.

Sarcasm uses irony as a weapon to hurt another. The principle of contrast appears in the difference between what the speaker says and what he means: "My, but you're an asset to this company!" Sarcasm, unlike other forms of irony, usually signals aggressiveness and hostility. Therefore use it at your own risk. Study this excerpt from an article on the New Left by a master ironist, Leo Rosten:

> During those historic months when the New Left was demonstrating its love of free speech by denying it to others, its devotion to peace by using violence, its love of Love by preaching hate against everyone from professors

to Presidents, its dedication to democracy by abusing it like Nazis, its thirst for education by wrecking classrooms and burning buildings, its sensitive soul by hurling obscenities, its superior thinking by silly slogans drawn from mushy ideologies, its non-conformity by playing sheep to unstable shepherds or demented demagogues — during these idealistic orgies (when the demand "Communicate!" meant "Agree with me!"), I conducted a series of interviews that would meet the most rigorous standards set by Lou Harris, George Gallup, and other seasoned takers-of-the-public-pulse. My scientific survey revealed that 28 per cent of the students, and only 24 per cent of the faculties, were nuts.

EXERCISE

A. Write an ironic paragraph or two, using these suggestions as a way of getting into a subject.

1. Student government: myth and reality.   2. Football and participatory democracy: why football coaches should be elected.   3. Teachers and labor unions: what would Socrates have said?   4. ROTC: center of the college curriculum.   5. The exploited doctor: why physicians need more money.   6. Medievalism on the campus: grades must go.   7. Environmental pollution: a national asset.   8. Film: an art form for morons. 9. Student power: why faculty promotion committees need it.   10. The television commercial: America's real art form.

18d.   How Do the Abstract and Concrete Blend?

S. I. Hayakawa, the semanticist, describes informal writing as moving up and down the "ladder of abstraction."[1] It is neither so difficult as to annoy the reader by not revealing what it is really about, nor so simple-minded and plain as to bore the reader with trivial details apparently directed to no end. Abstract writing would be appropriate for a technical journal in metaphysics or literary theory; a less abstract style could be just the thing for directions on how to bake a cake. But neither high nor low abstraction is in itself a virtue unless it is suited to the subject and the audience. Why use abstruse words, technical jargon, and lofty abstractions to tell someone to put out the lights? Nor is there any reason to insult the intelligence of an audience of specialists by using a primer vocabulary. Here is a writer unwilling to put simple ideas into concrete words:

---

[1] See S. I. Hayakawa, *Language in Thought and Action,* 2nd ed. (New York: Harcourt, Brace, Jovanovich, 1964), pp. 176 ff.

INAPPROPRIATELY HIGH LEVEL OF ABSTRACTION	REVISED TO A LOWER LEVEL
If one were to make even a cursory examination of pedagogic literature for its attitude toward the lecture, it would not be too difficult to find criticism in ubiquity.	A quick survey of pedagogic literature shows hostility to the lecture method.

Remember, however, that abstract prose is not in itself an evil. The writer seeks concreteness or abstraction appropriate to his purpose and subject. Paul Oskar Kristeller writes appropriately for specialists on the Italian Renaissance in a fairly abstract prose.

Ever since 1860, when Jacob Burckhardt first published his famous book on the civilization of the Renaissance in Italy, there has been a controversy among historians as to the meaning and significance of the Italian Renaissance. Almost every scholar who has taken part in the discussion felt it was his duty to advance a new and different theory. This variety of views was partly due to the emphasis given by individual scholars to different historical personalities or currents or to different aspects and developments of the Italian Renaissance. Yet the chief cause of the entire Renaissance controversy, at least in its more recent phases, has been the considerable progress made during the last few decades in the field of medieval studies. The Middle Ages are no longer considered as a period of darkness, and consequently many scholars do not see the need for such new light and revival as the very name of the Renaissance would seem to suggest. Thus certain medievalists have questioned the very existence of the Renaissance, and would like to banish the term entirely from the vocabulary of historians.	*Presupposes an informed audience, to whom the name* Burckhardt *and* Italian Renaissance *would mean something.* *Renaissance controversy not supported with specifics because of reader's supposed familiarity with topic.*

Effective prose may blend the abstract and the concrete; the writer will shift up and down the ladder of abstraction, moving from the general to the specific, or from the specific to the general:

The essence of Vassar is mythic. Today, despite much competition, it still figures in the public mind as the archetypal woman's college. Less intellectual than Radcliffe or	*Two lead sentences suggest capacity of the word* Vassar *to evoke an image in the public mind; high level of abstraction.*

Bryn Mawr, less social and weekendish than Smith, less athletic than Wellesley, less bohemian than Bennington, it is nevertheless the stock butt of musical-comedy jokes and night-club wheezes. It has called down thunder from the pulpit, provided heroines for popular ballads; even a girdle bears its name. Like Harvard it is always good for a knowledgeable smile from members of the population who have scarcely heard the name of another college. It signifies a certain *je ne sais quoi;* a whiff of luxury and the ineffable; plain thinking and high living. If a somehow know-it-all manner is typical of the Vassar student, the public has a way of winking that it knows all about Vassar, though this sly wink only intimates that there is something to know. For different people, in fact, at different periods, Vassar can stand for whatever is felt to be wrong with the modern female. MARY MC CARTHY

By direct comparison with other important women's colleges, the author makes specific what the mythic consists of. Abstraction drops a notch with *jokes* and *wheezes.* Systematically, Miss McCarthy gives more and more exact details for the mythic, moving steadily down the ladder of abstraction.

The French phrase ("I don't know what") moves up a rung on the ladder.
The myth now comes down to response of the general public. Once again the movement is up the ladder, away from a lower to a higher level of abstraction, as in generality about *people* and *periods.*

The relative frequency of key sentence elements, or pivotal words — subject, verb, object, and complement (see 26) — may tell something about a writer's level of abstraction and it will certainly make visible his stylistic habits. Usually a low frequency of pivotal words, which may be called either "kernels" or "key sentence elements," signal high abstraction and result in a grand style. Conversely, where many pivotal words are found, expect low abstraction and a plain style. Grand style and plain style were once called "Ciceronian" and "Senecan" after the stylistic practices of the Roman writers, Marcus Tullius Cicero (106–43 B.C.) and Lucius Annaeus Seneca (about 4 B.C.–A.D. 65). Cicero's orations and essays, written during ferocious political squabbles, set a lofty model of eloquence that was influential in western Europe for centuries. By contrast, Seneca, a playwright and philosopher, who as tutor to the Emperor Nero may even have modified that notoriously cruel man's behavior, earned a reputation for terse, epigrammatic utterance. John Milton, Cardinal Newman, and Henry James fit the grand style; Sir Francis Bacon, Mark Twain, and Ernest Hemingway, the plain style.

The grand style is expansive, studied, and sweeping; probably its most recent great practitioner in America was Senator Everett Dirksen of Illinois. It allows thought to flow out of the main clauses into the byways and detours of modifying and parenthetical elements. The plain style is pithy, often cumulative, and meant to appear casual. It concentrates thought within the limits of terse clauses. Divergence of meaning and pivotal elements suggest grand style; convergence of meaning and pivotal elements, plain style. In grand style, the action goes on in the subordinating and parenthetical elements in the sentences; in plain style, it happens in the main clauses. Grand style implies that the writer already knows the truth; plain style gives the illusion that we are watching the writer discover truth. Grand style was shown off in the traditional Fourth of July oration; plain style carries the bulk of modern prose.

Is it worthwhile for a student writer today to know this much about style? Yes, simply because it is a way of penetrating the mystery of style. Not only the style of others, but also of our own.

Learning the difference between such styles as the "grand" and the "plain" is usually treated as a subjective matter. But they can be uncovered objectively, by counting (quantitatively), with a simple procedure. In any passage of prose, label the key elements of the main clauses S,V,C, and O, meaning subject, verb, complement, and object; label key sentence elements in dependent clauses with lower-case s,v,c, and o. You can then find the ratio of the number of words in the passage to the number of key sentence elements, revealing some of the writer's habitual practices. In these excerpts from works by John Milton and Sir Francis Bacon, we can quickly see that Milton preferred subordinate elements and that Bacon leaned heavily on key sentence elements. A word count shows that Bacon packs 22 pivotal words into 7 main clauses in a passage of only 47 words. Milton uses only 6 pivotal words in 2 main clauses in a relatively lengthy excerpt of 109 words (if we count the clauses in Milton's subordinate elements, the ratio is 14 pivotal words in 5 clauses). The ratios 7–22–47 and 2–6–109 suggest a plain style for Bacon and a grand style for Milton. The method is not infallible; some writers are bound to make themselves exceptions to the rule. In general, however, it is a way of penetrating the elusive question of what style is. And studying another man's way of expression may teach us something about how we express ourselves.

HIGH FREQUENCY OF PIVOTAL WORDS

```
          S              V    C
The joys of parents are secret, and so are
              S        V
their griefs and fears; they cannot utter the
 O    S              V            O
one, nor they will not utter the other.
 S        V        O        S    V
Children sweeten labours, but they make
 O              C    S    V
misfortunes more bitter; they increase the
 O                  S    V          O
cares of life, but they mitigate the remem-
brance of death. SIR FRANCIS BACON
```

Bacon's sentences barely move away from the kernels of *subject-verb-object,* and *subject-verb-comple-ment.* He employs 7 kernels, 22 kernel words (or pivotal words) in only 47 words. The ratio is 7–22–47. He achieves a prose of great density and pithiness.

         S   V   C

The end then of learning is to repair
the ruins of our first parents by regaining to
know God aright, and out of that knowledge
to love him, to imitate him, to be like him,

    s   v

as we may the nearest by possessing our

              s

souls of true virtue, which being united to

              v

the heavenly grace of faith, makes up the
highest perfection. But because our under-

    s   v v

standing cannot in . . . this body found itself

              v

but on sensible things, nor arrive so clearly
to the knowledge of God and things invisible
as by orderly conning[2] over the visible and

              S

inferior creature, the same method is neces-

           V

sarily to be followed in all discreet teaching.
JOHN MILTON

Labels for pivotal words in main clauses are in capitals; those for subordinate clauses, lower-case, to show an alternative method of analysis. Milton in 2 sentences of 109 words relies on only 1 main clause in each sentence, 1 clause containing 3 pivotal words; the other, 2. The subordinate clauses contain 7 more pivotal elements (*cannot* construed as auxiliary to *found*). The ratio, then, is 2–5–109, if we consider only main clauses; 5–12–109 if we include the subordinate clauses.

Nearly half the words in Bacon's selection are pivotal, compared with about a tenth in Milton's. Habits of structure have as much to do with style as the choice of words. These paragraphs again illustrate the principle of low frequency and high frequency of pivotal words:

With the exception of the staircase, and his
lodger's private apartment, Poll Sweedlepipe's

    S   V   C   S

House was one great bird's-nest. Game-cocks

    V   S   V

resided in the kitchen; pheasants wasted the

    O

brightness of their golden plumage on the

         S   V   S

garret; bantams roosted in the cellar; owls

In 88 words Dickens uses 8 clauses with 21 pivotal words; the ratio is 8–21–88.

[2] Studying.

```
V        O                       S
```
had possession of the bedroom; and speci-
mens of all the smaller fry of birds chir-
```
V              V
```
rupped and twittered in the shop. The
```
   S       V      C
```
staircase was sacred to rabbits. There in
hutches of all shapes and kinds, made from
old packing-cases, boxes, drawers, and tea-
```
        S       V
```
chests, they increased in a prodigious degree.
CHARLES DICKENS

LOW FREQUENCY OF PIVOTAL WORDS

```
       V            S           s      v
```
There is another impediment, as time goes
on, to the rise of fresh classics in any nation;
```
      S    V      C              s
```
and that is the effect which foreigners, or
```
                       v           S
```
foreign literature, will exert upon it. It may
```
V                                  s
```
happen that a certain language, like Greek,
```
    v         v
```
is adopted and used familiarly by educated
men in other countries; or again, that edu-
```
      s              s   v    c          v
```
cated men, to whom it is native, may aban-
```
    o
```
don it for some other language, as the
```
    s
```
Romans of the second and third centuries
```
    v
```
wrote in Greek instead of Latin.
JOHN HENRY CARDINAL NEWMAN

In 3 main clauses, Cardinal Newman uses 7 pivotal words in 83 words for a ratio of 3–7–83. Obviously the action is not in the main clauses. If we count dependent clauses we get 22 pivotal words in 9 clauses, a ratio of 9–22–83. Either way, the frequency of pivotal words remains low.

Almost exact contemporaries, Charles Dickens (1812–1870) and John Henry Newman (1801–1890) had very different habits of prose structure. The 8–21–88 ratio for Dickens' passage supports an impressionistic judgment that it is writing of high density, with frequent concrete words. Words like *packing-cases, boxes, drawers,* and *tea-chests* have strong visual appeal. Newman, whose ratio here is 3–7–83, pushes most of his pivotal words into dependent clauses. Newman was fond of the anticipatory sentence (see 19). The gap between pivotal words and meaning is as narrow in Dickens' prose as it is wide in Newman's.

EXERCISES

A. Apply these procedures to the quotations:

1. Find the ratio for each passage, following the design demonstrated above (number of main clauses — number of pivotal words — total number of words). 2. Discover how wide or narrow the gap is between pivotal words and finished utterance. 3. Describe the distance between pivotal words and count the number of nouns and adjectives in each passage. 4. Drawing together all you've learned from your analysis, write a three-sentence summary about the style of each writer.

For everything there is a season, and a time for every purpose under heaven: a time to be born, and a time to die; a time to plant, and a time to pluck up that which is planted; a time to kill, and a time to heal; a time to break down, and a time to build up; a time to weep, and a time to laugh; a time to mourn, and a time to dance; a time to cast away stones, and a time to gather stones together; a time to embrace, and a time to refrain from embracing; a time to seek, and a time to lose; a time to keep, and a time to cast away. ECCLESIASTES 3:1–6

Hamlet: The King doth wake to-night and takes his rouse,
Keeps wassail, and the swaggering up-spring reels.
And as he drains his draughts of Rhenish down,
The kettle-drum and the trumpet thus bray out
The triumph of his pledge. WILLIAM SHAKESPEARE, *Hamlet* I. ii. 8–12.

Macbeth: To-morrow, and to-morrow, and to-morrow
Creeps in this petty pace from day to day,
To the last syllable of recorded time,
And all our yesterdays have lighted fools
The way to dusty death. Out, out, brief candle!
Life's but a walking shadow, a poor player
That struts and frets his hour upon the stage
And then is heard no more: it is a tale
Told by an idiot, full of sound and fury,
Signifying nothing. WILLIAM SHAKESPEARE, *Macbeth* V. v. 19–28

How are pivotal words distributed between main and dependent clauses in this passage?

It was as instrument maker that Tycho [Brahe] excelled all astronomers who had lived before him. Some of the devices he built were of his own invention but most were refinements of traditional types. The basic instrument of astronomy in his day was the quadrant, a quarter-circle that was normally sighted from the angle to the arc. One of the quadrant's arms was made precisely horizontal and the other precisely vertical. The whole instrument was usually pivoted so that it could be rotated 360 degrees. When the sighting arm, or alidade, was pointed at a star or planet, the altitude was read off the 90-degree arc and the azimuth off a 360-degree circle within which the quadrant revolved. JOHN CHRISTIANSON

B. Analyze the style of your last composition. Does it tell you anything about your unconscious habits of structure?

SOME OTHER ASPECTS OF STYLE

18e.   What Is Idiomatic Language?

By *idiom* we mean the unique way in which the words of a language are connected to express a thought. Thus idiomatic French allows "it's me" (*c'est moi*) but in English purists insist on "it's I" (with less and less success, admittedly). In French the expression is *Ici on parle français* ("Here one speaks French"), which translates into the American idiom "French spoken here." Idiom is therefore subtle, having to do with a culture's ways of expressing a thought. To be unidiomatic is to write a construction that is simply "un-English," or, worse yet, "un-American." Often the difficulty is rooted in misusing prepositions that support verbs, as in these instances (all unidiomatic):

NOT:	BUT:
They could be heard throughout AM-FM radio stations.	They could be heard on all **AM-FM** radio stations.
They fill a small need of today's culture.	They fill a small need in today's culture.
Antony attacks a Brutus statement without attacking the man.	Antony attacks Brutus' statement without attacking the man.
Many of today's television commercials attempt to strike at the viewer's sense of humor.	Many of today's television commercials appeal to the viewer's sense of humor.

18f.   Trivialities, Clichés, and Commonplaces

Whenever the writer's energy dissipates, the worn-out phrase or trite expression perches, ready to take over. Stories in one week's newspapers overworked the word *hailed* in these ways: "Officials *hailed* the news"; "Stockmen last week *hailed* the report"; and "The approach of spring was *hailed.*" Other journalistic favorites are "gutted by fire"; "guarded optimism"; "tinder-dry woodlands"; "flatly denied"; "racially troubled"; and "limped into port." Newspapermen, working against deadlines, have perhaps more excuse than college students for using trite phrases.

Cliché is a French word meaning a stereotyped word or block of words. Most clichés were once colorful and fresh, but they quickly grow dull from repeated use. Do you remember the line from a commercial: "I can't believe I ate the whole thing"? Here are some old standbys, all to be avoided.

CLICHÉS IN STUDENT THEMES

a well-rounded person   the rising middle class
intestinal fortitude   last but not least
there are many factors in this case the material rewards of life
it is interesting to note[3]   church of one's choice
this modern age of today   in this day and age

WORN-OUT WAYS OF BEING LITERARY

between Scylla and Charybdis   the immortal bard
halcyon days (*or* salad days)   sings his swan song
the alpha and omega   the Grim Reaper
the rosy fingers of dawn   with satanic glee
the villain cackled fiendishly   the voice of doom

DEAD SIMILES

fit as a fiddle   ate like a horse
red as a beet   drank like a fish
big as a house   fat as a pig
strong as an ox   happy as a lark
slept like a log   worked like mad

TEN BUSINESS AND NEWSPAPER STANDBYS

military posture   hardware (meaning computers)
bottom line   weapons systems
megaton capability   escalate
ballpark figures   détente
balance of terror   missile gap
timewise   police brutality
at this point in time   police-state mentality

18g.   Jargon and Argot

Argot is specialized talk, at one time associated with the private language of thieves. Jargon originally meant gibberish, something akin to reciting the Lord's Prayer backward. Today jargon is often the label attached to specialized kinds of languages that one does not understand. The social sciences have developed a jargon, though some of it, such as "peer group," and "deviant behavior," has its place. It is not entirely accurate to say that "peer group" is a fancy synonym for "gang" or that "deviant behavior" is an elaborate way of describing a "mean kid." The technical phrases avoid the subjective social condemnation in the popular ones. A science of human behavior needs a neutral language free of moralistic premises. Therefore, labeling indiscriminately every strange expression as jargon may be a form of anti-intellectualism. On the other hand, using technical language out of context when addressing laymen is equally

---

[3] Do not tell the reader something is interesting; show that it is interesting.

absurd. A teacher may report to colleagues, who will understand, that "reader reliability on this test was .89." He will tell students and parents that "the test was fairly graded." A physician may record for the hospital records that a patient suffered from "a neurasthenic circulatory condition tending toward arrhythmia and palpitation with some indication of cardiac arrest," but he may inform the patient that "you are awfully nervous and your heart skips around a bit." Here is a student who fell in love with important-sounding words:

ORIGINAL	REVISION
The factor which is responsible for this modern phenomena is the object of quite intensive discussion today. Some scholars believe that such an infatuation with death and violence is the culmination of the tensity and trepidation experienced by every human in the ominous shadow of the atomic age.	Modern man's preoccupation with death stems from living in dread of the nuclear bomb.

18h. Slang

Because slang is short-lived, it is unacceptable except when addressing an in-group audience. It is better suited to spoken than written communication. Occasionally yesterday's slang becomes today's standard diction: *pickpocket, picayunish, hoyden, carpetbagger,* and *hippie.* More usually, however, slang perishes. Shakespeare's rival playwright, Ben Jonson, in his zeal to employ "the language men do use" filled his plays with slang that is today impenetrable except by scholars (*vapours, Tobie's dogs, cutpurses, pimp-errant, stone-Puritan,* and *a child of the horn-thumb*). It is also unlikely that such current vogue words as *hassle, mickey-mouse, rip-off, pig, freak, up-tight, flipped out, turned on, get into,* or *rap* will outlast the century. On the other hand many have enough sticking power to creep into the written vocabulary of important writers. *Fink* seems to have outlasted many slang words, and certainly *hangup* threatens to enter standard usage. Very secure writers like Tom Wolfe may use slang as an ironic game when the audience understands that the writer is being playful. It is wise, however, to save slang for idle moments with friends. Nor is it acceptable to sneak slang into a paper by putting it in quotation marks. Readers somehow sense that the writer is merely substituting a faddish word embellished with punctuation for the harder task of finding the right word.

18i. New Words (Neologisms)

New words may or may not be slangy, depending on the context from which they spring. English has several ways of making new words. One interesting phenomenon is back-formation — one part of speech encourages the development of another part of speech similar in form. *Domination* has the verb *dominate;* by analogy, speakers develop *computate* as the verb for *computation* (though the conventional form is *to compute*). *Orientate* begins to replace *to orient* as the verb for *orientation*. Everywhere one hears or reads that new groups are about to be *orientated,* rarely *oriented*. The trend continues as department store advertising copy announces that a women's fashion show will be *commentated* on. True enough, the English language is constantly shifting and changing, but few readers are liberal enough to tolerate back-formation leading to such results as "they would *considerate* a challenge"; "students are *accreditated* by the faculty"; and "he *ascertaited* the problem."

Blending produces other varieties of words: *smog* (smoke + fog), *brunch* (breakfast + lunch), *motel* (motor + hotel). Other words, called "acronyms," grow out of the habit of stringing initials together, until no one remembers what the initials stand for: *radar, laser, scuba,* and *snafu*. The American language also has words that represent mergers such as *cheeseburger, taxpayer,* and *theatergoer*. Other words name historical personages and events: *gerrymander, bowdlerize, lynch, quisling*. And new words are made by shortening long words: *zoo, Frisco, lunch, auto, bus,* and *plane*.

18j.   Euphemism

A euphemism (from the Greek rhetorical term *euphimismos*) substitutes an agreeable or nonoffensive word for a disagreeable or offensive one. Society encourages euphemisms to conceal from itself some of the more unpleasant parts of reality. The guest at a party may ask where the "little boy's room" is, offending no one but enemies of euphemism. A study of British speech habits showed that upper-class persons were less committed than lower-class persons to euphemism. The British Brahman preferred "belly" to "tummy," "leg" to "limb," and "death" to "demise." In America, the public relations men of the funeral industry are notorious for mass-marketing such absurdities as "casket" for "coffin," and "resting one" for "corpse." Euphemism may be harmful when such evasive labels as "final solution" and "terminate with extreme prejudice" are used to describe genocide, or "benevolent incapacitator" is substituted for nonlethal poisoned gas. But euphemism is not in itself bad. It is a matter of taste in which the writer must steer the middle road between enough and too much. The danger in overworking euphemisms is in losing touch with reality because of over-squeamishness; the danger in bluntness is in losing friends because of excessive candor.

18k.   Denotation and Connotation

Words are symbols for persons, things, and ideas. The persons (such as Jack), things (such as chairs), and ideas (such as idealism) that words stand for are called "referents." Most words are both denotative and connotative. They denote, or designate, specific things or persons and connote a cluster of associations. The proper noun *Jack* designates a person, but it also conveys a myriad of associations. To some it conveys a suggestion of heartiness, good fellowship (during his youth the celebrated seventeenth-century poet-divine John Donne was known as "Jack" Donne); to others, it may even convey a whiff of the sinister, the malign (they may be thinking of Jack-the-Ripper). *Magnolia* stands for a tree but also connotes the Old South, gallant cavaliers and their ladies dancing on the eve of departure for war. *Hawaii* stands for the fiftieth state of the Union, but one also thinks of hula girls, orchid leis, and the surf at Waikiki. The capacity of words, almost any word, for triggering associations in our minds must be almost infinite. A practical precaution is never to use words in a context that will give them an unexpectedly unwelcome twist of meaning. To write that "the condemned ate his breakfast with relish" may cause some readers to wonder about the condemned's eating habits.

EXERCISES

A. Analyze these passages for triteness, euphemisms, and jargon:

1. From the rock-bound coasts of Maine to the sun-kissed shores of fair California, from the orange-scented balm of beautiful Florida to the pine-crested mountains of Washington — all Americans unite today in paying tribute to a great national hero, a great citizen, a great man — James P. Livermore.

2. Every red-blooded American boy who believes in the American Way as opposed to foreign ideologies will want to get out there on the field today and give his all for the old school.

3. "He does not seem oriented properly toward his peer group, displaying hostility and tendencies toward aggression that might be characterized as anti-social." "Do you mean he's a mean kid?" "No, I did not say that."

4. During that time we were financially embarrassed, so to speak, a bit short of liquid assets, but on the whole we looked forward to brighter prospects during the next year.

5. Little Johnnie had an accident at the movie theater and had to be rushed into the little boy's room by his daddy.

6. Shortly after that, my father obtained a position with a highly reputable concern engaged in the important and socially useful task of buying, storing, and selling metal parts that had outlived their usefulness.

7. She attended a school devoted to training young ladies in the social and professional skills required to function as executive assistants in large corporations.

8. That semester she worked like a Trojan at the books, but the pace was so swift that soon she was once again in danger of falling behind.

B. Examine these words for their denotative and connotative qualities:

abstract	red	door	integer	toothbrush
politician	yellow	tree	thief	monster
polo	green	rose	war	martini
folksong	shame	terrible	H-bomb	couch

*One can write nothing readable unless one constantly struggles
to efface one's own personality. Good prose is like a window
pane.*

GEORGE ORWELL, Why I Write, 1947

*For whosoever will write well of any matter must labor
to express that that is perfect, and not to stay, and content
himself with the meane.*

ROGER ASCHAM, The Scholemaster, 1570

6   The Writer's Devices:

Style as Artifice

19.   What Is Sentence Rhetoric?
Periodic, Loose, and Balanced Sentences

We have seen that style is functional — it responds to the demands of
the subject. There is yet another side of the coin, however. Style also grows out
of the way an author organizes the subject. Styling prose is a never-ending battle
between subject and author to see who will win control. One result of authorial
manipulation of language is the conscious or unconscious production of fairly
predictable types of sentences. These sentence patterns are not mere ornaments,
fancy ways of saying things. They have been used since Homer's time, gradually
programed into the human mind as the best ways of making one's ideas clear.
They are *artifice* or *art* only because most of us don't habitually use them; able
writers do and we can learn to also.

Sentence patterns can be given four names: (1) periodic; (2) loose; (3)
balanced; and (4) combined sentences, putting together periodicity or looseness
with parallel or balanced elements. The names seem archaic when we think about
today's prose styles, but they are useful, guiding us in restyling vague, incoherent,

123

or rambling sentences. The writer has to have a feeling for parallelism and balance in sentence structure; without it he loses himself and his audience in chaotic word-jumbles.

The periodic sentence, sometimes called the anticipatory sentence, holds the meaning in suspense until the last possible moment. *Periodic* suggests that the period ending the sentence and the revelation of meaning are coincidental.

> But I am certain that a state governed by the rules of justice and fortitude, or a church built and founded around the rock of faith and true knowledge, cannot be so *pusillanimous.* JOHN MILTON

Ultimate meaning is withheld until last word of sentence.

A more modern example of periodicity:

> If Ticknor, and even Everett, in his way, stood so calmly in their own shoes, and used their heads so shrewdly, during a four-years' tour of observation that might have flattered a diplomat, — as Ticknor's *Journal* was to prove in time, a picture of the Europe of these years that could hardly have been more full or more discerning, — it was because, with the Revolution behind them, they were engaged, and they knew it, and everyone knew it, in serving the purposes of the Revolution. VAN WYCK BROOKS

Until we reach "Revolution," masterfully held off, we remain in suspense.

Not all periodic sentences are long, however. In an address at Columbia University Dr. Robert Oppenheimer managed to build periodicity into a relatively brief sentence:

> For the truth is that this is indeed, inevitably and increasingly, an open and, inevitably and increasingly, an eclectic world.
>
> *very*
> *specialized*

Meaning remains in suspense (an excellent way of holding the ear of an audience) until the word *world* appears.

The loose or cumulative sentence is the opposite of the periodic because it yields its principal meaning at once and then proceeds to modify it. It relies for effect not on suspense but on revelation.

> He liked the evenings at the Grantham Theatre, idyllic interludes of celluloid, and soap, and flapdoodle, as the screen swarmed with the Technicolor images of Hollywood gods and goddesses, all of whom somehow warmed the innermost recesses of his withered soul.

In this student sentence, the main meaning is released in the first few words. Everything that follows is amplification.

A similar technique is used here:

[1] The dogs were there first, [2] ten of them huddled back under the kitchen, [3] himself and Sam squatting to peer back into the obscurity where they crouched, quiet, [4] the eyes rolling, and luminous, vanishing, and no sound, [5] only that effluvium which the boy could not quite place yet, of something more than dog, and not just animal, just beast even. WILLIAM FAULKNER

1. Main clause is completed in first 5 words of a 59-word sentence.
2. Appositional phrase picks up topic of dogs.
3. What might have been the subject — *himself and Sam* — is almost hidden in a participial phrase that seems almost digressive.
4. A subordinate clause modifies the previous participial phrase — and also incorporates a string of parallel elements (see 19a) into this loose pattern.
5. The final string of words is in apposition to the noun *sound*.

[1] These were distinguished visitors, but they did not outnumber the succession of simple, often touching, and sometimes afflicting callers, [2] mostly Americans, [3] who came to constitute a serious problem for Longfellow, but who were invariably received with courtesy and consideration — though some of them belonged in that category of "books, bores, and beggars" which even he came to count as one of the principal vexations of daily life. NEWTON ARVIN

1. Compound clause is completed in first 19 words of a 67-word sentence.
2. *Mostly Americans,* in apposition to *callers,* provides link between introductory main clauses and the great accumulation of modifying elements. Adroit use of parallelism (see 19a) in the string of adjectives modifying *callers.*
3. Compound clauses modify *Americans.*

EXERCISE

A. As we might expect many writers make use of looseness in sentence construction. Analyze these for that quality:

1. The mountain that was beyond the valley and the hillside where the chestnut forest grew was captured and there were victories beyond the plain on the plateau to the south and we crossed the river in August and lived in a house in Gorizia that had a fountain and many thick shady trees in a walled garden and a wisteria vine purple on the side of the house. ERNEST HEMINGWAY

2. I never went to New York without being bewildered by a whole crop of new "successes" of various kinds: great novelists, world-shaking drama-

tists, stupendous architects or financial geniuses, whose names and achievements were unknown to me. VINCENT SHEEAN

3. It was upon a mind [H. D. Thoreau's] still uncrystallized, but mature, flexible, and creative, that the powerful doctrine of the Hindu moralists broke and precipitated the resolve to be "unanimous" in his desire "to live deliberately, to front only the essential facts of life, and see if I could not learn what it had to teach, and not, when I came to die, discover that I had not lived." HENRY S. CANBY

Because it becomes epigrammatic, even fussy, today the balanced sentence does not appear so frequently as the loose and periodic. Nevertheless balance, proportion, and symmetry often rescue a long sentence from incoherence. Without their guidance, a sentence can crumble into a string of unrelated words, phrases, and clauses. In an older, more leisurely time, writers with classical educations like Thomas Babington Macaulay worked variations on the sentence patterns of Cicero or Seneca:

There a few resolute Puritans, who, in the 1 cause of their religion, feared neither the rage 2 of the ocean nor the hardships of uncivilized 3 4 life, neither the fangs of savage beasts nor the tomahawks of more savage men, had 5 6 built amidst the primeval forests, villages 7 which are now great and opulent cities but 8 which have, through every change, retained some traces of the character derived from their founders. THOMAS BABINGTON MACAULAY	Master of the grand style, Macaulay sets up two pairs of parallel phrases (1/2; 3/4) built around the disjunctive "neither . . . nor," builds into the verb (5), and achieves a climax with the periodic effect of *villages* (6). Remainder of sentence modifies *villages* and repeats balancing effect in two "which" clauses (7/8).

The parallel relationships among the clauses can be revealed graphically:

There a few resolute Puritans,
   who, in the cause of their religion, feared
     ||neither the rage of the ocean
     ||nor the hardships of uncivilized life,
     ||neither the fangs of savage beasts
     ||nor the tomahawks of more savage men,
   had built amidst the primeval forests, villages
     ||which are now great and opulent cities but
     ||which have, through every change, retained some traces of the character
     ||derived from their founders.

The Stanton delegation *met* with the Newburgh Chamber of Commerce on Tuesday, and the Newburgh people *agreed* to the Stanton contract.	The verbs *met* and *agreed* have been played against each other in cross-fashion.

In most sentences, like the Macaulay example, looseness and periodicity mingle with balanced elements. It is even possible to write a loose sentence, like this one, which ends by showing balance and by employing parallelism.

19a.   What Is Parallelism?

Parallelism imposes symmetry and proportion and/or balance on verbal structures. A fundamental way of organizing thought, it requires that like thoughts be presented in like syntactic patterns. *Parallelism,* by the way, is often used interchangeably with *balance.* Generally, however, balance means paired or contrasted elements as large as the clause or larger, and parallelism indicates shorter elements such as the phrase or smaller elements.

‖ The Stanton boys meet the Newburgh ‖ stranger ‖ and ‖ the Newburgh stranger rebukes the Stanton ‖ boys.	Balanced: the paired elements are both clauses.

The Stanton boys meet	‖ the stranger, ‖ the outraged head- ‖ master, ‖ and ‖ the Chief of the ‖ Newburgh police.	Parallel: deliberately placed elements are words and phrases only.

The sentence with parallel elements deliberately arranges a progression by putting the Stanton boys' experience in order of ascending importance, culminating in the Chief of Police. The number of words in each phrase also is increased incrementally to parallel the idea of advance in importance of ideas (the first phrase, *the stranger,* two words; the second, *the outraged headmaster,* three words; and the third, *the Chief of the Newburgh Police,* six words).

Some varieties of parallelism are (1) the complementary, (2) the antithetical, and (3) the climactic. The Book of Common Prayer version of the Old Testament Psalms shows how the patterns work:

Complementary Parallelism. The second clause (or phrase) adds further information to what has been said previously in the first clause (or phrase):

All beasts of the field drink thereof, *and the wild asses quench their thirst.*
PSALMS 104:11

He bringeth forth grass for the cattle, *and green herb for the service of men.* PSALMS 104:14

The Stanton boys meet the stranger, *and find at the same time a startling truth about life.*

Antithetical Parallelism. The second clause (or phrase) reverses or contradicts what has been said in the first part of the sentence:

In the morning it is green, and groweth up; *but in the evening it is cut down, dried up, and withered.* PSALMS 90:6

For the arms of the ungodly shall be broken, *and the Lord upholdeth the righteous.* PSALMS 37:17

The town fathers meet the opposition in the morning, *but the meeting will bring sorrow by evening.*

Climactic Parallelism. This variety stresses the increasing importance in the arrangement of clauses or phrases or words:

When thou hidest thy face *they are troubled;*
   When thou takest away their breath, *they die,*
      And are *turned again to their dust.* PSALMS 104:29

I will love thee, O Lord, *my strength.* The Lord is *my stony rock,* and *my defence.* PSALMS 18:1

As a result of the chairman's advice, he was *first troubled, then disoriented,* and *finally unnerved,* to the point of requiring psychiatric care.

19b. What Is Parallelism in Thought?

A series of parallel statements usually combine elements that are consistent with each other and belong to the same class of things.

NOT: There are new synthetics to be found,
           new types of cosmetics yet to be uncovered,
           improving our metals and plastics,
             and
           many other objectives to be reached.

Clearly *types of cosmetics* does not belong logically in the same class with *new synthetics* and *metals and plastics. Many other objectives* shifts from a low to a high level of abstraction.

BUT: Among the many challenges facing mankind today are the search
      for |||metals,
          |plastics,
          | and
          |even new synthetics.

Cosmetics has been eliminated. The progression has gone from the least to the most important kinds of discoveries.

Here is another example:

NOT: He spoke of the corrupt political situation,
           of the uneasy economic situation,
                and
           of how the social fabric of the country was becoming immoral and scandalous.

BUT: He spoke ‖ of the corrupt political situation,
                ‖ of the uneasy economic situation,
                ‖   and
                ‖ of eroding social conditions.

In these sentences the thought is parallel, but the diction is inappropriate:

NOT: The white man showed his hatred for the red man in the form of hangings
                                                                and
                                                                murders
                                                                by guns.

BUT: The white man showed his hatred for the red man by ‖ hangings
                                                          ‖   and
                                                          ‖ shootings.

The series of thoughts should progress logically from either the less important to the more important, or from the more important to the less important.

NOT: At the County Fair there were booths,
                lots of people,
                soda-pop salesmen,
                merry-go-rounds,
                pie-baking contests,
                    and
                other such things.

Making the last item in the series *other such things,* an abstraction, spoils the emphasis.

BUT: The County Fair featured ‖ gaily decorated booths,
                                ‖ swirling calliopes,
                                ‖ pie-baking contests,
                                ‖ soda-pop salesmen,
                                ‖   and
                                ‖ great crowds of people.

The last item in the series has been made more emphatic, and modification of nouns is more consistent. The series can be terminated, of course, by *and so forth* or *etc.,* but your readers begin to suffer if you use them more than once in five or six pages. President John F. Kennedy, in his speeches, was inordinately fond of the expression "and all the rest" ("higher wages, more help for the aged, better medical care, and *all the rest*") as a way of ending a series.

19c.   What Is Parallelism in Syntax?

Once committed to a syntactic framework, the writer must remain loyal to it. In this sentence, the third element veers away from the original commitment to prepositional phrases:

NOT: He spoke of the political situation,
              of the economic situation.
          and
              talking also about the military situation.

BUT: He spoke of the ‖ military,
                          ‖ economic,
                          ‖   and
                          ‖ political situation.

Avoid the *and who* kind of construction without a preceding parallel element.

NOT: He was very successful and who charmed everybody.
BUT: He was very successful and charmed everybody.

Keep sentence elements joined by making coordinating conjunctions parallel.

NOT: He prefers tennis
                and
              to play football.

BUT: He prefers ‖ tennis
                      ‖   and
                      ‖ football.

Keep clauses parallel and balanced.

NOT: He was the young man who had been cited for bravery
                            and
              after that being dropped into oblivion.

BUT: He was the young man ‖ who had been cited for bravery
                                ‖   and
                                ‖ who after that had been consigned to oblivion.

Make certain that verbs are parallel. A series of verbs should be consistent in tense and voice. Do not begin with the active voice and then inadvertently shift into the passive or begin in the past tense and then unexpectedly move into the present.

NOT: He passed,
                kicked,
                    and
            was able to accomplish some running.

BUT: He ‖passed,
            ‖kicked,
            ‖   and
            ‖ran.

Antithetical parallelism can be used for effect. Witty reversals meant to shock and surprise within a syntactically parallel framework cannot be called violations of parallelism. They are a form of antithetical parallelism, as in this gag attributed to Woody Allen: "They kill, they maim, and not only that, they call information for numbers they could easily look up themselves." Here are two other examples of parallelism with a reverse twist:

As an accountant, Mr. Greenshades was slow and methodical, but highly inaccurate.

The children were rosy-cheeked, golden-haired, well dressed, and completely vicious.

EXERCISES

A. Correct the errors in parallelism in these sentences:

1. He was a ruthless cut-throat who looted ships, sank them, and let the crew drown.   2. That is the kind of experience that comes to friends, animals, and John.   3. Johnny kicked, screamed, and permitted himself to indulge in crying when his mother called him to come home.   4. The students grew angry over the free-speech issue and who found themselves protesting against the school's policy.   5. The girls by the time they were ten knew how to sing and all about sewing.   6. The speaker described the government policy, the foreign aid program, and related it all in a funny voice.   7. Learning to write is a slow process in toil, sweat, and vast displays of intestinal fortitude.   8. Having passed the intersection for the third time and being frightened by the sight of the police car, the thieves sped away in the countryside.   9. He flew his airplane toward Topeka and thrilling every second of the way at the sight of the wheatlands below.   10. They were not only left sitting on the dock when the ship sailed but also finding themselves cheated out of the passage money by the unscrupulous travel agent.

B. Which of these apply to the sentences below? The sentence is distinguished mainly by: (1) its parallel structure; (2) its periodic structure; (3) its loose structure; (4) combining both periodic and parallel elements; (5) combining both loose and parallel elements.

1. Mrs. Halloway peered out over the blueness of the waters, watching the horizon and the white sail, sharp and clear like a folded dinner napkin, and wondering if the lighthouse would be there tomorrow.

2. They would the next day perhaps, almost certainly, though the possibility of rain always hovered over them, go, providing the children were well behaved and the cook could prepare a luncheon hamper, to the lighthouse.

3. All that morning Mrs. Halloway busied herself with preparations for the excursion to the lighthouse, sorting out the children's raincoats, sending the butler to town for a bottle of mosquito lotion, and checking weather reports with the captain of the small launch.

4. It was felt by all that the small launch would be more suitable than the Halloway yacht for a trip to the lighthouse, especially because the excursion could then be carried out in an informal way.

5. Ordinarily when cruising on the yacht, the children, because they had to wear their blue sailor suits, and because they were forbidden to run on the polished decks, and because they had to remain seated quietly inside the ornate mahogany-paneled salon, fretted and fussed.

6. A trip to the lighthouse in a small launch would not be without peril if a sudden squall came in from the east or if the August fog crept in between the launch and the lighthouse.

7. On the eve of the excursion, Mrs. Halloway gave final orders to the cook, maid, gardener, game-keeper, butler, chauffeur, tenant farmer, governess, and yacht captain.

8. The morning of the day planned for the trip to the lighthouse dawned grey and misty, the foghorns moaning beyond the breakwater and the whitecaps slapping against the sides of the bobbing launch down at the dock.

9. After consulting with the yacht captain and after catching a glimpse of the grey and white waves in the bay, Mrs. Halloway retired to her room, her head aching, to make a final decision on the day's activities.

10. Assembled by the governess and marched before their mother, the children — dressed informally in sneakers and blue shorts and wearing yellow raincoats — heard Mrs. Halloway say that the trip to the lighthouse would have to be canceled.

C. In these sentences, pick the word or phrase or clause that seems to you most appropriate for completing the sentence logically and effectively:

1. The "English old woman" found the servants insolent, the men uncouth, and (a) the city of Cincinnati to be a very unpleasant place; (b) the

situation in Cincinnati obviously the work of low elements; (c) the city of Cincinnati unpleasant; (d) was stunned by the city's lack of sanitation; (e) by careful inspection also discovered the city to be repugnant.

2. The meeting of the town council that Friday (a) brought about the conclusion that the law should be repealed; (b) ended in the reasoning that the law should be repealed; (c) was able to bring about the repeal of the law; (d) resulted in the repeal of the law; (e) effectuated action commensurable with the removal of the law from the statute books.

3. Mrs. Trollope liked to draw sharp portraits of the Americans, to reveal the folly of their customs, and (a) to be able to indulge in a feeling of superiority; (b) to revel in her own superiority; (c) was prone to finding herself superior; (d) was thought by herself to be able to discover within herself a certain superiority; (e) to be pleased with herself.

4. Charles Dickens found working girls in New England mill towns as well treated and well paid as they were (a) polite and showed pride in their culture; (b) being able to display with pianos and poetry their good education; (c) learned in social customs and well turned out in dress; (d) wholly opposed to any kind of influence which might undermine their moral and social values; (e) well dressed and well mannered.

5. As a grader of papers Professor McFootnote was extremely slow but (a) thought he had to search conscientiously for mistakes; (b) was endowed with the gift of promptly detecting the slightest flaw in either content or expression; (c) accurate; (d) never seemed to miss any inadequacies; (e) cackled with joy whenever he was able to spot a mistake.

6. After the defeat at Gettysburg, Confederate troops (a) moved backward with gathering momentum; (b) overcame the forces of inertia sufficiently well to march below the Mason-Dixon line; (c) retreated; (d) found themselves able to sustain a retrograde movement; (e) executed a tactical withdrawal of surprising efficiency.

7. Every day they tested the sports car by (a) accelerating to 150 miles an hour, checking the chassis, driving in low gear, applying the brakes, and trying out the ignition switch; (b) applying the brakes, accelerating to 150 miles an hour, driving in low gear, trying out the ignition switch, and checking the chassis; (c) driving in low gear, checking the chassis, trying out the ignition switch, applying the brakes, and accelerating to 150 miles an hour; (d) checking the chassis, trying out the ignition switch, driving in low gear, accelerating to 150 miles an hour, and applying the brakes; (e) driving in low gear, trying out the ignition switch, applying the brakes, accelerating to 150 miles an hour, and checking the chassis.

8. In dealing with his colleagues, the young physician was agreeable and pleasant but (a) trustworthy; (b) probably not to be relied on; (c) always charming; (d) oriented in the direction of taking care of himself before anyone else; (e) untrustworthy.

9. Charles Dickens was a man who wrote wonderfully effective novels, who had tremendous insight into the hearts of men, and (a) thinking to

learn more about people traveled to America; (b) who traveled to America in search of more knowledge about human nature; (c) being a writer was able to set down in words many things about human nature; (d) never once missed an opportunity to learn more about people; (e) being a gentleman felt great compassion for the plight of the poor.

19d.   What Good Are Models?

The great writers once held authority; their works were used as models by scholars learning to master rhetoric. Three centuries ago few schoolboys escaped the real or imaginary drudgery put on them by their masters, who drew out of them essays imitating Cicero's grand or Seneca's plain styles (they read the authors' Greek or Latin but wrote in English). Young Will Shakespeare and John Milton learned much about style by studying the masters very closely and imitating as well as they could. Sometimes they learned to imitate so well that they could turn out a parody not too inferior to the original but humorously overdone in one way or another. Today no authority — governmental, academic, professional, parental — can escape challenge or at least suspicion. Imitation is in disfavor in the schools today but it may be coming back. It is after all a proven first step toward individuality and a style of your own. Just sitting down and mechanically copying a polished work, word by tedious word, can force you to see and *use* literary structures none of us could create by ourselves. But don't confuse *imitation* with *copying*. Imitation builds sensitivity and encourages thought; mere copying is too easy to be productive. Imitative composition involves you with the manner of the model, not the matter. The remarkable, self-taught Benjamin Franklin explained how imitation worked for him:

> About this time I met with an odd volume of the *Spectator*. It was the third. I had never before seen any of them. I bought it, read it over and over, and was much delighted with it. I thought the writing excellent, and wished, if possible, to imitate it. With that view I took some of the papers, and, making short hints of the sentiment in each sentence, laid them by a few days, and then, without looking at the book, tried to complete the papers again by expressing each hinted sentiment at length, and as fully as it had been expressed before, in any suitable words that should come to hand. Then I compared my *Spectator* with the original, discovered some of my faults, and corrected them. But I found I wanted a stock of words, or a readiness in recollecting and using them, which I thought I should have acquired before that time if I had gone on making verses; since the continual occasion for words of the same import, but of different length to suit the measure, or of different sound for the rhyme, would have laid me under a constant necessity of searching for variety and also have tended to fix that variety in my mind and make me master of it. Therefore, I took some of the tales and turned them into verse; and, after a time, when I had pretty well forgotten the prose, turned them back again. I also sometimes

jumbled my collections of hints into confusion, and after some weeks endeavored to reduce them into the best order, before I began to form the full sentences and complete the paper. This was to teach me method in the arrangement of thoughts. By comparing my work afterwards with the original, I discovered many faults and amended them.

But it is easier to see how exercises in imitation work in examples.

THE BALANCED SENTENCE

MODEL: The Castilian of those times was to the Italian what the Roman, in the days of the greatness of Rome, was to the Greek.
THOMAS BABINGTON MACAULAY

IMITATION 1: The Vietnam war became to the Americans what the Wars of the Roses, in the feudal times of Britain, were to the English.

IMITATION 2: The Carnaby Street of modern London is to the Mod generation what Bond Street, in the 1930's, was to the admirers of Fred Astaire.

MODEL: Wives are young men's mistresses, companions for middle age, and old men's nurses. SIR FRANCIS BACON

IMITATION 1: Children are grandparents' treasures, joys for fathers, and mothers' headaches.

IMITATION 2: The Seven Deadly Sins are man's weaknesses, burdens to God, and the Devil's delights.

THE PERIODIC SENTENCE

MODEL: Those summer days which some of my contemporaries devoted to the fine arts in Boston or Rome, and others to contemplation in India, and others to trade in London or New York, I thus, with the other farmers of New England, devoted to husbandry. HENRY DAVID THOREAU

IMITATION 1: Those crucial days which some of my friends dedicated to bridge in the union or at the fraternity house, and others to beer and songfests, and others to picnics at Lone Star or Perry, I thus, with the other campus militants, devoted to protest.

IMITATION 2: Those interminable hours in which most of the delegates debated the question of Pakistan and India, and others quarreled over population control, and others analyzed foreign trade with China and Burma, I thus, with the other irresponsibles, gave over to high living.

MODEL: This distinctive character of our own times lies in the vast and constantly increasing part which is played by natural knowledge.
THOMAS HENRY HUXLEY

IMITATION 1: This frustrating aspect of the football season hinges on the unpredictable and erratic role which has been demonstrated by the offensive unit.

IMITATION 2: The unique achievement of the American university rests on its energetic and tireless commitment to matters of both theoretical and practical value.

THE LOOSE SENTENCE

MODEL: The great remedy which heaven has put in our hands is patience, by which, though we cannot lessen the torments of the body, we can in a great measure preserve the peace of the mind. SAMUEL JOHNSON

IMITATION 1: The chief weapon which the older generation has developed is the blacklist, by which, though they cannot entirely annihilate obstreperous militants, they can in great measure cut down on the size of their following.

IMITATION 2: The final resource which the football coach relies on is the forward pass, by which, though he cannot always score against the opponent, he can without question move the ball for long yardage at a single stroke.

MODEL: Writing a book is a horrible, exhausting struggle, like a long bout of some painful illness. GEORGE ORWELL

IMITATION 1: Baking a cake is a pleasant, challenging interlude, like a brisk whirl on the dance floor.

IMITATION 2: Being home at Christmas is warm and pleasant, like discovering the world all over again.

EXERCISES

A. Select two models from each group of sentences, which are arranged in rhetorical patterns, and imitate them.

PERIODIC

1. Aristotle, then, in his celebrated treatise on Rhetoric, makes the very essence of Art lie in the precise recognition of a hearer.
JOHN HENRY CARDINAL NEWMAN

2. Tall and thin, his white hair pushed straight back from his forehead, his long face reamed with wrinkles, his eyes sharp and commanding, Jackson was a noble and impressive figure. ARTHUR SCHLESINGER, JR.

3. The nasty old men, debauched and selfish, pig-headed and ridiculous, with their perpetual burden of debts, confusions, and disreputabilities — they had vanished like the snows of winter, and here at last, crowned and radiant, was the spring. LYTTON STRACHEY

4. As our life is very short, so it is very miserable; and therefore it is well it is short. JEREMY TAYLOR

LOOSE

1. The first indication of our approach to land was the appearance of this mighty river pouring forth its muddy mass of waters, and mingling with the deep blue of the Mexican Gulf. FRANCES TROLLOPE

2. I have fitted up in this farmhouse a room for myself — that is to say, strewed the floor with rushes, covered the chimney with moss and

branches, and adorned the room with basins of earthenware filled with flowers. LADY MARY WORTLEY MONTAGU

3. Lincoln had begun wearing broadcloth, white shirt with white collar and black silk cravat, sideburns down three-fourths the length of his ears. CARL SANDBURG

4. Now education, many people go on to say, is still mainly governed by the ideas of men like Plato, who lived when the warrior caste and the priestly or philosophical class were alone in honor, and the really useful part of the community were slaves. MATTHEW ARNOLD

BALANCED

1. I saw moreover that it did not so much concern us what objects were before us, as with what eyes we beheld them, with what affections we esteemed them, and what apprehensions we had about them. THOMAS TRAHERNE

2. Seeing there are no signs, nor fruit of religion, but in man only; there is no cause to doubt, but that the seed of religion, is also only in man; and consisteth in some peculiar quality, or at least in some eminent degree thereof, not to be found in any other living creatures. THOMAS HOBBES

3. The gold-lamé odalisques of Los Angeles were staring. The Western sports, fifty-eight-year-old men who wear Texas string ties, were staring. The old babes at the slot machines, holding Dixie Cups full of nickels, were staring at the craps tables, but cranking away the whole time. TOM WOLFE

4. As to the ratio of property to responsibility, Ben Franklin remarked that some of the worst rascals he had known had been some of the richest. EZRA POUND

B. Complete the series in each of these sentences. Experiment if you like with deliberate variations to combine rhythm and balance, and even surprise.

Sample: The Incas ate shrimp, bananas, and _____.
    The Incas ate shrimp, bananas, and *mushrooms.*
      or
    The Incas ate shrimp, bananas, and *missionaries.*
    (Notice how this sentence would change if "missionaries" came first.)
      or
    The Incas ate shrimp, bananas and, when we visited their village, often shared our canned *salmon.*

1. He liked rare stamps, fine music, bottled crickets, and _____.

2. The German High Command at no time felt sympathetic with either the aims of Adolf Hitler or _____.

3. Robert E. Lee remains a unique example in history of a general officer who fought without belief in his cause and _____.

4. I do not know if these matters can be settled, if these differences can be arbitrated, or _____.

5. Students, faculty, janitors, yardmen, visitors, and _____ all joined in protesting against the firing of Coach Biff McBlock.

20.   What Is Figurative Language?

Arbitrary distinctions between prose and poetry are tempting and easy to find but they mask the many techniques the two share. Many poetical devices color effective prose, as this passage by Elizabeth Hardwick shows:

> As you pass Big Swamp Creek, you imagine you hear the yelp of movie bloodhounds. The cabins, pitifully beautiful, set back from the road, with a trail of wood smoke fringing the sky, the melancholy frogs unmindful of the highway and the cars slipping by, the tufts of moss, like piles of housedust, that hang trembling from the bare winter trees, the road that leads at last to just the dead Sunday afternoon Main Streets you knew were there.
> ELIZABETH HARDWICK

Images of sound and sight, "movie bloodhounds"; personification, attributing human traits to frogs; simile "like piles of housedust."

Speech is more likely to come up with flashes of instinctive poetry than writing. Among primitive tribes inspired poetical utterance is normal, not exceptional. In cultures committed to the printed word, the poetic instinct shrivels. A poetical touch enlivens any writing except that which is technical or scientific. Of course effective poetical devices are not easy to invent and harder still to put in the right place without making prose look affected and silly. Use this review of figurative language to refresh your prose style.

20a.   Simile

A simile makes a comparison between two dissimilar things, as in "My love is *like* a red, red rose" or "My heart is *like* a singing bird." A simile works only if it makes the reader see an unexpected connection between two things that seemed unrelated.

20b.   Metaphor

A rough translation for the Greek word *metaphor* is "beyond belief." And so it is beyond belief that two unrelated things merely compared in a simile ("my love is *like* a red, red rose") should be actually identified in a metaphor ("my love *is* a red, red rose"). But the stock-in-trade of poets, lunatics, and lovers is wonder, the tiny miracles of life that go beyond belief. For our prosaic purposes, however, a touch of metaphor, or a part of one, is often sufficient to add color. A sportswriter may indulge in something like "Woozoloski sliced his way off tackle for one yard," using *sliced* in a metaphorical sense. He says that "Woozoloski is a bread knife." The next step is to leave off the "bread" and keep only the last part, so that all we hear about is the player's prowess as a knife.

20c. Synecdoche and Metonymy

Synecdoche is using a part to represent a whole. If we say "John is hitting the bottle again," *the bottle* suggests not just that he takes a drink now and then but that he falls somewhere on the high end of the drunkenness scale. In "I have all I can do to keep a roof over my family's head," *roof* stands for the whole burden of parental responsibilities. Robert Frost claimed that synecdoche is at the heart of poetry. In the poem "An Irish Airman Foresees His Death," William Butler Yeats writes that neither "law nor duty" made him fight, nor "public men nor cheering crowd." "Public men" and "cheering crowd" are parts of wartime experience that suggest the whole of war. In the same way we select details in prose very cautiously to convey a sense of our entire meaning. Frequently used with synecdoche is metonymy, using an attribute of a thing to stand for the thing itself, as in "by order of the Crown" for "by order of the King." Metonymy and synecdoche are so closely related that most people cannot distinguish between them.

20d. Mixed and Strained Metaphors

You make a mixed metaphor by illogically yoking together two unrelated images. Theoretically it is wrong to write "He clawed his way to the top with the bare knuckles of strength and energy." When did you last see anyone "clawing" with "bare knuckles"? Say instead "He fought his way to the top with bare knuckles." Likewise "The Republican elephant brays its final chorus" is questionable because elephants do not bray. A strained metaphor relies on images so excessively colorful as to teeter on the edge of ridiculousness, as "Man has climbed over a road of blood and violence, leaving his cape behind for his women to follow"; "Booze was John's Achilles heel and stood out like a sore thumb."

However, many writers of genius, including William Shakespeare and Charles Dickens, have mixed metaphors shamelessly. Shakespeare's Hamlet takes "arms against a sea of troubles" in the famous "To be or not to be" soliloquy. Can you imagine flailing at the sea with a sword or rapier? And yet who is to say that Shakespeare was wrong to insert this illogicality? His metaphor may be literally illogical, illogical on the surface, but in a more profound sense it does the job effectively. Does the mixed metaphor sometimes suggest the possibility of a higher logic? Charles Dickens goes into an ecstasy of mixed metaphors in describing the unloveable Mr. Gradgrind of *Hard Times:*

The emphasis was helped by the speaker's voice, which was inflexible, dry, and dictatorial. The emphasis was helped by the speaker's hair, which bristled on the skirts of his bald head, a plantation of firs to keep the wind from its shining surface, all covered with knobs, like the crust of a plum-pie, as if the head had scarcely warehouse-room for the hard facts stored inside.

Poor Mr. Gradgrind's head is variously likened to a clearing surrounded by a forest, the crust of a plum pie, and a warehouse. Mr. Dickens found uninhibited free association more exciting than cold logic, hard facts that is to say.

What is the answer? May we mix metaphors? When conditions are right, yes. Mixed and strained metaphors will always be conspicuous in a passage of objective, analytic prose, but they may very well fit the occasion in an impassioned argument or a description. Remember that language from the heart always looks uncomfortable alongside language from the head. The Gradgrindian world of hard facts and the modern world of computer language will have small tolerance for the mixed metaphor. If you do mix, be sure you know when and why you are doing so. Mix metaphors rarely, whatever the circumstances, and always be prepared for attacks from the literal minded.

20e.   Sound Imagery

Impressing the reader by manipulating sound in word patterns is an old technique carried over from oratorical rhetoric. Reading silently, we still "hear" the sound effects the writer planned for us. Some familiar kinds are alliteration, consonance, assonance, and onomatopoeia.

Alliteration is the deliberate use of similar-sounding consonants at the beginning of a series of words: "He *l*eft *L*aborador *l*ast night"; *W*e *w*ent *w*ith *W*illie *w*hen *w*ooing *w*as *w*aning." Obviously if we handle it badly this kind of thing can be silly, and overdone. Sometimes people do it accidentally too, with ludicrous results: "He is a *w*izened *w*izard *w*ith a *w*an visage."

Consonance is the use of sound patterns within words, a variation on alliteration: "He *pl*ays *pl*enty of ba*ll*, a cou*pl*e of peo*pl*e encouraging him."

Assonance is the deliberate and repetitive use of vowel sounds within a series of words: "The young m*ai*d was m*a*de to be afr*ai*d by the desire to ob*ey*."

Onomatopoeia describes words formed to imitate natural sounds: *crack, splash, boom, howl, yowl, weep.*

21.   Styling Sentences: How Do I Give Emphasis?

Sentences can be made powerful by the syntactic patterns, the planned assemblages of words, we build into them. The reader who has to thrash through an underbrush of obscuring words, phrases, and clauses, none of them chosen to give clear direction, is justified in cursing the writer, whose responsibility is clarity, conciseness, and proper emphasis. The well-wrought sentence leaves the reader clear about everything you have said because you have put up road signs emphasizing differences between its principal and qualifying elements. Diction, syntax, and sentence rhetoric give you templates to follow in writing those road signs.

21a.   Emphasis: Integration

You make sentences emphatic by applying the rules we've gone over here about parallelism, balance, and periods, also keeping an eye on looseness of structure. All these methods are called "integration," which means putting all parts of the sentence into relationships known to be effective. Use this *scale of modification,* which tells you how *not* to modify an element of the sentence. That is to say, never use a clause when a phrase will do the job:

NOT:	BUT:
It was obviously a low budget film and *it was of poor quality.*	*Of poor quality,* it was obviously a low-budget film.

Never use a phrase when an adjective or adverb will do the job:

NOT:	BUT:
During this film period, the romantic lover was very popular, *Hollywood stars being exalted.*	In the Hollywood era of *exalted* stars, the romantic lover was very popular.

Never use an adjective or adverb when the right noun or verb will do the job:

NOT:	BUT:
Senecan elements of horror *deeply* enter into the play.	Senecan elements of horror *penetrate* the play's entire fabric.

This simple but indispensable idea can save your sentences from misplaced emphasis and floundering rhythm. The reader who squanders energy hunting through irrelevant phrases and clauses for the sentence's real meaning quickly loses interest. Plan the whole sentence around the syntactic element you want to impress hardest on the reader.

21b.   What Are Subordination and Coordination?

Sorting out *coordinate* (main) and *subordinate* (supporting) ideas, and placing them in the logical syntactic unit (word, phrase, or clause), proves a writer's competence. As in parallelism (see 19a), ideas of equal weight deserve equal treatment; those of less importance need to be connected to the main thought as adjectives, adverbs, phrases, or subordinate clauses. These are equal:

These are unequal:

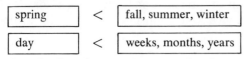

| spring | < | fall, summer, winter |
| day | < | weeks, months, years |

A main thought goes into a main clause; a subordinate thought into a subordinate clause:

NOT:
Each day brought fresh surprises into his life and the weeks, months, years went by with incredible speed.

BUT:
The weeks, months, and years went by with incredible speed, as each day brought fresh surprises into his life.

Join clauses that are equal in thought and in syntax with the coordinate conjunction *and*.

NOT:
He closely analyzed the economic influence of NATO in Western Europe during the last half of the decade *and he spoke clearly*.

BUT:
Speaking clearly, he analyzed the economic influence of NATO on Western Europe during the last half of the decade. [Here the clause has been reduced to a size appropriate to its significance by making it a participial phrase.]

OR:
He closely analyzed the economic influence of NATO in Western Europe during the last half of the decade and he concluded by making a long-range forecast of the contribution of NATO to the common market. [In this version, the second clause is equivalent both in thought and length to the first clause.]

21c.   Upside-down Subordination

Putting a main thought in a subordinate clause, and the subordinate thought into a main clause results in "upside-down subordination," reversing the usual relationship.

In some contexts, however, rhetorical rather than logical considerations may lead you to violate this "rule." The sentence about NATO in 21b could be justified as an attention-getting device, a way of alerting the reader to an important point about to follow. Only the context of the utterance can tell you if it is suitable.

NOT:	BUT:
The cotter pin worked loose, which caused the airliner to crash.	The airliner crashed when a cotter pin worked loose.
Longstreet may have disobeyed Lee, which caused the Confederates to lose at Gettysburg.	Because Longstreet may have disobeyed Lee, the Confederates lost at Gettysburg.

At the ends of your sentences, watch for the phrase or clause that seems an afterthought, something tacked on at the last minute. End strongly, on top of a peak and not down in a valley. You can make an exception when you deliberately want to give the feeling that the thought is trailing off into nowhere.

NOT:	BUT:
In a college course the student is naturally responsible for all that he can accomplish.	The college student is always responsible for his ultimate accomplishment. [Note the strong accent on the final word.]
The knowledge that we are wavering between a world of slavery and riches is known by every man, woman, and child who lives today in this modern world.	Today every man, woman, and child knows we live in a world wavering between slavery and riches. [Would it be known by any *deceased* men, women, or children?]

Occasionally a sentence can end in a valley rather than a peak. By ending on a muted rather than an accented note, this sentence breaks the news slowly and softly and lets the reader down gently:

> The syndics of the press regret to inform you that financial problems beyond the control of either the press or the university will make it impossible to continue with plans for publishing your manuscript at this time.

Stress verbs and nouns to give emphasis.

NOT:	BUT:
There is the necessity of *turning out* the *lights*.	*Please put out* the *lights*.

The unsatisfactory example gives you no opportunity to use emphasis. In the revision, four out of five words are solid points of reference.

Sometimes you can achieve stress by sacrificing a useless clause:

NOT:	BUT:
On the battlefield, Achilles was a swift and cruel fighter who gave no quarter to anyone.	On the battlefield, Achilles, a swift and cruel warrior, gave no quarter. [In this revision more stress falls on the verb *gave* than in the first version.]

21d. Cut Needless Repetitions

Leave out all repetitions that might obscure the ideas you want to emphasize:

NOT:

The stadium was the gift of Mrs. Jones of the class of 1903 of the same year of Daddy's graduation.

This course has given me a chance to develop self-discipline and to depend on myself for every bit of information I learn.

Nick Adams was told of the information in the message, after the door of Henry's lunchroom opened.

BUT:

The stadium was the gift of Mrs. Jones, a 1903 classmate of Daddy.

This course has taught me self-discipline and independent study habits.

Nick Adams was given the message, after the door of Henry's lunchroom opened.

21e. Using Subordinating Conjunctions

The correct subordinating conjunction (e.g., *when, which, that, although*) will establish a logical relationship between main and dependent clause.

NOT:

The picnic was canceled, *and* there was a tornado.

The medieval period was filled with superstition where men believed in witches.

The church members enjoyed the picnic and decided against having another one.

BUT:

Because there was a tornado, the picnic was canceled. [*Because* expresses cause and effect.]

The medieval period was a superstitious one *when* men believed in witches. [*When* expresses time.]

Although the church members enjoyed the picnic, they decided against having another one. [*Although* expresses qualification.]

21f. Placing Conjunctive Adverbs

Conservative usage discourages us from using such conjunctive adverbs as *nevertheless, however,* and *therefore* at the beginning of a sentence. They do their job better, theoretically, not at the beginning, but *near* the beginning, of the sentence. Many good writers seem to open sentences with such words, anyway. But the practice should be avoided in formal writing, if only because it is too easy to fall into a terrible habit: starting sentence after sentence with "However . . .; "Nevertheless . . ."

NOT:

However, he continued to begin sentences with conjunctive adverbs.

BUT:

He continued, however, to begin sentences with conjunctive adverbs.

21g.   Using *As, So,* and *While*

The catch-all *as* often is lazily used to take the place of a more precise subordinating conjunction.

NOT:	BUT:
The library will be closed *as* the furnace is out of order.	Because the furnace is out of order, the library will be closed.
As they have gone away, the party will be canceled.	Because they have gone away, the party will be canceled.

So is also overused as either a subordinating or coordinating conjunction.

NOT:	BUT:
The weather was bad *so* the picnic was canceled.	*Because* the weather was bad, the picnic was canceled.

So is useful as an intensifier, as in "the illness was *so* terrible that the teacher missed meeting Harold." In a result clause, the preferred usage is *so that:*

NOT:	BUT:
They were ill *so* they could not go.	They were ill *so that* they could not go.

So is used more and more by good writers to introduce independent clauses, as in "So then we must reconsider the choices." Observe the ancient rule: don't overdo it!

Like *as, while* is one of those subordinating conjunctions which are often used indiscriminately. *While* is used to mean *although* as in "While you may think so, I do not"; to mean *at the same time* as in "The house was burglarized while we were on vacation"; to stand for *but* as in "I like pizza while Jane likes hamburgers"; and even to stand in place of the conjunction *and* as in "I study German, Harry takes Greek, while Jim tackles Math." Notice the ambiguity of *while* in the last example where its meaning could be construed as either *and* or *at the same time*. Despite advice from such authorities on usage as H. W. Fowler, warning against the perils of using *while* ambiguously, most Americans use the word in all the senses mentioned here. Where you need clarity and exactness, however, it is better to substitute a more exact connective for *while*.

NOT:	BUT:
We saw the city *while* we did our business.	We saw the city *and* did our business.
While in the city, we saw a play. [We can't tell whether the *while* suggests cause and effect or time.]	When in the city, we saw a play.

21h.   Illogical Correlation

Faulty coordination with correlative conjunctions can lead to trouble:

NOT:
The students *were* not only mischievous but also *thinking* in terms of destruction. [Note the inconsistency of moving to a verbal in the second clause.]

BUT:
The students were not only mischievous but also destructive.

Either the malcontents will go or they say the situation will deteriorate.

Either the malcontents will go or the situation will deteriorate.

21i.   Compounding

A laundry list of facts, strung out as though all were of equal importance, is dull and confusing. Place more important ideas in main clauses and less important ones in phrases or clauses.

NOT:
The Girl Scouts assemble early and they walk over to Hughes Street and they see this little dog and the little dog wags its tail and it is really a hot day.

BUT:
After the Girl Scouts assembled, they all walked over to Hughes Street, where they saw a little dog wagging its tail in the terrible July heat.

21j.   Piling up Subordinate Clauses

If you let one subordinate clause modify another subordinate clause, which modifies another subordinate clause, you end up in what James Thurber called the "which mire."

NOT:
The troops moved out early which was what had been planned which was a good thing which the brass all realized later on.

BUT:
Later the brass all realized how fortunate it was that the troops moved out early, as planned.

The delegation met with Mr. Jones who came from Hughes Street which is over near Delancey which is the "street of a thousand sorrows" that the writer J. Struthington Fullwell wrote about.

The delegation met with Mr. Jones of Hughes Street, near Delancey, celebrated because of J. Struthington Fullwell's stories about the "street of a thousand sorrows."

21k.   Short, Choppy, Primerlike Sentences

Repeating many brief sentences or compounded clauses gives you a monotonous tone, because you don't distinguish between the trivial and important by subordination. Handled properly, though, for specific rhetorical purposes, this kind of writing can be rhythmic and effective. It is not ordinarily so when inexperienced writers try it.

NOT:	BUT:
He came from Illinois. He was a good athlete. He was born in 1945. We went to college together. His name was Bill Simmons.	I went to college with Bill Simmons, a good athlete, who was born in Illinois in 1945.

EXERCISES

A. Revise these sentence fragments into emphatic sentences.

1. Town commission to hear complaints about downtown parking. 2. Merchants outraged by parking meters. 3. Shopping centers to take away Main Street business. 4. Threat of chain stores frightening to local business community. 5. Hopes for improving parking good. 6. Police claiming merchants take up parking space themselves.

B. Look over each of these sentences and determine how you can improve emphasis.

1. The robber was caught by the police. 2. His last novel was considered his best by the experts. 3. The dog was driven into the street by Harry. 4. Their movement toward freedom was thought dangerous by the conservative element in the community. 5. We think this wrong. 6. Announcing the time of the picnic that was to be held on Thursday is about all that Tom Jones did while he was on the committee.

C. Correct the flaws in subordination in these sentences. Repair the bad connectives or revise to improve the sentence.

1. The assassination news came, when the stock market crashed shortly afterward. 2. The teacher told the boy to stay after school, which caused hard feelings. 3. The sails on the boat were flapping and there was a stiff breeze. 4. The Renaissance was a time where the Italian city-states came into their own. 5. The team won the game while it decided not to play Hillville High again. 6. Please come on time as a hot dish will be served at seven. 7. As time has run out, the examination is ended. 8. The boys were late so the play was delayed in starting. 9. While we visited in Paris, we enjoyed the opera. 10. While mathematics is fun, English is challenging. 11. The teacher explained to us the best way in which to connect two clauses. 12. The plan of Von Schleiffen called for German troops to swing westward toward the sea to outflank the French and he was a genius. 13. Not only was the German plan a failure but also the French scheme failing badly. 14. The picnic was at the park which was near the village of Stowe which is in Vermont

which is in New England.   15. I am going away so he will not find me in town.

D. Revise these sentences for greater emphasis by making the meaning and the pivotal words (Subject, Verb, Object, or Complement; see 26a, 30) converge.

Sample: The theme of the play, which demonstrates that the people of the lower class are satisfied with their poor position, is illustrated when members of the upper class and the lower class discuss money.

Remove all elements from the sentence except the pivotal words of the main clause to see what remains.

S   V

Theme is illustrated.

Ask if these pivotal words have any significance when removed from the rest of the sentence. The words *theme is illustrated* are cryptic and have no significance when taken alone.

Revise to make pivotal words and meaning coincide, so that pivotal words will function as an outline for the meaning of the whole sentence: "The dialogue between members of the upper and lower classes supports the play's attitude that the poor are satisfied with their station in life."

Remove everything from the revised sentence except the basic elements:

S   V   O

Dialogue supports attitude.

By outlining the sentence the pivotal words serve as a spine for the whole statement. The problem of emphasis has been solved. Carry out the same procedures with these unemphatic sentences:

1. More numerous in the first part than in the second part of *Pilgrim's Progress* is the number of Bible references given to supplement or explain the passages that precede them.

2. Thomas Lake Harris' *Epic of a Starry Heaven* is the epic poem that the writer, who later migrated to California to become a spiritualist and religious fanatic, wrote in a trance.

3. The middle class was rising at the time that the novel began to become popular in England during the eighteenth century.

4. It is not every woman who dresses to please men alone.

5. Between the shops along the Bowery are hotels where men may rent mattresses to sleep on in corners while men on Wall Street may rent luxurious apartments.

6. Instead of trying to analyze and solve their problems, Americans try

to discover a problem similar to theirs with a set pattern of facts for solution.

7. Full appreciation of the status of the verb in achieving sentence effectiveness requires appreciation of how the other parts of speech operate.

8. This patient acceptance that war is an unavoidable thing of the future can lead to nothing but a frightening feeling in individuals.

9. Mme. Beauvoir found that American college students are preoccupied with social and economic questions, and they specialize in these fields in order to base their careers upon them.

10. They spend many hours and dollars at the beauty parlor and dress shop, etc., trying to dress the correct way so that they will be accepted in the social groups that have become so important.

11. The speaker said that most college students whom she talked with concerning America's relationship with Russia were not well developed in their thinking because they favored a preventive war instead of a peaceful solution of the problem.

12. A key factor by which a woman displays her disposition and personality is her dress.

21l.   Emphasis: Isolation

Integration connects the elements in the sentence to highlight the core of meaning. Isolation gives just the opposite: a striking point is made to stand out all by itself in a word, phrase, clause, or brief pithy sentence. Here are some samples:

> It has been widely argued that the critical estimate of Orson Welles' *Macbeth* has been high. *Whose?* I have searched in vain for anyone whose printed remarks suggest unrestrained enthusiasm for that strange film.

> Not a soul had a good word to say about him. *Which is exactly my point.* He never once in his career thought of anyone but Jim Harrington.

> *So far, the disease.* As to the cause, I have delivered a few hints. I now describe it particularly. It is, in brief, a defect in the general culture of the country. H. L. MENCKEN

> Clearly, the Ventura was chosen for what it feels like to the driver, not for its back seat. And considering its performance, driver comfort and general quality, it feels like the most car for the money in this whole group. *That makes it the winner.* CAR AND DRIVER

21m.   Emphasis: Repetition

Deliberate repetition for rhetorical effect sometimes has a kind of hypnotic effect, which can be just the right prescription. Even the much-maligned *it is* and *there is* may have a positive use, as in this example from *The New York Times Magazine:*

According to his memoirs, which he is [now] writing..., there was, for example, the time he caught a rich drunk on Sutton Place who had broken a window in a bar, and he shook the guy down in his home for $1,000.

There was the time he found a Puerto Rican beaten up in the gutter, found the guy who did it, took $1,500 for not arresting him, and gave the Puerto Rican $400 to forget about it.

There was the time he found another beating victim, located the man who did it, took $500 for not arresting him, then collected $900 from the victim for telling him where to find the guy who beat him up.

There was the time he found a man shot in the shoulder, found the man who did it and collected $3,000 to let him go.

There was the time he captured a hood who had helped break up a restaurant, locked him in a room at the station house, then told him he had been identified through a one-way mirror, and received $3,000 for not arresting him.

There were the times he was assigned to investigate homicides and other sudden deaths in the precinct, and contacted a certain undertaker before the families of the deceased could make other arrangements, receiving a 10 per cent commission for each funeral he arranged. RAY SCHULTZ

21n.   Emphasis: Variation

A string of sentences with unrelentingly similar structure lulls the reader to sleep, unless of course it has been constructed deliberately for rhetorical effect, like the Schultz paragraphs. Raising a question or several questions halfway through a block of declarative sentences (if the questions do not disrupt the flow of the paragraph) is a way of breaking the string:

> Be that as it may (prophecy, as George Eliot once observed, is gratuitous folly), the lyric has had its successes in this century and in the nineteenth. And the lyric is a great form, perhaps the greatest after the epic and the tragedy. But some hard questions still need asking.
>
> What has happened to longer poems? Or to the multiplicity of kinds within the general kind of lyric? Why has poetry shrunk? In its kinds as well as in its audience?
>
> The historical answer is, of course, not easy. The shift of major attention to prose fiction, the collapse (in many minds) of a religious and meaningful world view, the narrowing path of advancing individualism, the progress of an "unpoetic" industrialism and the growth of a mass society, romantic rage against order, the fragmentation of pluralism and relativism — all are possible if not entirely consistent answers; all have some truth. PAUL RAMSEY

But lively writing often is done by deftly alternating and varying sentence types and lengths. Alan Paton puts variation to work in amplifying just one paragraph:

What does the Afrikaner Nationalist believe? He believes that God made separate peoples, and that He wants them to stay separate. He often blames visiting sailors for the existence of a million and a half colored people. But we never had that many visiting sailors. In any case, white men still break the fierce Immorality Act. Hardly a day passes but that some white man — some white man's family — is ruined because he has been caught breaking this iron law.

Begins with a rhetorical question. Second sentence is complex and uses parallelism. Fourth sentence deliberately isolates thought by its brevity. Last sentence, again long and complex, suggests labyrinthine Apartheid policy in South Africa.

As these examples show, English syntax offers many alternative resources for starting a sentence.

WORDS AND PHRASES

Hating is Hamlet's favorite pastime.

From Elsinore to London is Hamlet's route into exile.

Hating Claudius, Hamlet schemes the destruction of the king.

To hate Claudius after he has murdered Hamlet's father is not difficult.

To have hated Claudius is to perform a noble role.

To have been hated by Hamlet is to be guaranteed immortality.

Learning the truth from the ghost of his father, Hamlet hates Claudius.

At the end of the play-within-the-play, Hamlet hates Claudius for excellent reasons.

In summary, Hamlet hates Claudius.

CLAUSES

That Hamlet hates Claudius is well known.

If Hamlet hates Claudius, he must also dislike Gertrude.

Because the ghost complained of being poisoned, Hamlet hates Claudius.

Although Hamlet hates Claudius, he is uncertain of Claudius' guilt for a long time.

When Hamlet discovers Claudius' real guilt at the play-within-the-play, he is very angry and mad.

After Rosencrantz and Guildenstern have been disposed of, young Prince Hamlet returns to Elsinore.

EXERCISES

A. Using the devices just outlined, compose twelve beginnings for two of these statements:

1. Oedipus loves his mother.   2. Oedipus killed his father.   3. Petrarch worships Laura.   4. Dante admires Virgil.   5. Michelangelo was a sculptor.   6. Lucretius was a stoic.   7. Stoics uphold virtue.   8. Pleasure can be harmful.   9. Elvis Presley is still great.   10. The Bay of Pigs was Kennedy's disaster.

B. Rewrite this paragraph, putting greater variety into the beginnings of the sentences. Use as many of the devices for beginning a sentence as you can, consistent with good sense.

Fraternities play a key role in college and university life. They serve as a meeting place for the most gifted and talented students. They encourage the development of character. Boys without manners and not knowing how to dress can find out in a fraternity how to do those things. A fraternity man is smooth in the way he approaches people. The future leaders of America will come from fraternities. The fraternity provides important contacts for business. The educational role of the fraternity in university life is therefore more important than most books and courses a student takes.

C. As you saw in the inventory of phrases and clauses above, the possibilities for interchanging the elements of a sentence to achieve pleasing variety are infinite. Re-ordering phrases and clauses can produce nuances and subtleties in thought and emphasis, depending on the point you are making. One way to acquire flexibility with words and to make the habit instinctive rather than deliberate is to practice manipulating sentences. Write several alternate versions of the sentences below, transposing elements in each version.

Sample: Caught up in the passion for scientific certainty, the structural linguists, overturning the value systems of the humanistic camp, have set out in search of the ultimate laws underlying the manipulation of language.

Alternate versions:

a. The structural linguists, caught up in the passion for scientific certainty, have set out in search of the ultimate laws underlying the manipulation of language, overturning the value systems of the humanist camp.

b. Setting out in search of the ultimate laws underlying the manipulation of language, the structural linguists, caught up in the passion for scientific certainty, have overturned the value systems of the humanist camp.

c. In search of the ultimate laws underlying the manipulation of language, the structural linguists in a passion for scientific certainty have overturned the value systems of the humanist camp.

d. Overturning the value systems of the humanist camp, the structural linguists, caught up in a passion for scientific certainty, have set out in search of the ultimate laws underlying the manipulation of language.

e. The structural linguists, whose indifference to the value systems of the humanist camp matches their passion for scientific certainty, have set out in search of the ultimate laws underlying the manipulation of language.

f. To search for the ultimate laws underlying the manipulation of language, the structural linguists have scrapped the values of the humanist camp in favor of the certainty of modern science.

g. Have you heard how the structural linguists, caught up in a passion for scientific certainty, have set out in search of the ultimate laws underlying manipulation of language, thereby overturning the value systems of the humanist camp?

h. See how the structural linguists, caught up in a passion for scientific certainty, have set out in search of the ultimate laws underlying the manipulation of language, thereby overturning the value systems of the humanist camp!

i. That they might discover the ultimate laws underlying the manipulation of language, the structural linguists, caught up in a passion for scientific certainty, have overturned the value systems of the humanist camp.

1. Arguing that "style is the man" many students of language dispute the wisdom of formal instruction in composition, in the expectation that style will follow naturally from wisdom and maturity.

2. To protect themselves from a searching estimate of their abilities, many teachers of English in the past relied on the rigid and inflexible dogma of Latinate grammar, a prescriptive approach that placed great value on forbidding and interdicting improper modes of expression.

3. While he returned often to the great city, John Smathers never ceased to find the endless and shifting vistas exciting and stimulating, the perspectives changing from moment to moment as the sunlight played out its role of genial supervisor over the whole vast, man-made enterprise.

4. The arrival of the swan completed, Lohengrin, dressed in golden armor, appears to the assembled people, a picture of knightly virtue and virility, ready to champion the cause of the wronged maiden.

5. Angered by Prince Hamlet's reluctance to accept the hand of friendship, King Claudius, suspicious and resentful, enlists the support of the garrulous Polonius in the search for Hamlet's true motives, all the more difficult to fathom because of Hamlet's decision (in the classic pattern of the revenge-play) to fake madness.

22.   Sentence Styling: How Do I Find Clarity, Conciseness?

To make concise sentences, you control the syntactic elements in the sentence, wisely choosing among the many ways of putting parts of sentences together. But conciseness, like clarity, also depends on choosing specific, concrete words. The old Aleutian proverb "Wind is not a river; sooner or later it must stop" holds hope for every writer casting about for the exact word. Inflated prose, the opposite of concise writing, is built on many things, one of which is deadwood.

22a.   What Is Deadwood?

Deadwood, which grows under the pen of the writer who can't be concise, means substituting words for thought, and comes from errors in syntax, hidden repetitions, excessive use of verbs, or inexact diction. Any sentence into which you've put such common symptoms of wordiness as *case, nature, situation, there is, it is, areas, fields, so, important, element, factor, things, individual, etc.,* forms of the verb *to be,* passive verbs, and any repetitions needs an extra look to be sure that you can find no better way of getting the idea across. In these examples, the writers have successively fallen into these traps: redundancy, excessive reference to self, inexact diction, and unnecessary *there is* and *of* constructions.

NOT:	BUT:
I was convinced of the validity of the argument that he presented.	I was convinced that his argument was valid.
Personally speaking, I think it is important for me to study English composition because it can enable me to express myself clearly in a manner that will be comprehensible.	I think the study of English composition is vital to clear and lucid written expression.
The boys, who are noisy and quarrelsome, often come over to our side of town on nights that are hot to ascertain if they are able to pick a fight with us.	The noisy and quarrelsome boys come to our side of town on hot nights, eager to pick a fight with us.
There is much evidence that the American public is aware of the threat of atomic war, and there is also awareness of the destruction of atomic war.	There is much evidence to show the American public's awareness of the destructive threat of atomic war.

22b.   Wordy Connectives between Phrases and Clauses

Wordy connective clauses destroy sentence clarity and emphasis (see 21). Almost always you can fix them by finding an appropriate and precise subordinating conjunction.

NOT:	BUT:
They are going to show us the way in which to climb a cargo net.	They are going to show us how to climb a cargo net.
It was then made plain that the reason why we had been denied an interview was because of our long hair.	We were plainly told that we had been denied an interview because of our long hair styles.

22c.   Clumsy Verb Phrases

When verbs and verbals proliferate, a condition called "overpredication" (and a linguistic kind of overkill), your emphasis weakens and disappears. Get rid of cluttering, nonfunctional verbals, and auxiliary verbs.

NOT:	BUT:
Caesar's riches would be able to go to benefit the people.	Caesar's riches would then benefit the people.
The same people had enough love and respect to try to make Caesar king.	The same people loved and respected Caesar enough to want him as king.
The interest of the reader is greatly increased by the irregular time sequence Faulkner used. [The terminal adjective clause *Faulkner used* is superfluous.]	Faulkner's use of an irregular time sequence greatly increases the reader's interest.

22d.   How Do I Use Active and Passive Verbs?

Active verbs such as *smash, hit,* and *put* generally carry more force than their passive forms, *is smashed, is hit,* and *is put.* Colorful, lively writing usually has many active verbs. It also has few linking verbs (forms of the verb *to be*). The paragraph on the left contains no active verbs; the one on the right has been revised to make greater use of active verbs. What are the differences?

Theologically speaking, Camus's *The Stranger is* a novel about a world from which God has withdrawn Himself, and in which there *is* a possibility of neither Revelation nor Redemption. Melville's *Moby Dick is* about the brutish passions of men in a world whose Christian God of mercy and love *has been replaced* by an anti-Christ of mindless force. At another level, Wharton's *Age of Innocence is* about the pride at the heart of man. Newland Archer *is* small in stature because — except for the sacred interval of the marriage sacrament at Grace Church — his world *is bound* by secular convention.	Theologically speaking, Camus's *The Stranger shows* a world from which God has withdrawn Himself, in which the possibility of neither Revelation nor Redemption *exists.* Melville's *Moby Dick portrays* the brutish passions of men inhabiting a world deprived of a Christian God of mercy and love, a God who has been replaced by a mindless anti-Christ. At another level, Wharton's *Age of Innocence explores* the pride at the heart of man. Newland Archer *shrinks* in stature because — except for the sacred interval of the marriage sacrament at Grace Church — his world *remains* in the grip of secular convention.

Choosing a passive verb can completely change the meaning of a statement, as politicians and diplomats have always known. The journalist who wrote about an actor who had "*blunted* his career in the 1950's by refusing to testify about alleged communist associations before the House Committee on Un-American Activities" makes a political judgment, perhaps unwittingly. Many would prefer to say the actor's career "*was blunted* by the House Committee on Un-American Activities." This difference between the active and passive forms of a verb goes far deeper than style.

It is not always wrong to use a passive verb. A passive verb does the same kind of job in prose that an unstressed syllable does in poetry. It gives a pause, a rest, between peaks, plus variety and the appearance at least, of objectivity. It gives variety by offering alternatives to unbroken sequences of active and linking verbs. For scientific and technical writing it suggests detachment and precision. Laboratory reports, for example, must be analytical, free from subjectivity.

NOT:	BUT:
The sulfur should be mixed with hydrochloric acid (an exciting combination) and then ever so gently heated over a Bunsen burner.	Sulfur *is mixed* in a beaker with hydrochloric acid. The solution *is* then *heated* slowly over a Bunsen burner.
The visitor is met by the committee. The situation is discussed and the terms of the contract are agreed upon.	The committee met the visitor to discuss the situation. Following this meeting, the terms of the contract were agreed upon.

Too many linking verbs, forms of *to be,* make reading tedious.

NOT:	BUT:
My home town *is* in the northern part of the state. It *is* cold there. People *are* often very anxious to head south in the winter, away from the bitter winds and frozen lakes.	In the winter, people in my home town in the northern part of the state become anxious to head south, away from the bitter winds and frozen lakes.

EXERCISES

A. Read Orwell's "Politics and the English Language" in George Orwell, *A Collection of Essays* (New York: Doubleday Anchor, 1953). This brief essay contains excellent suggestions about effective writing.

B. Write a composition in which you use only active verbs and no adverbs or adverbial phrases. This exercise will make you verb-conscious, even though normally you should use passive and linking verbs as variations from the active form.

C. In these sentences the original verb has been removed, or the original wording has been rephrased. See if you can discover the original sentence.

1. The various codes which were presented to you at Crossgates — religious, moral, social, and intellectual — were contradictions to each other if you worked out their significance.

2. Life is a stain on the white light of eternity.

3. In the beginning, the heavens and the earth were created by God.

4. The silence of these empty spaces is something that I find makes me feel terrified.

5. I am thinking; therefore I must have some kind of existence.

6. Therefore, I must ask for the liberty to know, to utter, and to speak, according to my conscience.

7. Human beings operate under optimum conditions when fully aware of their inner thought processes.

8. People who are maladjusted in relationship to their peer group often identify with other persons who are maladjusted to their peer group.

I think, therefore I am.
RENÉ DESCARTES, Principles of Philosophy, 1637

"Please your Majesty," said the Knave, "I didn't write it, and they can't prove I did: there's no name signed at the end."
"If you didn't sign it," said the King, "that only makes the matter worse. You must *have meant some mischief, or else you'd have signed your name like an honest man."*
LEWIS CARROLL, Alice's Adventures in Wonderland, 1865

7 The Writer's Thoughts:

Logic, Rhetoric, and Argument

23. What Are Facts and Opinions?

You can verify — prove — a *fact* by observation (seeing the evidence that proves it true) or by authority (going to someone or something that can reliably prove it true). But you can't verify an *opinion* because it comes from belief, not factual knowledge. Facts are the data you see in a report describing a scientific experiment (people who smoke heavily are more likely to have heart trouble than those who don't); in a historical document (the Soviet timetables for demilitarization are clearly itemized in the published minutes of the Strategic Arms Limitation Talks); and in public records (Mayor Curley spent *x* dollars on his last victorious campaign). These are some clear-cut samples:

FACT: George Washington was the first president of the United States.
OPINION: Washington was our greatest president.

FACT: Sir Francis Bacon wrote lucidly about inductive logic.
OPINION: Bacon had the mightiest influence in moving men from medieval superstition to modern enlightenment.

FACT: Anthony Trollope wrote *Barchester Towers*.
OPINION: *Barchester Towers* was Trollope's greatest novel.

But please don't think that anything is wrong with having opinions. Where would our country or the world be without people who have *informed* opinions and are willing to speak them? Opinion is dangerous only when we confuse it with fact — when we aren't sure which is which, confusing illusion with reality. These two paragraphs show how the same ideas can be transmitted factually (giving the straight facts) or subjectively (coloring the story with opinions):

FACTUAL STATEMENT	SUBJECTIVE STATEMENT
In 1741 the Russian explorer, Vitus Bering, was commissioned by the Czar to explore the possibilities of an eastward passage to America. Besides discovering the straits and sea that now bear his name, Bering also found four of the westernmost islands in the Aleutians. Three of these (Attu, Kiska, and Amchitka) were called the "Near" island group because of their proximity to Russia. The fourth was designated the Commander (*Komandorskie*) Island; it remained in Russian hands following the Alaskan purchase. At the time of these explorations in the eighteenth century, the Aleut population, which numbered 25,000, maintained its own independent and unique culture. Unhappily for the Aleuts, however, the price of Bering's discoveries was the gradual extinction of the Aleuts themselves by Bering and his followers.	By 1741 the Russians had foreseen the danger of American encroachment on their territories. For that reason, the Czar commissioned Vitus Bering to explore the possibilities of setting up listening posts along the eastern borders of the nation. A result of this exploration was the discovery of four of the westernmost Aleutian islands. Three of these the Russians called the "Near" group (Attu, Kiska, and Amchitka) because of their proximity to the Motherland. The fourth, designated the Commander (*Komandorskie*) Island, remained in Russia's hands after the Seward purchase. The Russians cleverly retained this key outpost as a wedge into American territory. Significantly, the Aleut population, which maintained its own culture, numbered 25,000 at the beginning of these explorations. Very soon, however, the Russians had deprived the Aleuts of their culture and even their lives. The Aleuts would have fared much better had they fallen under American rather than Russian control.

23a.   What Is Logical Argument?

In theory, argument and persuasion are not quite the same, though in practice they often overlap. Pure argument is high-minded debate, the arguers supporting formal propositions by offering logical proofs; persuasion may also rely on logic, but more often than not emotion is the proof it offers. Argument convinces the audience of the truth; persuasion merely wins approval. Two scholars engaged in a lofty dispute about how to pronounce final *e* in Middle English may be arguing, but a television commercial identifying automobiles with sexy girls may be said to be merely persuasive. Oversimplifying a little, we'll say that *argument* convinces but *persuasion* seduces.

The "factual" statement about the Aleutian islands is limited, except for the last sentence, to a straightforward, nonjudgmental account of their discovery. The last sentence, of course, implies a condemnation of the Russian explorers for their activities. The second statement, objective on the surface, grows out of a paranoid assumption that from 1741 the Russians had been in deadly fear of American encroachment. See the word *danger* in the first sentence. The "cause" of this danger — American imperialism — brings about the "effect" in the next sentence of having the Czar set up "listening posts" along the Siberian shore (electronic listening posts had not been thought of in the eighteenth century). Later, the Russians "cleverly" retain these listening posts, again crediting the Russian czars of two hundred years ago with diabolical foresight. The final sentence is a comparison that almost anyone would admit is biased at worst, unprovable at best.

This paragraph amounts to a very bad argument, and not even much of an exercise in persuasion — except to the most fanatical chauvinists. How might it have been improved? For one thing, a basic principle of argument demands that the proposition to be asserted or defended must be *probable;* it must lie somewhere in the range of plausible human experience. As the fate of the North American Indian may suggest, it is difficult to accept as probable the thesis that the Aleuts would have fared better in American hands. The first thing you need for a good argument is a defensible (probable) proposition. Without that all the proofs (examples and logical arguments) in the world are useless. A defensible proposition on this topic might well be "The Aleutian islands have never been of any real value to the United States"; or, "The fate of the Aleuts was sealed when the white man arrived." You could develop plenty of proofs for either proposition — examples, comparisons, and logical statements.

We can give three examples for the first proposition: "The Aleutian islands have never been of any real value to the United States": (1) they have no agricultural value; (2) all workers are unskilled; and (3) they cost more to administer than they yield in tax revenues. We can find many comparisons to support this proposition: Hawaii, Puerto Rico, the Alaskan mainland. How much more they have contributed to the United States than they have cost! The opinions in this paragraph prove indefensible precisely because they are improbable (two centuries of history make them sitting ducks for the opposition). Effective argument takes far more than strong opinions ("that's *your* opinion" is a familiar retort); it also demands propositions that can stand up to the test of experience.

Not only do these propositions require proof by examples, comparisons, and logical development but they must also be limited enough to be defensible. The narrower you make the topic the more easily you can find workable examples and comparisons. The proposition that the "Aleutian islands have never been of any real value to the United States" at once drains the quagmire built into the first topic — you'd need to be clairvoyant to get into the minds of eighteenth-century czars for its defense.

23b. How Does Argument Work?

To convince others that a proposition is true you need to give proof by examples, details, and comparisons, and by demonstrating causes and effects (see paragraph amplification, Section 17). When developing paragraphs, it is almost impossible to develop a few sentences around these principles without creating an embryonic argument. As soon as we make a statement ("I think the Redskins will win the Super Bowl"), we are forced into giving reasons (proofs), for example (1) "they pray in the locker room"; (2) "they have better backs"; (3) "they are the underdogs." Comparisons also come crowding to mind: "They are more experienced than the Chiefs, who won the Super Bowl several years ago."

Aristotle defined three kinds of "proofs" that are at work in almost any argument: the *ethical,* the *emotional,* and the *logical.* He meant that we can win a point by establishing our credibility (absolute honesty or expert knowledge of the subject, or both); by using emotional appeals, logical fallacies, and half-truths (see 24); and by the sheer logic of our position. The Greek and Roman rhetoricians even arranged patterns of argument into specific inevitable steps that would come up in every argument. Even today most writers will find themselves falling instinctively into this sequence: *exordium* (introducing the argument); *narratio* (stating circumstances); *propositio* (further stating the issues); *partitio* (dividing up the causes); *refutatio* (arguments against opposing positions); *confirmatio* (arguments supporting one's position); and *peroratio* (conclusion). The names may be antique but the techniques are as current as today. Ayn Rand, a popular essayist, develops a case against modern American culture. Do you think her arguments are ethical, emotional, or logical?

When a man, a business corporation or an entire society is approaching bankruptcy, there are two courses that those involved can follow: they can evade the reality of their situation and act on a frantic, blind, range-of-the-moment expediency — not daring to look ahead, wishing no one would name the truth, yet desperately hoping that something will save them somehow — or they can

Introduction

identify the situation, check their premises, discover their hidden assets and start rebuilding.

America, at present, is following the first course. The grayness, the stale cynicism, the noncommittal cautiousness, the guilty evasiveness of our public voices suggest the attitude of the courtiers in the story "The Emperor's New Clothes" who professed admiration for the Emperor's non-existent garments, having accepted the assertion that anyone who failed to perceive them was morally depraved at heart.

Let me be the child in the story and declare that the Emperor is naked — or that America is culturally bankrupt.

In any given period of history, a culture is to be judged by its dominant philosophy, by the prevalent trend of its intellectual life as expressed in morality, in politics, in economics, in art. Professional intellectuals are the voice of a culture and are, therefore, its leaders, its integrators and its bodyguards. America's intellectual leadership has collapsed. Her virtues, her values, her enormous power are scattered in a silent underground and will remain private, subjective, historically impotent if left without intellectual expression. America is a country without voice or defense — a country sold out and abandoned by her intellectual bodyguards.

Bankruptcy is defined as the state of being at the end of one's resources. What are the intellectual values or resources offered to us by the present guardians of our culture? In philosophy, we are taught that man's mind is impotent, that reality is unknowable, that knowledge is an illusion, and reason a superstition. In psychology, we are told that man is a helpless automaton, determined by forces beyond his control, motivated by innate depravity. In literature, we are shown a line-up of murderers, dipsomaniacs, drug addicts, neurotics, and psychotics as representatives of man's soul — and are invited to identify our own among them — with the belligerent

Statement of circumstances

Use of parable

Full statement of the proposition

Examples and comparisons

Intellectuals have deserted their posts

Proofs against opposing positions

1. Philosophy

2. Psychology

3. Literature

assertions that life is a sewer, a foxhole, or a rat race, with the whining injunctions that we must love everything, except virtue, and forgive everything, except greatness. In politics, we are told that America, the greatest, noblest, freest country on earth, is politically and morally inferior to Soviet Russia, the bloodiest dictatorship in history — and that our wealth should be given away to the savages of Asia and Africa, with apologies for the fact that we have produced it while they haven't. If we look at modern intellectuals, we are confronted with the grotesque spectacle of such characteristics as militant uncertainty, crusading cynicism, dogmatic agnosticism, boastful self-abasement and self-righteous depravity — in an atmosphere of guilt, of panic, of despair, of boredom and of all-pervasive evasion. If this is not the state of being at the end of one's resources, there is no further place to go.

Marginal annotations:
- 4. Politics
- Comparison with USSR
- Argument supporting position
- Tentative peroration

EXERCISES

A. Arguing on both sides of an issue (with different opponents or audiences) usually gives you excellent training in expression. John Milton's treatment of lightheartedness in "L'Allegro" ("Hence loathed Melancholy / Of *Cerberus* and blackest midnight born"), and melancholy in "Il Penseroso" ("Hence vain deluding joys, / The brood of folly without father bred") is a good example of an old-fashioned rhetorical exercise in which an author treats both sides of a question. A contemporary of Milton, Robert Burton, in *Anatomy of Melancholy* (1628) did much the same thing in making a brilliant case for and against marriage:

FOR MARRIAGE	AGAINST MARRIAGE
1. Hast thou means? thou hast one to keep and increase it.	1. Hast thou means? thou hast one to spend it.
2. Hast none? thou hast one to help to get it.	2. Hast none? They beggary is increased.
3. Art in prosperity? thine happiness is doubled.	3. Art in prosperity? thy happiness is ended.
4. Art in adversity? she'll comfort, assist, bear a part of thy burden to make it more tolerable.	4. Art in adversity? like Job's wife, she'll aggravate thy misery, vex thy soul, make thy burden intolerable.

5. Art at home? she'll drive away melancholy.

5. Art at home? she'll scold thee out of doors.

6. Art abroad? she looks after the going from home, wishes for thee in thine absence, and joyfully welcomes thy return.

6. Art abroad? If thou be wise, keep thee so, she'll perhaps graft horns in thine absence, scowl on thee coming home.

7. There's nothing delightsome without society, no society so sweet as matrimony.

7. Nothing gives more content than solitariness, no solitariness like this of a single life.

8. The band of conjugal love is adamantine.

8. The band of marriage adamantine, no hope of losing it, thou art undone.

9. The sweet company of kinsmen increaseth, the number of parents is doubled, of brothers, sisters, nephews.

9. Thy number increaseth, thou shalt be devoured by thy wife's friends.

10. Thou art made a father by a fair and happy issue.

10. Thou art made a cornuto [cuckold] by an unchaste wife, and shalt bring up other folks' children instead of thine own.

11. Moses curseth the barrenness of matrimony, how much more a single life?

11. Paul commends marriage, yet he prefers a single life.

12. If nature escape not punishment, surely thy will shall not avoid it.

12. Is marriage honourable? What an immortal crown belongs to virginity!

Using Burton's *pro* and *con* arguments, write a theme either supporting or attacking marriage as an institution.

B. Write argumentative essays on these topics. Use the Rand essay as a model and take either the *pro* or *con* side. You might also aim the essay toward one of these: a convinced socialist, a dropout, a campus leader, a university president, a factory worker, a professional athlete, a small-town banker.

1. Giving the vote to eighteen-year-olds has not helped America.   2. Presidential campaigns should be underwritten by the taxpayers.   3. America needs a far Right and far Left.   4. Big-time college football is a useful institution.   5. Socialized medicine is badly needed in the United States. 6. Labor unions are socially useful.   7. Students should govern universities.   8. Grades should be abolished.   9. The sale of drugs should be legalized.   10. Police should be given more power.   11. ROTC should be abolished.   12. The federal government should subsidize the arts. 13. Detroit automobile manufacturers should produce a small, economy car.   14. The Supreme Court has crippled law enforcement.   15. Busing is an offense to American values.   16. Abortion should be legalized.

17. The jury system should be abolished. 18. Euthanasia should be legalized.

23c. What Is Deductive Thought?

All the patterns that we follow in writing prose make us go through the procedures for thinking known as "deduction" and "induction." Deductive writing leads us to prove a thesis; following the inductive method brings us to the thesis itself. In deductive thought you use *inference,* coming to a conclusion by reasoning from beliefs or from evidence; the conclusion you reach necessarily follows from the premises you chose. Deduction makes thinking much easier. It lets us conclude that *this* three-sided geometrical structure is a triangle because we've memorized the "hidden premise" which tells us that three-sided objects are triangular. Without that premise in mind we'd have to start thinking all over again every time we ran into a three-sided thing before we knew what to call it. People learn from experience that they can safely invent and apply all kinds of generalizations (premises) to their daily lives: "All English instructors like to have papers written legibly" looks like a fairly universal truth. "All pedestrians should be careful crossing streets at busy intersections" probably would seem valid to most people.

This procedure for thinking becomes clear when we state it as a syllogism:

MAJOR PREMISE: All three-sided objects are triangular.
MINOR PREMISE: All these objects are three-sided.
CONCLUSION: Therefore, all these objects are triangular.

To be valid, a syllogism must have major and minor premises (that is, propositions antecedently supposed or proved as a basis of argument), as well as a *middle term* that appears in the first part of the major premise and in the second part of the minor premise. The syllogism takes this form, Z being the middle term:

MAJOR PREMISE: All Z are Y.
MINOR PREMISE: All X are Z.
CONCLUSION: Therefore, all X are Y.

The syllogism shows a truth that we also find in the mathematical principle that "things equal to the same things are equal to each other." That principle works in these syllogisms, too:

MAJOR PREMISE: All *sporting events* are athletic contests.
MINOR PREMISE: Football is a *sporting event.*
CONCLUSION: Therefore, football is an athletic contest.

MAJOR PREMISE: All *good students* are hard workers.
MINOR PREMISE: Mary C. is a *good student.*
CONCLUSION: Therefore, Mary C. is a hard worker.

MAJOR PREMISE: All *airline flight attendants* are polite and well groomed.
MINOR PREMISE: Lizzie G. is an *airline flight attendant.*
CONCLUSION: Therefore, Lizzie G. is polite and well groomed.

23d.   What Are Deductive Fallacies?

Prose of course is not made up of formal syllogisms all strung together. But the bits and pieces of syllogisms, the premises and the conclusions, are the raw material from which we build an argument. Aristotle called these parts of syllogisms *enthymemes* and gave elaborate directions for classifying them. Almost any kind of assertion we make grows out of unstated premises, things we know but take too much for granted to mention them. "Final examinations should be abolished" points back to some kind of unstated proposition that "all examinations are detrimental to the young." Behind the statement "we are independent; therefore we are outspoken," is the unexamined (and unmentioned) major premise that "all independent people are outspoken." Some readers, finding outspoken people merely obnoxious, may resent this aggressive persuasiveness. If you know these hidden patterns of thought you will have no trouble in spotting some logical traps that can spoil compositions.

Sometimes an illogical major premise can lead to an absurd conclusion, even though the steps along the way follow flawless logic. When men believed the earth was flat, it was logical for them to conclude that mariners were in peril if they sailed too far to the west. The illogical major premise zealously applied to the wrong situations leads to bureaucratic thinking in our day. Joseph Heller's ironic novel about World War II, *Catch-22,* shows how airmen in a flight squadron got into all kinds of absurdities because they could not escape from a prison cell of sweeping generalizations. In it, Doc Daneeka, the flight surgeon, can ground any pilot who shows signs of insanity. To be grounded (released from the hazards of combat missions), however, a pilot must make formal application. But according to the surgeon-general's office, such an application is a cardinal sign of sanity because only a lunatic would *not* want to be released from combat duty. There, the double-cross that Heller calls "Catch-22" goes to work: the pilot continues to fly. The absurdity is brought on by the blind acceptance of the proposition that "all pilots who ask release from combat duty are sane." In syllogistic form:

MAJOR PREMISE: All pilots who ask for release from flight duty are sane.
MINOR PREMISE: This pilot has asked for release from flight duty.
CONCLUSION: Therefore, the pilot must be sane.

If the conclusion is valid, the pilot cannot be released from flight duty. It is maddening that, formally, the logic is impeccable. The syllogism is sound; the middle term ("release from flight duty") is there. But this faulty generalization builds into a chain of lunatic conclusions.

Another deductive fallacy is the sweeping generalization, a broad and unqualified statement about large categories of persons and things. It reveals the writer's poverty of thought and it can cause active harm to others. Bigotry thrives on such allegations as "all people of dark complexion are lazy and shiftless." Any statement prefaced by *all,* a *universal affirmative,* needs careful examination and perhaps qualification. *Some* is almost always a safer word than *all.* The courts have ruled against the doctrine of guilt by association; one lunatic in a city does not prove that the city is a madhouse. Compare the differences between these statements:

SWEEPING STATEMENT	MODIFIED STATEMENT
All redheads are hot-tempered.	*A few* redheads have hot tempers.
All basketball players are smarter than football players.	*Some* basketball players are smarter than some football players.
People who drink to excess are *always* security risks.	People who drink to excess are *usually* security risks.
College graduates *inevitably* earn more money than other people.	College graduates *normally* earn more money than other people.

A third deductive fallacy, the fallacy of the *undistributed middle,* can be detected easily when put into a syllogism:

MAJOR PREMISE: All dollars are currency.
MINOR PREMISE: All nickels are currency.
CONCLUSION: Therefore, all nickels are dollars.

Even though nickels and dollars share the common fate of being currency, they are by no means identical. Remember that the syllogism is invalid unless the middle term appears in the first part of the major premise and in the second part of the minor premise. The same faulty reasoning shows up in this syllogism:

MAJOR PREMISE: All automobiles are wheeled vehicles.
MINOR PREMISE: All hay wagons are wheeled vehicles.
CONCLUSION: Therefore, all automobiles and hay wagons are identical.

That two things have one thing in common does not mean that they have all things in common. Because both Republicans and Communists advocate breathing oxygen does not mean that Republicans are Communists. Examine these syllogisms[1]; see if you can detect the fallacy of the undistributed middle term:

MAJOR PREMISE: All police detectives have large feet, wear snap-brim hats, and look hard-eyed.

---

[1] For further readings on logic, see John C. Sherwood, *Discourse of Reason* (New York: Harper & Row, 1964), and Monroe C. Beardsley, *Thinking Straight,* 3rd ed. (New York: Prentice-Hall, 1966).

MINOR PREMISE: This man has large feet, wears a snap-brim hat, and looks hard-eyed.

CONCLUSION: Therefore, he is a detective.

MAJOR PREMISE: All ball-players are good fellows.

MINOR PREMISE: John is a good fellow.

CONCLUSION: Therefore, John must be a ball-player.

EXERCISES

A. Comment on the soundness of these syllogisms. Are the premises valid? Is there any evidence of an undistributed middle term?

1. All teachers are warm and friendly people. He is a warm and friendly person. He is a teacher.

2. All football coaches build character. The minister also builds character. He is a football coach.

3. All fraternity men enjoy fellowship and good company. He enjoys fellowship and good company. He is a fraternity man.

4. All mathematical geniuses possess a remarkable power for abstract analysis. Jack has a gift for abstract analysis. He is a mathematical genius.

5. All athletes develop great physical skill and stamina. He has great physical skill and stamina. He is an athlete.

6. All planetary systems above the orbit of the moon are spherical. The earth is not above the orbit of the moon. The earth is flat.

7. No heavenly bodies except the sun rotate. The earth does not rotate. The earth is not a heavenly body.

8. All green-eyed people are notoriously malicious. Betty is not green-eyed. She is not malicious.

9. All residents of New York City love noise, din, and rudeness. I am a resident of New York City. I love noise, din, and rudeness.

10. No member of the Democratic party ever advocates a tax reduction. He advocates reducing taxes. He is not a member of the Democratic party.

B. These are implied syllogisms. State whether the major premise, minor premise, or conclusion is missing.

1. As a Boy Scout, I shall do my duty to the sick and the elderly.

2. People who cannot read signs in parks get into trouble. You can't read the signs in the park.

3. Everyone who was here last night is part of the conspiracy. You were here last night.

4. "Early retirement for automobile workers would open up many new jobs in that industry, for the benefit of all," said the union leader.

5. Every ship built by the Parker yards has for one reason or another gone to the bottom within one year. Parker built this ship last month.

6. I never travel on a ship manned by foreign crews because of their known habit of becoming excited, blowing up at the slightest hint of trouble, racing for the lifeboats, and abandoning the passengers.

23e.   What Is Induction?

Another tool that very often helps in argument is *induction,* which leads you from particular instances to general ideas, just as deductive thought goes from generalizations to specifics. The inductive way of thinking amasses for you the examples and details that will help you support a proposition. Deduction and induction are as important to thinking as exhaling and inhaling are to life. Induction leads you to truth through a number of events that seem to work in analogous or parallel ways. When a first-grader has been shown that one apple and another apple add up to two, and one pear and another pear add up to two, and one chair and another chair add up to two, he may discover (infer) from all these events (which he sees forming a pattern) that one and another of anything add up to two. The first-grader is working out for himself the law of probability: events repeating themselves in a predictable way during a specific time will probably (though not inevitably) continue to follow that pattern. The child's arrival at this understanding is called the "inductive leap," the logician's name for common sense. From this law we get the argument that if ten students from a school show ignorance, the *chances* are that an eleventh one will too. We stress the word *chances* because the eleventh might turn out to be a scholar. Of course, in scientific experiments no such chances happen. Water heated to 212° Fahrenheit will boil for us the first ten times we heat it, and will also boil the eleventh (if we stay at sea level).

The inductive method has been actively exercised in the scientific revolution. Some people assume that most scientists sit around busily observing, sorting, comparing endless ranks of minute data. And those working in the earth sciences still do, though in some mathematical sciences methods have changed since the nineteenth century. Physics has gone through many advances, often set off by a theory or hypothesis leading scientists into inductive verification by minutely examining experimental data. Einstein's theory of relativity has been verified and reverified many times over in just this way.

John Stuart Mill in his celebrated *System of Logic* (London, 1851) cites four types of inductive thought: (1) the method of agreement; (2) the method of difference; (3) the method of residues; and (4) the method of concomitant variation. To understand how each works, imagine two groups, A and B, of six boys each.

The method of agreement. Think of group A as brilliant students, all on the Dean's List, and group B as dunces, all in jeopardy academically. What cause accounts for this difference? Comparing the two groups reveals that all members belong to fraternities, own automobiles, and have steady girl friends. But one element they do not share is a capacity for hard work. That, then, is the key variable discriminating between groups A and B. Other elements are not causative factors in academic success, and they can be eliminated from consideration.

The method of differences. Imagine group A on a hike. Suddenly one member falls over dead. When an autopsy reveals a bullet in his body, no profound thought is needed to pinpoint the cause of death. In this case, however, the bullet is the variable that cannot be eliminated, distinguishing the dead person from his live companions.

The method of residues. This more complicated method closely resembles the mode of paragraph amplification called "eliminating alternatives" (see 17j). Assume again that group A has gone on a hike. A report comes in that they have vanished from sight. Search parties venture into the wilderness, tracking down leads. Several weeks of hard work go by without the trained investigators turning up a clue — not a footprint, a bent twig, a discarded knapsack, not even a trace of the party. Systematically excluding every possibility pushes the investigating team toward the only conclusion that is left over, which is residual: the original report of the disappearance was false. Happily it turns out to be so.

The method of concomitant variation. Most people would call the fourth method a "persuasive coincidence." Once again group A and group B are active, this time on a college campus where every Friday night for five months a major riot has erupted. The Dean of Students, with the aid of the university traffic and security office, has noticed that immediately before a riot, group A always leaves its fraternity house to head for the house occupied by group B. Because this phenomenon has occurred seventeen times, there seems to be some ground for concluding that the coming together of groups A and B has a causal connection with the riots.

EXERCISE

A. What kinds of inductive thought are needed in solving these problems?

1. It has been observed that all the lights in the building except one are on.

2. Following weeks of investigation, the detectives on the homicide squad still cannot solve the alleged murder of Robert Jones because they cannot find the corpse of the murdered man.

3. Every time a tall, dark man in a grey fedora meets a short, squat man in a homburg at a cocktail lounge on Q Street, a major robbery occurs shortly afterward in that portion of the city.

4. Extensive research with two groups of middle-aged men shows that Group A, made up of heavy smokers, is far more susceptible to cancer and heart disease than group B, made up of nonsmokers.

5. A novel is not philosophy and not history, and, therefore, it is literature.

24. What Are Logical Fallacies?

Slipshod thinking makes faulty prose. The students who created these sentences were only half awake:

All people are naturally good, but all contain a subconscious desire for bad or wrong.	*If people are* naturally good, *how can they be bad too?*
It follows then that the argument can be grasped by anyone with a common, ordinary kind of job, a glass-blower, for example.	Anything so esoteric as glass-blowing is probably not a good example.
She baked some of the most delicious pies I have ever tasted but she won the first prize at the county fair.	The logic calls for a causal (*because*) relationship rather than an adversative (*but*).

24a. Begging the Question

The question-begging statement (*petitio principii*) contains the fallacy of assuming in the premise of an argument that which needs to be proven.

The failure of the public schools has resulted in an avalanche of poorly trained stenographers.	The question is begged because the sentence implies what is really a surmise: that the public schools have failed.

24b. Faulty Causation

Confusing mere chance, coincidence, with a logical chain of events may lead to the fallacy of faulty causation, called *post hoc ergo propter hoc* (after this therefore because of this).

Proof of the witch doctor's powers came immediately after the dove-strangling ceremony, when there was a great clap of thunder.	Gullible persons ascribe to occult powers an event that was doubtless a lucky coincidence.

24c. Argument at the Man

Slanderously attacking the morals or credibility of one's opponent to distract the audience from the real issues is called "argument at the man" (*ad hominem* argument). Many otherwise intelligent persons don't seem able to see through this shabby subterfuge.

A candidate for public office, unwilling to discuss the sales-tax issue, makes the following comments about his opponent: "Wayne G. Smathers was at one time a racist, a member of the Klan, and later a candidate for Congress on a communistic ticket."

These charges, aimed at the man instead of at the issues, are designed to distract the voters from the sales-tax issue and put all their attention on Smathers' character.

24d.   Slanting

Omitting key facts by quoting out of context or by rearranging the facts can mislead a reader. Compare these versions of a film magazine interview:

WHAT LIZ LAWHIZZ SAID AT THE INTERVIEW

Cooking is my secret vice! I just love to cook! If I ever lost my recipe collection I'd kill myself.

HOW IT APPEARED ON THE MAGAZINE COVER

Liz LaWhizz speaks of suicide! Her secret Vice revealed at last. Learn the shocking facts about her real love!

Rearranging unrelated events casts suspicion on the innocent. What does this news story imply about the mayor of Boonville?

Police today raided a gambling and bookmaking parlor located at the rear of the Homer T. Rising Barber Shop at Eleventh and Scroop. Taken in the raid were electronic communications equipment, a stock of numbers slips, and a roulette wheel. Rising was charged with failure to hold a Federal Gamblers Tax Stamp. Rising has long been a close friend and associate of John H. Dailey, mayor of Boonville.

24e.   Headline Hysteria

The technology that spawned the headline — in which a copy writer must stuff a big idea into a few words in a small space — results in oversimplification. Headlines may be the only source of news for the average, harassed man. What can he possibly make out of such fragments as these?

Democrat "Spending Spree" Nixon Target in L.A.
Judge Kills Bid to Subpoena Aide in Watergate Hearing
State Declared by Congo Reds
2 Jets Boosted as Knee Injury Slaps Namath
Dora Lashes Florida

24f.   Ignoring the Question

I do now, as I have always, advocate the right of all Americans to live out their lives privately without interference from government snoopers or meddlers.

Charged with indifference to public welfare, a speaker opposing medical care for the aged avoids discussion of the issue by ignoring (ignoratio elenchi) the real question: Is medical care needed for the aged?

24g.   Non-observation

Hastily examining a thorny problem may lead to superficial and even erroneous conclusions.

To keep the American economy alive and healthy, it is the duty of consumers to spend every nickel they make, of industry to turn out shoddy goods in a program of "planned obsolescence," and of government to pump money into the economy by means of public-works projects. In this way, full employment will be guaranteed.

The writer overlooks the fact that the man who saves his money is also providing jobs through the various firms he has indirectly invested in. Firms that turn out well-made products also conserve natural resources.

24h.   Mistaken Observation

When we wrongly interpret the information our five senses report to us, we can call the result *mistaken observation*. John Stuart Mill, the nineteenth-century philosopher, thought the best example was the understandable error people in the Middle Ages made when they looked at the sky and thought they saw the sun traveling around the earth. "People fancied they *saw* the sun rise and set, the stars revolve in circles around the pole. We now know that they saw no such thing; what they really saw was a set of appearances" (*A System of Logic,* II, 340). And the medieval doctor of medicine believed the arteries in our circulatory system were filled with "aery spirits." Because when people died their arteries collapsed, he assumed those spirits had left the body, deflating their containers. Only in 1637, when William Harvey explained how blood circulates, was this ancient myth exploded. Distinguishing between what we think we see and what is really true is tricky. Henry James's ghost story *The Turn of the Screw* hinges on the witness's reliability. Did the governess really see a ghost, or was the ghost only in her hysterical imagination?

STATEMENT OF A WITNESS

Then I turned and there was a great white object floating there in the dark outside the window of my bedroom. It swayed, made a tearing sound, came closer to the window. I screamed and then I must have fainted, for when I awoke it was dawn and light outside.

FACTS

The neighbor's bedsheet blew off the clothesline. The wind in the trees made a weird noise, and the witness became hysterical.

24i.   It Doesn't Follow

The fallacy in reasoning that we tumble into when we state a conclusion that can't possibly follow from the premises we started with is formally a *non sequitur*. Translated, it is "that which does not follow," another kind of faulty syllogism.

The athletic program is booming. State has been winning games steadily. Doubtless the grateful alumni will contribute great sums of money to the school.	It does not follow that the alumni who are addicted to football and the alumni who are interested in education are identical. Perhaps neither group will contribute.
Although this type of man may seem very intelligent and educated, he is always a better risk than the man who thinks for himself.	What logical connection is there between the dependent clause and the main clause?

24j.   Name-calling, or Appeal to Emotion

A kind of catch-all fallacy, calling the opposition names, plays on the fears of the less informed, who are supposed to be easy targets for slick but wrongly reasoned arguments. Here is a handy list of bogeymen:

yellow peril, red menace, black terror, foreign elements from outside, meddling do-gooders, bleeding hearts, wild eyed radicals, unwashed hippies, male or female chauvinist, crackpot theorists, long-haired potheads, dangerous doctrine, subversive thinkers, capitalist jackals, capitalist wolves, bloated plutocrats, parlor pinks, brass hats, teen-age juvenile delinquents, cadillac Democrats, effete corps of impudent snobs, white racist pigs.

24k.   Black or White or Sometimes Gray

Many people think that any argument must break down into the most fundamental choices — one side has all the right so the other must be wrong. Wiser debaters know that no person, organization, or nation has a monopoly on truth or good or their opposites. They will suspect that the truth may be neither black nor white but somewhere between them, maybe gray; that no one is either completely right or completely wrong in every discussion.

I am in this fight to the end. Everyone who is not with me is against me. I call upon you to stand up and be counted.	Assuming that one side is completely right and the other completely wrong forces a false choice on the audience.
When a sovereign vessel of the U.S. Navy is attacked, the nation either must retaliate instantly with a nuclear attack or itself run the risk of annihilation.	Most military men would agree that between nuclear holocaust and abject surrender some viable option will turn up.

24l.   Overcomplicated Hypothesis

Experts in logic say that the best hypothesis is the simplest, yet it manages to explain all the known facts. Any complicated explanation is always suspect. A sudden headache doesn't *always* mean you have a brain tumor; it generally is a sign of fatigue.

> A mother failed to hear from her son, who was away at school, for three weeks. She worried and worried about the boy and concluded that he had probably been studying too hard, had suffered an attack of extreme fatigue in his room, had fallen helpless to the floor, had lain suffering for several days unable to call for help, and was therefore near death from malnutrition. She hastened to call the dean's office at the university.

The boy had not written because of acute laziness.

24m.   Appeal to Illegitimate Authority

Advertisements often lean on learned authorities to boost a product. The tobacco industry quotes endorsements by physicians for the alleged health-saving values of a cigarette or of its filter:

> Doctors everywhere testify to the merit of Mildacin as a reliever of pain and distress.

"Doctors everywhere" is vague enough to suggest widespread approval of Mildacin, though in fact many M.D.'s think it is a quack medicine.

> Our political party has the support of Dr. Harry T. Tremone, the respected educator, in its effort to ban the fluoridation of water in this community.

Dr. Tremone's status as an educator (but not an M.D.) does not qualify him as an authority on public health, though of course he has a right as a private citizen to express an opinion on any topic.

24n.   Arguing from Analogy

Analogies are useful to illustrate ideas in your writing, but you must keep yourself from tying together two kinds of experiences that aren't logically related. A workable analogy connects experiences that are covered by the same laws of causation (the reason for one must be the same as the reason for the other). For example, the analogy comparing the sun-centered universe with the nucleus-centered atom helps the high-school physics teacher explain (very roughly) the atom's structure. On the other hand, making an analogy between logically disconnected ideas can be intentionally misleading.

> Because the planet earth is inhabited by human beings, it follows that all other planets in our universe must be inhabited.

Even though planets share the property of being in the same universe, it does not follow that all planets are alike.

Competition in the world of business is like the competition of beasts in the jungle for survival: the weak must perish.

Human beings are not beasts in a jungle. Civilization is threatened by such an assumption.

EXERCISES

A. These statements contain logical fallacies. Read each one to find which type of fallacy each shows:

1. All soldiers are ramrod straight. This man is ramrod straight. He is a soldier.

2. I saw two of the Higgins boys steal apples from the orchard, and I know that all of the boys in that neighborhood are a bad bunch.

3. Distinguished physicians throughout the United States recommend Garglewell, the mouth astringent with the special tang.

4. My opponent dares to speak on the issue of water fluoridation, knowing full well that his record of softness toward left-wingers, friendliness with the gambling element, and espousal of radical ideas lurks in his background.

5. And therefore I can say without fear of contradiction that the Mudville Heights subdivision will enjoy a great success by the year 2010.

6. Following your initiation into the brotherhood of Blenseheim, all worldly sin and tendencies toward moral weakness will vanish.

7. The failure of our politicians to support the police in the difficult task of cutting down juvenile delinquency has brought about the present sorry mess.

8. In reply to my opponent's charge that I do not support aid for the sick and aged, may I say that I have in fact on several occasions come out for a sales tax to support the construction of a new baseball stadium on the west edge of town.

9. His alliance with the Leffingwell forces during the fight over the school-bond issue makes him singularly unsuitable to comment in any way on the present controversy over the hiring of a new fire chief.

10. Failure to vote for John Ransom may mean a fresh wave of terror in the streets, further attempts by insidious forces to infiltrate our government, and an orgy of spending in the nation's capital.

11. By and large, people who don't belong to fraternities and sororities are a dull crowd. I'm surprised therefore to learn that Jack is not a Greek. Anyway, I suppose a good deal of what he talks about is dull.

12. Doubtless the attempt to steal your garbage cans reflects a deep mistrust in the community of your political beliefs and religious convictions, a mistrust probably now hatching into a full-scale conspiracy of terror and harassment.

B. Read this letter and answer the questions following it:

TO THE EDITOR:

Mr. James Jones, whose spiteful tirade against fraternities unaccountably found its way into last week's letter column, has convinced himself that "fraternities . . . do more harm than good and should be abolished. . . ." In so doing, the befuddled Mr. Jones has been wrong-headed enough to question the value of that sacred heritage of institutions and traditions which our predecessors have preserved for us because they found them good and useful. That these institutions and traditions are beneficial and serviceable is proved by the fact that our wise predecessors have taken such care to pass them along to us. How, then, can any person who has an interest in the welfare of his fellow students suggest the abolition of those fraternities which are an important part of our heritage? It is obvious that persons who do not have the best interests of their fellows at heart are the ones who attack good institutions. No persons who do not have the best interests of their fellows at heart are worthy of respect; therefore no persons who attack good institutions are worthy of respect. Certainly, Mr. Jones, with his hypocritical pretense of "offering constructive criticism," is not only unworthy of respect, but is richly deserving of contempt.

Mr. Jones seems to think that his is the voice of reason personified, but to less deluded ears his dreary fault-finding much resembles the whine of an outcast animal. It is evident that this carping critic is unable to enjoy life here in the natural, wholesome way in which you and I enjoy it. A well-adjusted student at this college may be defined as one who understands and honors its institutions and traditions. As we have seen, Mr. Jones neither honors nor understands them, and I am accordingly forced to conclude that he is not a well-adjusted student. Further, all misfits are students who are not well-adjusted. Mr. Jones is not a well-adjusted student, and it will therefore be evident to every just reader that Mr. Jones's trouble is that he is a misfit at this college.

One naturally pities a homeless cur, though it snarls at you, but this does not make the beast any less dangerous, nor you any less justifiably fearful. Frankly, I fear Mr. Jones and his kind because I know there is no such thing as a partial misfit. If one tries to fit a square peg into a round hole, he will be unable to make any part of the peg fit. Mr. Jones is just such a square peg, and we know what to expect from "squares." It follows from this that he cannot and will not fit into our way of life on this campus in any way whatsoever. Furthermore, every observant person knows that misfits are frustrated; and, because frustrated persons commonly turn upon the cause of their frustrations (as my roommate, who has taken a course in psychology, says), Mr. Jones can be expected to turn upon our college and its institutions and subvert them whenever he can. It is malcontents of this stripe who not infrequently advocate the uprooting of sound, domestic traditions in favor of the dark seeds of alien philosophies.

We are now in a position to appraise Mr. Jones's dogma that "fraternities are undemocratic. . . ." Every democratic organization which the world has ever known has been based upon brotherhood; and fraternities, by definition, are based upon brotherhood. Who can deny, therefore, that all fraternities are democratic organizations? While some misguided persons tend to forget the basis of the democracy in which they profess belief, no fraternity man ever forgets the basic principle of his fraternity. For brotherhood is not just the foundation stone of every fraternity; it is the *same thing* as fraternity. We may dismiss as embarrassingly naive the remainder of Mr. Jones's statement that "fraternities are undemocratic because they practice discrimination. . . ." What individual or social group, sensible reader, can afford to be indiscriminate?

Mr. Jones would also like to trick us into believing that fraternities are wicked because they are "exclusive." Of course they are, and we are proud of it. In a capitalistic society the rewards justly go to the ambitious, hard-working, successful citizens. Just so, on our campus, each student by his own merit determines his reward. If he has the ability to succeed, he is entitled to recognition and reward in the form of membership in an organization which alone can make possible to him the full benefits of a college career. Those who believe that "fraternities . . . do more harm than good and should be abolished . . ." (even though they add, as Mr. Jones does, "in their present form" as an escape hatch) damage the American way of life. Perhaps it is charitable to assume that Mr. Jones is a fool rather than a knave.

Finally, I would like to say that I fail to see any reason why non-fraternity students on this campus cannot have normal, full, and happy college careers. Mr. Jones cannot, because he is consumed by anger at not having made the grade. However, I number among my acquaintances two or three students who do not seem to suffer noticeably from being non-fraternity men. This should be enough to prove my point. But this opinion received further support at a recent meeting of the twenty-man inter-fraternity council (which includes a non-fraternity representative) when 95 per cent of the group responded "no" to the question, "Is a student's career at this college adversely affected by his failure to be admitted to a fraternity?" The conclusion to all this is simple. All students can be happy provided they are well adjusted. But because a few students are not well adjusted, they cannot be happy. Nothing can be done about Mr. Jones, but we can profitably ignore his childishly petulant attack on those very fraternities by which he would be only too glad to be accepted.

JOHN A. ALLEN

In this letter find:

1. Five examples of slanted language. What impression of Mr. Jones is the writer trying to create?

2. One example of quoting out of context. What false impression does it make?

3. One definition in a circle. Why is it circular (see 13b.)?

4. One example of argument from analogy. What is compared and how can you attack the analogy?

5. One black-or-white fallacy. What is the oversimplification?

6. One impromptu definition. What's wrong with this definition (see 13b.)?

7. One inconsistency. What is the inconsistency?

8. One distraction by the *ad hominem* argument. Why is this point irrelevant?

9. One distraction by alarm. What fear is it aimed at? Why?

10. Two distractions by flattering or identifying with the audience. Explain these devices and their purposes.

Part Two   USAGE

When the age of our people, which now use the tung so well, is dead and departed there will another succede, and with the peple the tung will alter and change.

RICHARD MULCASTER, Elementarie, 1582

8 The Writer's Words

25. Where Did English Come From?

The ancient Greeks' word for "general" was *strategos*; the ancient Romans' word for "farmer" was *agricola*; an old but still used French word for "cup" is *gobelet*; the Germans' word for "child" is *Kind*. The English language has taken over these words, sometimes directly and sometimes by adapting their spelling, and so we have *strategy, agriculture, goblet,* and *kindergarten.* Some words have been forced on the language, as in the eleventh century, when the Normans invaded England, imposing the French language on the natives. English too has been forced on other peoples, as in the colonies occupied by the British Empire during its days of expansion. But it is always remarkably open to immigrant or invader words, unlike other less hospitable languages. The French government recently purged 347 English expressions from the French language, freeing French from words like *hit parade* and *zoning,* and giving the people a purer but maybe a stingier language. Legislation like that isn't likely to be dreamed of in the United States or the United Kingdom.

Some people are astonished when they learn that English was once a local dialect of the German language. More or less "real" English words are hard to sort out from the foreign ones, which have changed along with the native words. As new words have come into the language, spelling and pronunciation of the old words have changed, and the language has gone on changing. Old English (or Anglo-Saxon, A.D. 500–1066) became Middle English, which worked its way into Early Modern English (1500–1660), eventually coming to its current state, Modern English. The prodigious difference between English in the Anglo-Saxon days (the fifth to the eleventh centuries) and today's language is completely unknown to people who haven't studied its history.

Through all these centuries the language has strengthened despite change because its adaptability let people adjust it to their own uses, generation by generation. Flexibility (and a little help from the grand days of the British Empire) has elevated English from a minor dialect into a worldwide means of communication.

The Old English period began when the Anglo-Saxon tribes from northern Europe invaded the British Isles, driving the Celtic inhabitants from the land and making their own language dominant. Old English came to an end in 1066 when the Norman victory at Hastings established French as the court language, Latin as the scholars' language, and English as the plain people's. After Henry VIII broke with the pope in Rome in 1534, nationalistic feeling loosened the foreign influences in England and prepared the way for Modern English. During the Reformation, which separated the protestant churches from the Catholic church, the Latin scripture and liturgy were translated into English, giving the native language new importance. Watch the opening words of the Twenty-third Psalm change across the centuries:

> Dominus gerecht me (Old English, about A.D. 950)
> The Lord governeth me (Middle English, about 1381)
> The Lorde is my shepherde (Early Modern English, 1535)
> The Eternal shepherds me (Modern English, 1922)

25a.   How Do I Find the Right Word?

To speak fluent, literate English, you need a good-sized vocabulary. Reading requires a still larger store of words, but fluent writing takes a huge stock. To pick the right word for each new idea, you must have plenty of alternatives to choose among. George Bernard Shaw, English playwright, boasted that he never had to go to a dictionary — a good share of the English vocabulary was right in his head. Without this talent, most of us need at least a good desk dictionary and a handbook of usage. But the best way to build a vocabulary is wide and energetic (thoughtful) reading, keeping a dictionary handy to go to instantly for the new words that come up. Students have been known to keep a list of the new words they find in reading, listening to public or classroom lectures, or conversing with people who care about the world of language and literature. Remember for the future that the size of a child's vocabulary and his success in school are often in direct proportion to the size of his parents' library.

25b.   Which Dictionary?

A collection of books isn't a library until a dictionary is part of it. Don't sell that dictionary when you're done with your English course — that is as sensible as pawning a stethoscope when you complete medical school. Six desk-sized "collegiate" dictionaries, abridged to keep them compact and decently priced and prepared for the student market, are sold in any large bookstore. Here they are, arranged by date of the most recent edition:

> *Webster's Eighth New Collegiate Dictionary* ([1973], more conveniently designated the *NCD*)
>
> *Webster's New World Dictionary of the American Language.* Second College Edition ([1970] *NWD*)
>
> *The American Heritage Dictionary of the English Language* ([1969] *AHD*)
>
> *The Random House Dictionary of the English Language.* College Edition ([1968] *RHD*)
>
> *Funk & Wagnalls Standard College Dictionary* ([1963] *SCD*)
>
> *The American College Dictionary* ([1947] *ACD;* this is the old Random House dictionary, now distributed by Harper and Row)

Any of these is useful and will make a respectable addition to your library. But the "future shock" we and our language are subjected to today means you should probably choose the most recent dictionary, if only because it will have words that weren't current when older dictionaries were published. *Hangup,* meaning something like "obsessions" or "psychological block," isn't in *ACD, SCD,* or *NCD* Seventh Edition because it was just coming into wide usage when the *NCD* Seventh was published in 1965. The more recent *NWD* and *RHD* have the word but cautiously call it "slang." The liberal *AHD,* revealing fewer hang-ups, so to speak, upgrades the word from "slang" to "informal." The new Eighth *NCD* has it along with 22,000 other new words not in the 1965 Seventh edition, making no comment about the word but defining it as a "source of mental or emotional difficulty." Randomly checking other faddish expressions (*uptight, cool, no way, with-it*) you will find similar trends.

The greatest dictionary of the language is the *Oxford English Dictionary* (*OED*), on which the Clarendon Press of Oxford University in England began work halfway through the last century, finishing it only in 1928. The editors analyzed five million quotations picked by informants everywhere. In one of its twenty-eight volumes you'll find as much as two full pages of examples showing how a word as simple as *bow* has been used from Anglo-Saxon times until now. The dictionary is now published in a two-volume micro-edition complete with magnifying glass for reading the tiny print photographically reduced from the full-sized dictionary.

A major current American dictionary is *Webster's Third New Interna-*

tional (1961), on which the shorter *NCD* is based. This edition enraged many purists because its editors described American usage without prescribing (dictating) which usages were correct and which wrong. An unwillingness to call all uses of the word *ain't* illiterate made conservative linguists furious. A competitor, *The Random House Dictionary of the English Language,* is another of unabridged (huge) size. The Random House editors, unlike Webster's, prescribe, telling you which usages they believe are correct, a practice carried over into their shorter college edition (*RHD*). Of *ain't* they warn that "it should be shunned by all who prefer to avoid being considered illiterate." *Webster's Third* appeals to the linguistically self-confident who want to know how the language is being used; the *Random House* attracts people who want to be told how to use the language.

Still valuable by the way, if you can pick up a set in a secondhand bookstore, is the old *Century Dictionary* (1888–91). It is the closest thing in American lexicography to the British *OED*.

The more recent abridged dictionaries, *Webster's New Collegiate,* Eighth Edition, and *Webster's New World,* Second Edition, also go back to labeling good and bad usage. Morris Bishop writes in the *American Heritage Dictionary* about the " 'scientific' delusion that a dictionary should contain no value judgments." The Eighth *NCD* gives "status labels," telling whether a word lies outside normal boundaries of time (*Obsolete*), region, or social acceptability (*Slang*). Whatever you think of prescriptive or permissive dictionary-making, you can't deny that the editors of *Webster's Third* were courageous in risking so much to defend the study of language as a scientific enterprise.

25c.   How Do Desk Dictionaries Compare?

Looking at the word *version* in the four most recent standard dictionaries, we find interesting facts, differences, and similarities. Of course, economy in writing is the first virtue in any reference book, and all show that.

Second, all four agree on how to pronounce the word, preferring the voiced *z* to the voiceless *sh,* though the *NCD* truthfully informs us that "the presence of variant pronunciations simply indicates that not all educated speakers pronounce the word in the same way." And yet not too long ago a school board insisted that people applying for teaching jobs use only the voiceless *sh* pronunciation of *version* or be denied employment. (Hardly anyone outside the school pronounced it that way.) Before you set out to correct anyone's faulty pronunciation, go to a dictionary so that (1) you'll be right and (2) you'll have an authority to back you up. Habits in pronunciation change; one that was out a decade ago may be in today. So long as we have no Academy for the Preservation of the Status Quo in American English, sensible people should be tolerant about minor unorthodoxies.

Each dictionary gives a fascinating etymology (history) of the word

ver·sion \'vər-zhən, -shən\ *n* [MF, fr. ML *version-, versio* act of turning, fr. L *versus*, pp. of *vertere*] **1 :** a translation from another language; *esp* : a translation of the Bible or a part of it   **2 a** : an account or description from a particular point of view esp. as contrasted with another account   **b :** an adaptation of a literary work <the movie ~ of the novel>   **c :** an arrangement of a musical composition   **3 :** a form or variant of a type or original <an experimental ~ of the plane>   **4 a :** a condition in which an organ and esp. the uterus is turned from its normal position   **b** : manual turning of a fetus in the uterus to aid delivery — **ver·sion·al** \'vərzh-nəl, 'vərsh-, -ən-ᵊl\ *adj*

Webster's New Collegiate Dictionary. Eighth Edition.

ver·sion (vûr'zhən, -shən) *n. Abbr.* **v., ver. 1.** A description, narration, or account related from the specific or subjective viewpoint of the narrator: *Her version of the accident differed from his.* **2. a.** A translation. **b.** *Usually capital* **V.** A translation of the entire Bible or of a part of it: *the King James Version.* **3.** A variation of any prototype; variant: *"At home we played soccer . . . and sometimes a version of hurling"* (Brendan Behan). **4.** An adaptation of a work of art or literature into another medium or style: *Lamb's version of Shakespeare.* **5.** *Medicine.* **a.** Manipulation of a fetus in the uterus to bring it into a favorable position for delivery. **b.** A deflection of an organ, such as the uterus, from its normal position. [Old French, from Medieval Latin *versiō*, conversion, translation, from Latin *vertere*, to turn, change. See **wer-³** in Appendix.*] —**ver'sion·al** *adj.*

American Heritage Dictionary.

ver·sion (vʉr'zhən, -shən) *n.* [Fr. < ML. *versio*, a turning < L. *versus:* see VERSE] **1.** *a)* a translation   *b)* [*often* V-] a translation of the Bible, in whole or part [the Douay and King James *versions*] **2.** an account showing one point of view; particular description or report given by one person or group [the two *versions* of the accident] **3.** a particular form or variation of something, esp. as modified in a different art form [the movie *version* of the novel] **4.** *Med.* *a)* displacement of the uterus in which it is deflected but not bent upon itself   *b)* the operation of turning the fetus during childbirth to make delivery easier —*SYN.* see TRANSLATION —**ver'sion·al** *adj.*

Webster's New World Dictionary. Second College Edition.

ver·sion (vûr'zhən, -shən), *n.* **1.** a personal or particular account of something, possibly inaccurate or biased. **2.** a particular form or variety of something: *a modern version of an antique lamp.* **3.** a translation. **4.** *Med.* the act of turning a child in the uterus so as to bring it into a more favorable position for delivery. **5.** *Pathol.* an abnormal direction of the axis of the uterus or other organ. [< L *versiōn-* (s. of *versiō* a turning) = *vers(us)* (ptp. of *vertere* to turn) + *-iōn- -*ION] —**ver'sion·al,** *adj.*

Random House Dictionary. College Edition.

version, though they emphasize different parts of it. In the eyes of the *AHD, NCD,* and *NWD,* French played a decisive role, although they agree with the *RHD* in seeing Latin *vertere* as the ultimate source. For those with scholarly interest, the *AHD* gives a bonanza — an elaborate appendix tracing the origins of English words back to their ultimate Indo-European roots. A cross-reference to *wer* in the appendix yields a harvest of precedents for senses of "turn" in Germanic, Old English, Old High German, and Old Norse. That's more than most readers will need or want, but it is impressive.

These differences among the dictionaries tell us something about etymology, which is always subject to debate. No one can be sure just where some old words came from or how they changed as they went through the minds, hands, and mouths of our ancestors.

Two dictionaries choose as their first meaning (definition) for *version,* "a particular account," qualifying it with "possibly inaccurate or biased" (*RHD*) and "from the specific or subjective viewpoint of the narrator" (*AHD*). The *NWD* and *NCD* agree on "a translation from another language." But why should dictionary editors choose different first meanings for a word? They explain in their prefaces, *NCD* saying that historical precedent set the sequence, and "the sense known to have been used first in English is entered first" (page 17a). The *AHD* editors say that their "first definition is the central meaning about which the other senses may be most logically organized" (page xlvii).

The medical sense of *version* is adequately treated in all the dictionaries. The *NCD* goes into the most detail in treating the sense of *version* as "an adaptation of a literary work [the movie ~ of the novel]"; "an arrangement of a musical composition"; and "a form or variant of a type," though the *AHD* is not far behind. All handle the adjectival form *versional* by running it into the noun entry instead of entering it separately. The *AHD* gives a lively example from the writings of a contemporary author, Brendan Behan. For help in finding synonyms, the *NWD* gives a cross-reference to *translation*; the others remain silent. All the editors ingeniously compose versions of the same definition, somehow never quite repeating one another.

What dictionary should you buy? They all offer something of value. The *AHD*'s format is handsome, with its outside column of illustrations; the *NWD* has a 1970 second edition, and a handy "Phonoguide" record for studying pronunciation; the *RHD* has a canny middlebrow approach that restores usage labels, and offers attractiveness; and the 1973 Eighth *NCD*, a zeal for scientific research into language, at least according to its editors. Moreover, Merriam-Webster, publisher of the *NCD*, is acknowledged by the Modern Language Association as *the* authority on American spelling. It is indeed an embarrassment of riches, though all other things being equal, the *AHD* is the most fun to work with.

25d.   How Do I Use the Dictionary?

Dictionaries have traditionally bristled with cryptic schemes of notation requiring long explanations by the editors and frequent looking back by those using them. It was revolutionary when the *AHD* editors abandoned dictionary shorthand and spelled out all definitions, except for such obvious things as *n.* for noun and *v.* for verb. If all dictionary-makers did the same, the kind of explanation that follows would become obsolete. The word *essence* from the *NCD* shows how a conservative lexicographer now handles these problems.

The Main Entry. The word *essence* in boldface type is the main entry, which shows how the word is spelled and how it is broken into syllables. Word division is important to a writer or typesetter or proofreader, who must know where to break a word at the end of a line. Clearly *essence* divides into *es-sence,*

es·sence \'es-ᵊn(t)s\ *n* [ME, fr. MF & L; MF, fr. L *essentia,* fr. *esse*
to be — more at IS] **1 a :** the permanent as contrasted with the
accidental element of being   **b :** the individual, real, or ultimate
nature of a thing esp. as opposed to its existence   **c :** the properties
or attributes by means of which something can be placed in its
proper class or identified as being what it is   **2 :** something that
exists :   ENTITY   **3 a** (1) : a volatile substance or constituent (as of
perfume)   (2) : a constituent or derivative (as an extract or
essential oil) possessing the special qualities (as of a plant or drug)
in concentrated form; *also :* a preparation (as an alcoholic solution)
of such an essence or a synthetic substitute   **b :** ODOR, PERFUME   **c**
: something that resembles an extract in possessing a quality in
concentrated form   — **in essence :** in or by its very nature
:   ESSENTIALLY, BASICALLY <accusations which *in essence* are well-
founded —*Times Lit. Supp.*> — **of the essence :** of the utmost
importance :   ESSENTIAL <time was *of the essence*>

*New Collegiate
Dictionary. Eighth
Edition.*

not *ess-ence,* as the unwary might think (even professional proofreaders find that
syllabification demands constant checking with the dictionary). Some words have
alternative spellings also, as *theater* (Am.) and *theatre* (Bri.); if so the main entry
will give this information. Check your dictionary for the syllabification of *meta-
morphosis, stumble,* and *leisure*; if you have an *American Heritage Dictionary,*
look up *syllabification.* What alternative spellings are given for *catalog, medieval,
ideology, judgment, draft, plow, esthetic, analyze, glamour, sulfur, flavor, extol,
program, through,* and *although*?

Pronunciation. The editors tell you how to pronounce *essence* between
the two slashes (reverse virgules) that follow the main entry. The "Guide to
Pronunciation" at the front of the dictionary and the key to pronunciation at the
bottom of each page will decode the notational system for you. For this word,
the mark just before and above the *e* shows that you put the stress on the first
syllable. The *t* in parentheses just means that some speakers use a *t* sound in
pronouncing the word and others do not. The editors make no judgment about
which is preferable. Many words break into syllables differently for printing and
pronouncing: *escape* is printed *es-cape* but is pronounced *e-scape.*

Your pronunciation depends on both your social and your regional surroundings — who you are and where you come from. The *NCD* editors, more
than any of the others, have kept from calling differences of any kind *substand.*
(substandard). Not that they have no standards, or low ones, but they simply
decided that the dictionary should describe, not prescribe. That they have standards shows when they describe an obviously illiterate pronunciation like
"drownded" (for "drowned") as *substand.* Pronunciation, like most other parts
of our lives, ought to be as free of regulation as possible, but there is a limit
— we have to pronounce our words so that people will understand us. Saying
"boid" for "bird" may seem funny in Kansas City but it upsets very few New
Yorkers. Pronouncing "pen" in Brooklyn as it usually is said in Kansas City
would get you a pin, not a pen. Which of these words has more than one usual
pronunciation: *eschatology, roof, renaissance, neither, quay, plethora, athlete,
miscegenation, poinsettia, Norwich, habeas corpus, Oepidus, sacerdotal*?

Functional Label. The letter *n* tells you that *essence* functions like a noun; it does all the things in speech and writing that nouns are expected to do. The editors don't mention the exceptions. Context may change the word's function from noun to adjective: *barn* door, *village* idiot. The editors may add the words *often attrib.* (attributive, functioning like an adjective) or create a separate entry for the word as an adjective.

Inflectional Forms. Words that change their spelling (see 25f) as they are inflected (changed in person, tense, or number) show this information after the functional label. For people who don't remember or know the rules of orthography (spelling) it is useful to find that the dictionary helps by saying that the plural form of *goose* is *geese* and that the other principal parts (the past and present participles) of *to pit* are *pitted* and *pitting*. As you see in the entry, *essence* has no such difficulties.

How do these form their plurals: *mother-in-law, ability, woman, Negro, calf, n, Smith*? How do you form the principal parts of these verbs: *swing, sneer, flog, freeze, promulgate, estimate*?

Capitalization. Some words that have more than one meaning show the difference by capitalizing one of the forms. *Scaramouche* is the name of a character in an old Italian comedy and pantomime; his name has a capital *S*. But a *scaramouche* is a shiftless person and starts with a lower-case letter. Words that are always capitalized appear that way in *NCD*. Others are marked *often not cap.*, meaning "as likely to be lower-cased as capitalized."

When should the following be capitalized: *west, nature, romantic, renaissance, republican, navy, reb, rem, pta, dauphin*?

Etymology. The boldfaced square brackets [ ] following the inflectional form give the word's history. Where it came from another language the source is in *italics*. The meanings inside these brackets are the ones the word had when it was used in Middle English, Old English, or whatever language or form of a language the editors cite for it. The etymology for *essence* tells us that the word came into the language during the Middle English period (ME), that it came in by way of Middle French (MF), and that it got into Middle French from the Latin (L) word *essentia*.

We are told more: *essentia* was derived by the Romans from *esse*, the Latin infinitive form of *to be*, about which we can find more information in the entry *is*. If you are interested in going beyond this brief historical sketch under the entry itself, you can do so in *AHD*'s appendix.

What is the etymology of these words: *Lenten, ether, gravel, cordovan, battalion, flaccid, robot, sandwich, tragedy, dollar*?

Status Labels. Many words are placed in time and usage — the editors tell us where they stand today. If *NCD* editors label a word *obs.* (obsolete), it hasn't been used in standard English since 1755. They also tell us if a word is *archaic* — it is out of date but still used occasionally; *slang* and *substandard* mean it isn't used in formal English; *nonstandard* — educated speakers use it but it is questionable; and *informal* — it is acceptable in all but formal occasions.

What status labels are attached to these: *goon, betwixt, fink, goof, creep* (n.)?

Subject Label. Three dictionaries tell us *essence* is often used in *Philos.* (philosophy), but *NCD* omits the label. Other categories are *Law, Chem., Class. Myth., Anat., Music, Geom.* Abbreviations and subject labels are listed at the front of the book.

Sense Division. One of the dictionary-maker's most intricate jobs is sorting out the senses in which words are used. The word *run* seems simple enough but it has more than a hundred senses — it can have meanings in different contexts. Three main meanings are given for *essence*, each marked by a boldface number. The editor has explained these meanings by dividing them into elaborate subdivisions. Senses 1 and 3 are subdivided into senses labeled a, b, and c. Sense 2 has one meaning, *entity*, but the first sense under 3, a, is divided into two further meanings. Each definition of a meaning is signaled by a boldface colon (symbolic colon), which means "is here being defined as. . . ."

The three philosophical meanings *NCD* gives for *essence* will certainly satisfy you unless you're a full-time professional philosopher. Number 2 brings up a new meaning, "something that exists," and a synonym, ENTITY. The small capitals used for that word are the signal for "here's a synonym," inviting you to see the definitions of that and possibly other synonymous words elsewhere in the dictionary. Number 3 combines the word's meanings for the technological and fashion worlds, with more cross-references in small caps.

How many meanings can be given to these: *rhetoric, epicene, talk, so, sage, factor, pedant, peg?*

Cross-references. Under the word you look up you'll often find references to similar or synonymous words elsewhere in the dictionary to learn about other subjects you had never read of. Beware — this can get to be a habit, turning you into a word nut and inspiring you to start your own vocabulary explosion. Tracing the *is* reference brings you the unconnected but intriguing information that *esse*, the Latin root of *essence,* also is related to Old High German *ist* and Greek *esti.*

Run-on Entries. The phrases *in essence* and *of the essence,* plus the quotation from the (London) *Times Literary Supplement,* give still more information about how the word is used.

Synonyms. Along with the cross-referenced synonyms, some dictionaries give a *synonymy,* a very convenient list of synonyms.

talk·ative \'to-kət-iv\ *adj* : given to talking — **talk·ative·ly** *adv* — **talk·ative·ness** *n*
syn TALKATIVE. LOQUACIOUS. GARRULOUS. VOLUBLE *shared meaning element* : given to talk or talking **ant** silent

New Collegiate Dictionary. Eighth Edition.

Find synonyms for these: *terror, sin, happiness, sorrow, pity, friend, assistant, secret, tricky, old, vertical.*

Usage Notes. Sometimes the editors will give extra help with idiomatic usage, for example, tying the right preposition to a noun or a verb. The *RHD* tells in its entry *derivative* that the word is "usually fol. by from."

Suffixes and Prefixes. Dictionaries usually give combining forms (prefixes and suffixes that combine with words to make new words) and roots (words from which other words are made). Prefix and suffix syllables such as *per, in, and, sub* will be listed in their expected alphabetical places.

Abbreviations and Proper Nouns. Common, widely accepted abbreviations often are listed alphabetically within the dictionary itself (LP = long-playing record). Biographical nouns are in *NCD*'s appendix, except for names that apply to religion, myth, or legend, which are in the dictionary proper. The *RHD* and *AHD* list names along with all other entries, which is convenient.

Supplementary Material. Every dictionary has a healthy collection of serviceable extras at its back and front. Each dictionary has something unique, though none seems superior in every way. The *NCD* offers an elaborate biographical section, listing most names you'd be likely to look up. The *NWD* has a chart on the origins of Western languages, plus the phonoguide to pronunciation. Both the *RHD* and *NWD* have brief manuals of style for preparing research papers, neither of them agreeing with the 1970 Modern Language Association's *MLA Style Sheet,* on which stylistic advice in this book is based. The *AHD* presents essays on language and usage by outstanding contemporary authorities on language. Several dictionaries have tables of weights and measures, proofreading charts, and devices for building your vocabulary; the *AHD*'s charts are worked directly into the dictionary itself. Spend some time with the front and end matter of your dictionary as soon as you get it home, and run through it again occasionally to keep you from forgetting that there's more to the dictionary than the word list.

25e.   Other Reference Works

More specialized dictionaries and handbooks of American usage also give the writer such advice as whether to use *different from* or *different than,* or whether to apply *Frankenstein* to the monster or his creator. Unfastened from its British moorings, the American language is anything but static, exposing these handbooks to possible obsolescence almost on the day they are published. A solid standby has been Bergen and Cornelia Evans, *A Dictionary of American Usage* (New York: Random House, 1957), though Roy H. Copperud's *American Usage: The Consensus* (New York: Van Nostrand, 1970) is more up-to-date. For other books on American English, see Wilson Follett, *Modern American Usage* (New York: Hill and Wang, 1966) and Margaret W. Bryant, *Current American Usage* (New York: Funk & Wagnalls, 1962), which offer sound advice. Helpful in ferreting out synonyms and antonyms to keep the reader from complaining about seeing a word used again and again is *The New Roget's*

Thesaurus (New York: Crowell, 1961). Use it with caution, though. You are better off overworking a common word than to misuse a recondite word. A teacher asked a student to use five new words every day; she was rewarded with this naive note: "Dear Miss Jones, May I have an assignation with you tomorrow after school to talk about my vocabulary list?" Here are some important aids for the writer:

> *Webster's Biographical Dictionary*. Rev. ed. Springfield, Mass.: Merriam, 1972.
>
> H. L. Mencken, *The American Language*. New York: Knopf, 1963.
>
> *The New Roget's Thesaurus in Dictionary Form*. Ed. Norman Lewis. New York: Berkley, 1972.
>
> *Webster's New Geographical Dictionary*. Rev. ed. Springfield, Mass.: Merriam, 1972.
>
> *Webster's New Dictionary of Synonyms*. Springfield, Mass.: Merriam, 1968.
>
> *The Complete Rhyming Dictionary*. Ed. Clement Wood. New York: Garden City Books, 1936.
>
> *Dictionary of American Slang*. Ed. H. Wentworth and Stuart B. Flexner. New York: Crowell, 1960.
>
> *Sisson's Synonyms*. Ed. A. F. Sisson. West Nyack: Parker, 1969.

25f.   What About Spelling?

Some of history's finest authors suffered from poor spelling, the plague of the detail-hater. Of course, English spelling is known to be unscientific, even illogical. A minor war on the language's disorganized ways of spelling was begun in the eighteenth century, but it ended too soon and we still have an unstandardized mess. Then as now, people were confused by such pairs as *sense-cents, low-lo, faint-feint, die-dye*. Another problem is words that used to be spoken as they were spelled, which have evolved so that now the spelling has nothing to do with the pronunciation. The *kn* and *gh* in *knight* and *brought* used to be spoken. Then too, regional pronunciations can be confusing: remember *pen-pin*; *drought* (pronounced *drout*) is pronounced *drouth* in the Midwest. And we occasionally run into British varieties of words that can look very different from American spellings: *theatre-theater* and *tyre-tire* are among the more easily recognizable.

Everything you read here about spelling is reinforced by implied or explicit information in your dictionary. But even the dictionary won't give you the last word every time.[1] The disagreements in dictionaries gave an author

---

[1] Lee C. Deighton, *A Comparative Study of Spellings in Four Major Collegiate Dictionaries* (Pleasantville: Hardscrabble Press, 1973).

enough material for a book. He found they disagreed on the spellings of two thousand words, such as: *per cent-percent, chaperone-chaperon, programmed-programed, reexamine-re-examine*. In spite of these minor indecisions, you can depend on your dictionary's authority for any questionable spelling. You can then claim that your spellings, though they disagree with those in other dictionaries, are consistent, because you found them in a dictionary. To give you a little more help, here are five relatively simple rules:

1. The old jingle about *i* before *e*:

> Write I before E
> Except after C
> Or if spoken as hay
> As in neighbor and weigh

IE	EI
piece, besiege, wield, wiener, relieve	After C: deceive, ceiling, conceive. When sounded as A: veil, reign, deign

EXCEPTIONS: Neither, height, leisure, seize, weird.

2. Losing final *e*

Drop the final *e* when the suffix begins with a vowel, as in *home-homing*. Retain final *e* when the suffix has an initial consonant, as in *spine-spineless*, or *hope-hopeful*. As always, the exceptions make the rules maddening: *changeable, loveable* (lovable is also acceptable), *courageous, noticeable, awful, judgment* (*judgement* is British), *truly.*

3. Double final consonants before suffixes when they are preceded by a single vowel, as in *fit-fitting, dot-dotting*. When two vowels come before it, however, the final consonant is not doubled, as in *leer-leering*, or *beat-beating*. In words with more than one syllable, when the last syllable is stressed, the final consonant is also doubled, as in *extol-extolling* or *compel-compelling*. Finally, if you can remember, when a root word ends in two consonants, the final consonant is not doubled, as in *send-sending*, or *twist-twisting.*

4. Add *s* and *es* to make plurals of most nouns, as in *boy-boys*, or *tent-tents*; and add *s* to nouns ending in *o* that are preceded by a vowel, as in *ratio-ratios*, or *cameo-cameos*. But be sure to add *es* to words that take an extra syllable in the plural, as in *witch-witches*, or *pitch-pitches*. With exceptions (consult the dictionary), a word ending in *o* preceded by a consonant will take *es* in the plural: *tomatoes, heroes, potatoes*, but *dominos* or *dominoes.*

5. Finally, *y* preceded by a consonant is changed to *i*, before *ed*: *fry-fried, spy-spied*. When *y* is preceded by a vowel, no change occurs, as in *convoy-*

convoyed, or in *array-arrayed.* Nor does *y* change when it falls between a consonant and *ing,* as in *try-trying,* or in *fly-flying.*

25g.   Look-alike and Sound-alike Words

Words that are identical in sound and spelling but different in meaning may confuse (as the verb *pool* and the noun *pool*) but they are less likely to cause spelling problems than words identical in sound, as *hole* and *whole.* Another trouble-maker is the suffix or prefix that gives a word a meaning different from the one you may have wanted. What is the difference between "disinterested" and "uninterested?" They cannot be used interchangeably. Compare the differences in meaning between these pairs of words:

except — accept	see — sea
Calvary — cavalry	sorted — sordid
lingering — loitering	feline — felon
site — sight	effect — affect
innate — inert	do — due
limpid — limped	repent — regret
incite — insight	click — clique
humanitarian — humanism	whole — hole

25h.   Oops! Made-Up Words (Spoonerisms)

Composition and speech done under pressure can push people into new and colorful transpositions of prefixes and suffixes that usually happen when they are most embarrassing. These words don't often get into dictionaries. If you become a talented Spoonerist (W. A. Spooner, 1844–1930, was an English clergyman celebrated for such slips), you might praise someone's "stick-tuitiveness," or "shutter to think" of something, "titter on the brink of disaster," deplore the number of "crimesters" in your city, or laugh about the "crime minister" getting mixed up in a scandal. Amusing, but they won't improve your academic reputation.

25i.   Misused (*Mal à Propos*) Words

Mrs. Malaprop was invented by British playwright Richard Brinsley Sheridan for his play *The Rivals* (1776). She was unerringly able to find the wrong word. She says that if she "reprehends" anything in the world it is her "oracular tongue," and she wouldn't hesitate to lay her "positive conjunctions" against anyone who steps out of line. Earlier, Shakespeare had created two characters, Dogberry of *Much Ado About Nothing* and Mistress Quickly of *Henry V*, both of whom could pull a perfectly good malapropism out of nowhere, but the later lady's name caught on, along with her habit, showing us all how a little slip can make us look.

EXERCISES

A. This spelling list is made up of words that have proved troublesome for many college freshmen. How many can you spell without difficulty?

abate	canon	fiat	increment	parenthesis
abet	caprice	firmament	ineffable	pauper
abeyance	caricature	fixation	inordinate	pecuniary
abjure	choleric	folio	jennet	pilfer
ablution	dabble	fulminate	jog	ptomaine
abnegation	debase	furbish	jubilee	rabies
abrogate	deciduous	fusillade	jurisprudence	ransack
abscond	declaim	galvanize	kaleidoscope	remission
abstract	deference	gambol	labial	reprisal
access	defile	germane	lachrymal	repute
aggressive	delineate	gibbet	languid	roadstead
adduce	denomination	gradation	lineament	rubric
asceticism	dexterity	gripe	maggot	scaffold
ballad	dogma	grisly	mammoth	scruple
bane	ecclesiastic	groundling	mannerism	sedition
barbarism	efferent	guerdon	marauder	tepid
bassinet	ejaculate	hamper	mattock	theology
bate	embellish	hiatus	neuralgia	therapeutic
battlement	enigma	homily	nether	unguent
bayou	entomology	humdrum	noisome	unique
benighted	equanimity	hydra	nucleus	viands
bevy	erotic	hydrometer	orthography	vibrate
caesura	estuary	hyperbole	osmosis	vicar
caliber	expedient	imbroglio	ostracism	vigil
calk	fantastic	immemorial	overrule	wharf
canvas	ferule	incisive	panegyric	wheedle
canvass	fetish	incontrovertible	pantomime	zoology

B. Look up the following words in the dictionary and classify them according to their derivations:

schlemiel	galore	scar	scapegoat	knockwurst
wrath	psalm	homily	fiend	pizza
psychology	peruke	gallant	churl	scenario
vichyssoise	flugelhorn	witch	umlaut	limpid
immutable	accurate	piracy	nautch	sequin
gallows	both	pyrogenic	fandango	icon
synecdoche	metonymy	lumbar	wonderful	

C. Using your dictionary, expand the following lists by finding ten words derived from each of the seven languages shown. Which languages seem to have given the most to English?

English	Greek	Latin	French	Scandi- navian	Spanish	German
gift	epiphany	agricul-	battalion	skirt	fandango	kinder-
groom	philos-	ture	chic	smorgas-	matador	garten
	ophy	carnival		bord		zeppelin

D. Some Spelling Problems (apply the rules outlined in this section).

Fill in the correct spelling for these words: perc——ve; n——ce; f——gn; s——ze; inv——gle; f——nd.

Add suffixes to these: donate + ing; tire + less; denote + ing; lone + liness; console + ation; serene + ity; define + able; apprehend + ing; home + ing; fine + ly; wince + ing; sole + ly; fit + ing; dub + ing; bear + ing; defy + s; overlay + s; decry + s; decry + ing.

Put these nouns into plural form: sex; ditch; fix; hippopotamus; piano; hero; thesis.

All of us have a grammar. The fact that we use and understand
English in daily affairs means that we use and understand,
for the most part unconsciously, the major grammatical
patterns of our language.
   HAROLD WHITEHALL, Structural Essentials of English, 1956

9   Problems in Usage:

A Brief Grammar

26.   What Is Grammar?

Once you have worked up an interest in words and have some control over them, your struggle for lucid expression is half won. Then you need practice in connecting the words into meaningful patterns, which grammar may help you to do. A grammar for written language is not the same as a grammar for speech, though. Written English is so different from spoken that it is almost like another dialect. Its conventions (they used to be called "rules") are set by serious nonfiction prose authors and by editors of newspapers, magazines, and books, among others. Ignore the standards that these practitioners set at your own risk; your audience will expect you to stick to them as a condition for reading what you write. For that reason much of what is said here is really a guide to linguistic etiquette, the accepted way of using standard, factual prose. How you handle *spoken* English, and how authors of imaginative prose (fiction) handle dialogue and narrative, can be entirely different.

26a.   How Do I Know a Sentence When I See One?

A sentence must be complete, except when a planned fragment (26b).

It has a subject (S) and a finite verb (V): Billie Jean excels. It may also have an

$$\text{S} \qquad \text{V}$$

object (O): Billie Jean crushes Bobbie; and an indirect object (o): Billie Jean

$$\text{S} \qquad \text{V} \qquad \text{O} \qquad\qquad\qquad \text{S}$$

gave us a victory (note that *o* and *O* refer to *different* things); or an objective

$$\text{V} \quad \text{o} \quad \text{O}$$

complement (OC): Billie Jean found Bobbie a pushover (here *O* and *OC* refer

$$\text{S} \qquad \text{V} \qquad \text{O} \qquad \text{OC}$$

to the *same* person); or even a complement after a linking verb (C): Billie Jean

$$\text{S}$$

is a champion. Another basic form is the anticipatory construction introduced by

$$\text{V} \qquad \text{C}$$

there is: There is a redfaced male chauvinist. Almost any sentence is an expan-

$$\text{V} \qquad\qquad\qquad \text{S}$$

sion or variation on these six patterns. For example, the passive "A victory was given to us by Billie Jean" simply reworks pattern three.

A sentence may be simple, with only a single clause: "Billie Jean annihilates Bobbie in tennis." It may be compound, with two or more clauses joined by a conjunction: "Billie Jean destroys Bobbie and women's lib declares a national holiday." It may be complex, with a main clause and one or more dependent clauses: "Billie Jean deflated male egos when she flattened Bobbie in the Astrodome"; or compound-complex when a compound sentence takes on one or more dependent clauses: "Bobbie's lobs were short and Billie Jean's overhead game was devastating, a situation that guaranteed the best man would not win."

The basic sentence patterns get more complicated as we add phrasal and clausal elements. These modifying elements, called *phrases* and *dependent clauses,* can act like nouns, adjectives, or adverbs (see 29). Phrases are strings of words without a subject or predicate, often introduced by prepositions such as *with, by, in, to,* and *for.* In the sentence "John loves Mary with tenderness," *with tenderness* is an adverbial phrase. In "John sought a girl with brains and beauty," *with brains and beauty* is an adjective phrase. A phrase that modifies the whole sentence functions absolutely (it modifies everything), or as a sentence modifier: "*In fact,* the invasion came in 1819, not 1821." A participial or infinitive phrase is introduced by a participle (*loving*) or an infinitive (*to love*), verbs that act like adjectives or nouns: "*Calling* on Mary, John felt embarrassed." These nonfinite verb forms can be confused with finite verbs. A finite verb makes an assertion ("John *loves* Mary") but a nonfinite verb, some-

times called a "verbal," does not make an assertion (*"Loving* is a good quality"; *"To love* is good").

Sentences get even farther from the basic patterns when we add dependent
clauses, clusters of words that may have a subject and a predicate (as an independent clause does), but that cannot stand independently. They form part of
a sentence and may act like an adjective ("The lads *who joined the regiment*
were very young"), an adverb ("They didn't know *how the flag should be
folded*"), a noun ("I give help to *whoever needs it*"), or an absolute (*"As I have
already said,* John loves Mary"). Words that tell the reader that a dependent
clause follows are: *who, when, if, since, because, although, as, so, that, which,
after, while, unless, in order that, yet.*

26b.   When Can I Use Fragments?

The ancient law that says thou shalt not write sentence fragments has
not been strictly enforced for a decade or so because practiced writers have used
them more and more. Fragments set off the short sentence from those of normal
length, giving a little extra *emphasis.* Advertising copywriters have found the
device irresistible for touting everything from the lowliest paper napkin to the
snobbiest luxury car. The most popular fragment for the moment is a dependent
clause cleverly introduced by *which,* as in this shampoo advertisement: "All it
will do is what we said it would do. Which is plenty." This kind of relaxed
writing uses constructions that are meant to make the reader feel comfortable.
They put spontaneous expression, or the appearance of it, above the ancient
rules. Even those who dwell in the citadels of literature now affect fragments.
Michael Wood wrote this for the *New York Review of Books:*

> Pound, like Proust, like Musil, was a man who discovered at the mid-point
> of his life a work that would occupy him until he died. Which is a way of
> saying he had started a work he would never finish, had invented a form
> which his whole life would feed but which only his death could close.

Just remember that most people who deal professionally with writing
and reading (including instructors) are conservative about fragments; they prefer
to see you restrain yourself and stay with complete sentences, at least until
you've established your own niche in the literary world. These examples show
a more conservative use of fragments, clearly designed to stress a point.

They were thought to have come from the Adreanof Islands by many authorities on Eskimo tribes. *Not so at all!* Anyone could tell that their ultimate identification could hardly be Mongoloid.	The fragment means of course *"this* is not so at all."
They claim then to have found Aleutian artifacts near the Arctic Circle. *Possible?*	A one-word question has been inserted as a rhetorical device.

Hardly, as anyone will agree who remembers
how the Slater expedition of 1902 went over
that ground.

Sometimes you make a fragment result by confusing a verb and a verbal.

NOT:	BUT:
He made extraordinary claims for the success of the wonder drug Marginol. Having the evidence in hand proving his success.	He made extraordinary claims for the success of the wonder drug Marginol. He had the evidence in hand proving his success.
	OR BETTER:
	Having the evidence in hand, he made extraordinary claims for the success of the wonder drug Marginol.

Improperly punctuated parenthetical elements (see 36) also make fragments.

NOT:	BUT:
He is a great man. To say the least.	He is a great man, to say the least.

26c.   Comma Faults

One helpful way to keep your punctuation from getting disorderly is to learn how to know an independent clause when you see one. An old watchword still works: A sentence (or clause) is a complete thought. In "The Watergate hearings were held, they proved nothing" two separate thoughts have been crammed into one sentence. For adequate separation, something more than a comma is called for — at least a semicolon and maybe a period. When you think you have a dependent clause but you really don't and you put a comma after it instead of a period or semicolon (see 36, 37) you fall into the *comma fault* or *comma splice*.

NOT:	BUT:
He met the boys and the stranger, they were coming home.	He met the boys and the stranger. They were coming home.
	OR:
	He met the boys and the stranger; they were coming home.

You can also solve the problem by making one clause dependent: "He met the boys and the stranger, just as they were coming home."

26d.   "Fused" Sentences

Not getting the punctuation right can also lead you into running a batch of clauses together, "fusing" them when punctuation should make them stand apart. Like fixing the comma fault, you can repair the fuse by revising your punctuation (see 36, 37), or be drastic and recast the sentence to straighten out the subordination.

NOT: BUT:
He saw the boys with the goalpost   He saw the boys with the goalpost.
they were coming home the police   They were coming home. The police
were hot on their trail.   were hot on their trail.

                                               OR BETTER:
                                               He saw the boys headed home with
                                               the goalpost, the police hot on their
                                               trail.

EXERCISE

A. Correct the fragments, comma faults, and run-on sentences in these sentences. See 36–40 for a guide to punctuation.

1. The testimony, which they had listened to all day, ebbed and flowed as the afternoon waned, the jury dozed on the hard benches.

2. Making his way slowly and painfully, dragging his crippled body over the sharp stones, he was in overwhelming pain from rope burns around his wrists, Snopes worked his way, pulled his way, up the side of the cliff.

3. The jury came in and it was hot in the courtroom. Blev Snopes, cursing and spitting, watching them.

4. Only a liar telling you that.

5. School is tough, the only chance for survival is by release of tension.

6. The picadors came out of the ring and the bull was there, blood spotting the dust under him, and the silence came over the crowd Manuel came forward with the cape to seek out the moment.

7. I told them that there could be no compromise with corruption. That there could be no equity without justice. And that there could be no net gain without losses.

8. By the fifth round he was very tired, at the gong his trainers having to push him out of the corner into the ring. Where Battleship O'Flanigan waited with stone fists.

9. Mrs. Halloway peered out over the blueness of the waters the white sail on the horizon sharp and clear like a folded dinner napkin, she turned, eyes apprehending the exquisite silhouette of the tea party, wondering if the lighthouse would be there tomorrow.

10. Then they were on the highway, the lights of St. Louis were behind them and the blur of neon along Route 66 was ahead of them, the migrant workers in the trucks were singing and laughing, Dean Moriarty wanted to lean out and tell everybody how great it was to be on the road.

11. Before a crowded audience and augmenting his remarks with colored

plates, Boswell Johnson, explorer, author and lecturer, speaking last night before the fifth annual meeting of the Lawrence Bird-Watchers, an organization devoted to the wonders of birdlore.

12. After taking into consideration the testimony of the witness, evaluating the laboratory reports of the police (always alert in these matters), listening to the hearsay gossip of the neighbors, and analyzing the confession of the accused (a person of unquestioned integrity prior to this sad misfortune), the jury finding the defendant innocent.

27. What Are the Classes of Words (Parts of Speech)?

Four classes of words (parts of speech) carry most of the sentence's meaning: *noun, verb, adjective,* and *adverb*. They are supported by the *function* words: *determiners, intensifiers, pronouns, prepositions, conjunctions,* and *interjections*.

Identifying these kinds or classes of words isn't hard. Just put together a dummy sentence with a space where the word or phrase seems to fit naturally. The space in "The _____ heard a startling lecture" calls out for a noun. In "The girls _____ a startling lecture," a verb is clearly suitable. Next, "The _____ girls heard a startling lecture" needs an adjective. Last, "The girls listened _____ to a startling lecture" is filled by the other kind of qualifier, an adverb. Filling in these holes in the dummy is painless because you can't fit the wrong word in without inventing a nonsense word or destroying the sentence's pattern by making it incomplete. "The *with* heard a startling lecture" or "The *is* heard a startling lecture" are senseless because prepositions and verbs can't fit where nouns are expected. You can write "The *pretty* heard a startling lecture," but only because you change some adjectives to nouns by changing their places in sentences.

We can also make a dummy sentence with slots into which only *function* words will fit. *Determiners,* also called "articles" (*a, an, the*), always precede and determine nouns unless an adjective comes between them. Along with adjectives, they fit into "_____ girls heard a startling lecture." *Intensifiers* (called "adverbs" too), words like *really, very, so,* and *pretty,* fill the blank in "He was a _____ good lecturer." *Prepositions,* such as *in, at, to, for,* or *with,* go into "They heard the lecture _____ Bailey Auditorium." *Conjunctions* join words, phrases, and clauses. They can be coordinating (*and, but, or*); correlative (*either . . . or, both . . . and*); subordinating (*who, which, that, when, while, so, so that, yet, as, since, because, if, although, what, whenever*); or adverbial (*however, therefore, moreover*). The coordinating and correlative conjunctions, respectively, fit into "The girls _____ boys heard the lecture," or "_____ the boys _____ the girls heard the lecture." The *interjection* is a nonsyntactic (not part of the sentence) kind of utterance such as *Wow! Ah! Oh! Yeccch!*

28. How Do I Use Pronouns?

Pronouns generally are used as noun equivalents; we put them where a noun would otherwise be used. Personal pronouns stand in place of a noun. In the sentence "She gave me the ball," *she* and *me* stand for proper nouns such as *Mary* and *Tom*. Other kinds of pronouns can't be so neatly packaged: relative (*who*); intensive (*I, myself*); reflexive (*I said to myself*); indefinite (*one, someone*); interrogative (*who?*); demonstrative (*these, those*); and reciprocal (*one another, each other*). We can feel that in "They harangued one another" and "One looks in vain for accuracy" *one another* and *one* work a little differently from *she* in "She gave me the ball." A very practical difficulty was left to us by the Anglo-Saxons, whose system of inflections (cases) still affects our personal and relative pronouns. We can see the remains of the system in *I, he, who* (nominative case); *me, him, whom* (objective case); and *my, mine, his, whose* (genitive case). These inflections are troublesome for everyone who wants to be reasonably meticulous and correct, but especially for the ones whose zeal for preciseness may smother any creativity they might have. That condition is called "hypercorrectness" — don't come down with it.

Very few still distinguish between *who* and *whom* in speaking (some have suggested that we abandon it altogether) but most language specialists including instructors don't go that far. In writing we're still better off with the antique but correct case-determined pronouns.

28a. Pronouns: Nominative Uses

1. When a pronoun is used as a subject it must be in the nominative case. Few people will tolerate "Us is going to the store" or "Them are the teachers."

2. Use the nominative case after *than* or *as* when the verb is understood.

NOT:	BUT:
They are taller than us.	They are taller than *we* [are].
He is as good as me.	He is as good as *I* [am].

3. It happens rarely, but when you use the verb *to be* in written work, the nominative case should be applied after the verb, even though educated speakers often say "it's me" (as in the French *c'est moi*) rather than the frigid "It is I":

NOT:	BUT:
It is *me*.	It is *I*.
It was *him*.	It was *he*.
The man at the door seems to be *him*.	The man at the door seems to be *he*.

4. Use the nominative case even when the pronoun seems to introduce a noun clause that is the object of a preposition or of a verb in the main clause. The key to the case you should choose is how the pronoun functions in its own clause.

NOT:	BUT:
I recommend him to *whomever* needs an excellent clerk.	I recommend him to *whoever needs* an excellent clerk.
I shall reward *whomever* finds my child.	I shall reward *whoever finds* my child.

5. Use the nominative case when the pronoun functions as a *predicate nominative* (that is, a noun or pronoun that follows a so-called linking or copulative verb such as *is* or *are,* and verbs of sense such as *taste* or *feel*) in a subject-verb-complement sentence.

NOT:	BUT:
They imagine that is *them* on the screen.	They imagine that is *they* on the screen.

28b.   Pronouns: Possessive Uses

1. Generally the possessive case is best for animate things, but an *of* phrase (*periphrastic genitive*) for inanimate things.

NOT:	BUT:
The *table's leg,* or the *mountain's peak.*	The *leg of the table,* or the *peak of the mountain.*
The *leg of* John; the *head of* John.	John's *leg;* John's *head.*

This rule needs tactful handling. Let your decision depend on sentence rhythm and idiom. Because "the leg of John" is a bit more leisurely than the snappy "John's leg," it may fit better the tone you want. Also, when you're talking of time, you would of course say "a month's work" or "an hour's toil," instead of "the work of a month" or "the toil of an hour" — usually.

2. Don't use the apostrophe to show that a personal pronoun is in the possessive case; do use an apostrophe to form the possessive of an indefinite pronoun.

NOT:	BUT:
It's[1] fender was damaged.	*Its* fender was damaged.
Their's not to reason why.	*Theirs* not to reason why.
It's *anybodys* guess.	It's *anybody's* guess.

---

[1] A mistake that far too many people make is not distinguishing between *it's,* a contraction for *it is,* and *its,* the possessive form of the indefinite pronoun.

3. Use the possessive pronoun before gerunds (non-finite verb forms used as nouns).

NOT:
I dislike *him* driving.

BUT:
I dislike *his* driving.

4. This rule applies to nouns as well as pronouns.

NOT:
I dislike *John* driving.

BUT:
I dislike *John's* driving.

But plural nouns aren't often given the possessive case ending: "They all watched the girls marching when the bands all came to town for the contest." If the word after the noun or pronoun is serving as an adjective (*participle*) instead of a noun (*gerund*), then the noun or pronoun stays in the nominative case. Here the case changes the meaning: "I dislike *him* driving"; "I dislike *his* driving." In the first you don't like the person who's driving; in the other it's the driving that bothers you.

5. Use *whose* as a substitute for *of which* whenever the latter looks awkward.

NOT:
We found a class the teacher *of which* was excellent.

BUT:
We found a class *whose* teacher was excellent.

28c.   Pronouns: Objective Uses and the *Who–Whom* Dilemma

1. Earlier forms of English were full of inflections, case endings changing the words to fit their place and meaning. For better or worse, as the language grew it shed the inflections, replacing them with a new system that used particles instead of endings: separate words, such as articles, prepositions, and conjunctions, doing the same job. But a few inflections have held on through the eight hundred years or so, paining almost everyone. You may even catch Mr. Pompous saying "Just between you and *I,* you used *who* incorrectly in that sentence." A writer in *The New York Times* flayed English novelist Graham Greene for faulty casework in writing "I wonder *whom* it could be." Greene felt the *it* between the *whom* and the verb, and fell into the trap of thinking the pronoun had become the direct object of *wonder.*

Here is how you can get them right. Use *whom* when the pronoun is the direct object of a preposition ("To *whom* are you speaking?"), or when it plainly looks back at a noun in the position of an object ("We identified the man *whom* we met last year"). Use *who* when the pronoun is the subject of a clause ("I met the man *who* donated the laboratory"), or, as above ("I wonder *who* it is"); use *who* in interrogative sentences when no preposition goes before the pronoun

("*Who* gave you the watch?"), or where the case of *who* is decided by the verb that follows, not the preposition ("Give the book to *who*ever asks for it"). Here are more illustrations:

NOT:	BUT:
He saw the man *whom* was arrested for assault.	He saw the man *who* was arrested for assault.
He saw the man *who* we met last year.	He saw the man *whom* we met last year.

When long intervening elements make the relationship hard to remember, however, only a purist will insist on *who*.

NOT ONLY:	BUT ALSO:
He saw the man *whom* many of us believe was responsible for the assault.	He saw the man *who* many of us believe *was* responsible for the assault.

2. In an interrogative sentence, *who* is acceptable unless a preposition comes before it.

NOT:	BUT:
Whom did you see there?	*Who* did you see there?
To *who* did you talk?	To *whom* did you talk?

3. Use the objective case after *than* and *as,* when the pronoun is the object of an understood verb.

NOT:	BUT:
I wrote the girls as well as *they*.	I wrote the girls as well as [I wrote] *them*.
She dislikes us even more than *he*. (This is acceptable if you intend to say "she dislikes us even more than he dislikes us.")	She dislikes us even more than [she dislikes] *him*.

4. Use the objective case for pronouns that are the objects of finite verbs, nonfinite verbs (sometimes called "verbals" and made up of infinitives like *to know,* and participles and gerunds like *loving*), and prepositions.

NOT:	BUT:
He warned *we* boys to be silent.	He warned *us* boys to be silent.
Just between you and *I*, the election was rigged.	Just between you and *me*, the election was rigged.
No one could save them now but *I*.	No one could save them now but *me*.

Choosing the case for the pronoun when you face compound objects is very unpleasant. Those who would never dream of writing "He liked I" get trapped into writing "He liked Jim and I."

NOT:	BUT:
He presented Mary and *I* with the gift certificates.	He presented Mary and *me* with the gift certificates.
Walking Mary and *I* home, he told us the story.	Walking Mary and *me* home, he told us the story.

EXERCISE

A. Correct the wrong choices of case in these sentences. If you find no "error," explain why you let the sentence stand.

1. They did not know the handwriting of John.   2. For who are you speaking?   3. You were told to give the gift to who?   4. They are the ones who I have reason to think make the annoying telephone calls. 5. Just between you and I, the whole school is corrupt.   6. The principal spoke to we boys and girls about Americanism.   7. You need the extra work more than me.   8. It was to us exactly as to they.   9. None of us was wild about him leading the class.   10. It's anybody's guess so far as we are concerned.

29.   What Are Adjectives and Adverbs?

Adjectives modify (qualify or limit in meaning) nouns, and adverbs modify verbs, adverbs, and adjectives. Both are inflected, changing their form in the positive, comparative, and superlative forms or degrees: *slow, slower, slowest; good, better, best; badly, more badly, most badly.* Some adjectives (*leisurely, lovely, manly*) use the *-ly* ending of adverbs. You can write "He dined leisurely" if you don't mind being corrected by the purist, who prefers "He dined in a leisurely manner," or "His dining was leisurely." A few "flat" adverbs don't take the *-ly* ending: "He is *doubtless* wrong"; "He walks *slow*" or "He walks *slowly*" — either is right.

The adjective fits into the dummy sentence somewhere near the noun it modifies: "He carried a _____ box." The adverb often comes just before the verb: "He _____ finds defects in her work." But it can go elsewhere in the sentence: "Quickly, she stooped," or "She stooped quickly."

1. Pick an adverb (not an adjective) to modify a verb.

NOT:	BUT:
He chatters *nervous* all the time.	He chatters *nervously* all the time.

2. Use the *comparative* form of the adjective to describe the relationship *between* two persons or things, the *superlative* form for the relationship *among* three or more.

NOT:	BUT:
She is the *best* of the *two* girls.	She is the *better* of the *two* girls.
She is the *better* of the *three* girls.	She is the *best* of the *three* girls.

3. Modify other adverbs and adjectives only with adverbs.

NOT:	BUT:
It was *terrible* badly done.	It was *terribly* badly done.
The play was *unbelievable* bad.	The play was *unbelievably* bad.

There are always exceptions. *Real good* seems to be forcing its folksy way into general circulation in place of *really good*. But the latter is still better in writing, unless you have an audience of bumpkins.

4. For downward comparisons (*brave, less brave, least brave*) use the same forms as in upward comparisons (*cowardly, more cowardly, most cowardly*).

NOT:	BUT:
She was the *least* skilled of the two sisters.	She was the *less* skilled of the two sisters.
He was the *less* talented of the five quarterbacks.	He was the *least* talented of the five quarterbacks.

5. After a linking verb use an adjective. The English language has at least sixty linking verbs and adds to our trouble by making them act like linking verbs in some places, connecting subject and predicate ("The hinge worked [became] loose"), and like intransitive verbs in others, when the verb takes no object ("The hinge worked loosely"). No easy formula covers all varieties. Generally, any verb like *to be, to seem,* or *to become* is linking and takes an adjective, not an adverb. The adjective modifies the subject of the sentence, not the verb.

NOT:	BUT:
The whole enterprise smelled *badly* to me.	The whole enterprise smelled *bad* to me.
The sauna felt *well*.	The sauna felt *good*.
He stood *four-squarely* for truth.	He stood [is] *four-square* for truth.

6. For the placement of adverbs, see Modifiers, 35e.

EXERCISE

√A. Correct the adjectives and adverbs in these sentences.

1. Her bridge game looks well to me.   2. Mary C. was often unconscious funny.   3. Liz is the most obedient of the two girls.   4. Little Ann is the faster runner of the three.   5. He did not seem real good-natured about it.   6. The apple tasted sweetly to Eve.   7. He walked home as rapid as possible.   8. She knows the least of the two.   9. John is the most bitterest of all.   10. We all thought Jack had done a real good job.   11. John conducted himself good.

30.   What Is a Verb?

The verb is the word in a sentence that moves; it is kinetic, not static. In the dummy sentence, "The football team _____ the game," the verbs *won* or *lost* will fit. Or in "The Dean is _____ing today," *leaving* goes nicely; any other part of speech would look silly.

The verb has kept more of the ancient inflections than any other part of speech. It changes according to the person, number, tense, mood, and voice of its subjects.

Person describes the subject of the verb, which can be first person (*I*), second (*you*), or third (*he, she, it, they*), as in *I walk, you walk, he walks, we walk, you walk, they walk.*

Number tells us whether the verb is *singular* (one subject) or *plural*. Its forms show up best in third person singular and plural of the verb: *he walks* shifts to *they walk*. The third person singular almost always ends with an *s* or *es* (he *sits* or he *does*).

Tense generally means *time* — when did the subject take the action the verb describes? The six tenses we use most often are *past* (I *said*), *present* (I *say*), *future* (I *shall say* or I *will say*), *past perfect* (I *had said*), *present perfect* (I *have said*), and *future perfect* (I *shall have said,* or I *will have said*). *Perfect* means the verb's action is completed or "perfected." But because English tenses don't always have anything to do with time, the Roman grammarians' wonderfully complete catalog of names for all their Latin verb forms doesn't go quite far enough for English. Present tense *may* mean something happening now ("I sit down at the counter"), but it can carry some past feeling, too ("I am sitting down at the counter when Harry walks in"), which is the *historical present*. The present tense can also have some future in it ("I visit my uncle this weekend"). And the present can go on indefinitely ("I run a mile every morning before breakfast"). Some tenses need a descriptive grammarian to name them ("Your mittens could have been being washed"). Some special usages complicate tenses so thoroughly that you would have to go beyond formal syntax into logic to figure them all out.

The tense of the verb or verbal in the main clause controls all verbs that follow in subordinate clauses, infinitives, and participles. All have to be logically related for a natural *sequence of tenses.* This sequence ("He *was walking* home from the game when he *sees* the tornado's funnel") isn't logical — he can't see now (present tense) something that happened to him in the past (unless you mean in his imagination). Shift the verb in the subordinate clause from present to past ("He *was walking* home from the game when he *saw* the tornado's funnel"), or even ("He *is walking* home . . . when he *sees* the funnel"). Sequence of tenses varies to follow the logic in your thinking.

I *think,* therefore I *am.*	All present tense.
After we *had planned* the party, we *realized* that the Rolling Stones *are* the entertainers we need, and we *expect* they *will accept.*	Logic calls for shifts from past perfect to past to present and then to future.
We *will organize* a student senate because we *feel* that this move *has been needed* for years.	Here the sequence calls for future tense to present to present perfect passive.

The sequence of tenses is off here:

NOT:	BUT:
If he *thought,* he *could have overcome* the problem.	If he *had thought,* he *could have overcome* the problem.
When you *know* him, you *admired* him.	When you *know* him, you *admire* him.
	OR:
	When you *knew* him, you *admired* him.

30a.   Verbs: Tense in Infinitives and Participles

You can always tell when you see a *present infinitive* that the action is going on at the same time as that of the main verb.

NOT:	BUT:
They would very much have liked *to have seen* you.	They would very much have liked *to see* you.

The *perfect infinitive,* though, means an action that happened before that of the main verb.

NOT:	BUT:
Our pilots *were known to have* bombed civilians.	Our pilots *are known to have* bombed civilians.

Participles are like infinitives. The *present participle* means action that happened at the same time as that of the main verb; the *perfect participle* shows the action took place before that of the verb.

NOT: BUT:
Having expected to achieve success,   *Expecting* to achieve success, *he en-*
he enrolled in a correspondence   *rolled* in a correspondence course.
course.

Now *being convinced* of his failure,   *Convinced* of his failure, he *re-*
he resigned from the committee.   *signed* from the committee.

30b.   Verbs: Mood

Moods are the inflectional reflex to an author's attitude toward his thoughts and audience. The three English moods are *indicative, subjunctive,* and *imperative.*

INDICATIVE: The battalion *marches* at dawn toward Siberia.
SUBJUNCTIVE: I suggest the battalion *march* at dawn toward Siberia.
IMPERATIVE: *March* the battalion at dawn!

The indicative mood tells us that the information is factual — ("this *is* truth") leaving no room for hesitancy, doubt, fantasy, or indecision; the statement is a plain assertion. The subjunctive suggests the nonfactual, the uncertain, the doubtful, the hesitant, the diffident, the wishful. The imperative mood commands, giving direct orders. The word *mood,* by the way, doesn't mean emotions, or moods; it is a synonym for *mode* and grammatically both have to do purely with telling what function the verb performs.

English has gotten away from the old inflections in some ways at least — the subjunctive and indicative are no longer easy to tell apart. You can almost always use the indicative, which saves a little worry. In these pairs you would use the subjunctive if you wanted to be formal; the indicative if you felt you could be relaxed.

SUBJUNCTIVE: I wish that I *were* a graduate too.
INDICATIVE: I wish that I *was* a graduate too.

Sometimes the subjunctive is just too stilted:

SUBJUNCTIVE: If this *be* a known fact, then you are obliged to testify.
INDICATIVE: If this *is* a known fact, then you are obliged to testify.

At other times, with forms of the verb *to be* in the dependent clause, you're forced to use the subjunctive by correct usage (social pressure), which won't accept the indicative:

NEVER: If I *was* you, I would ignore him.
BUT: If I *were* you, I would ignore him.

Very formal ceremonies also call for the subjunctive: installing presidents, graduation speeches, funeral eulogies, or legal proceedings. These often have some kind of demand or request in the main clause:

> I move that the council table the resolution pending further discussion.
> I ask that the distinguished Senator from Ohio yield the floor.

Or in passive form:

> I ask that the defendant, the shiftless, no-account, Lem Snopes, be found guilty.
> Let it be here firmly resolved in solemn assembly that the 12th day of October be declared henceforth and forevermore Columbus Day.

After the subjunctive in the dependent clause, be sure to pick the logical *auxiliary verb* to make your sequence of tenses follow through.

NOT:	BUT:
If I were you, I *will* go.	If I were you, I *would* go.
If that be the case, then I *go*.	If that be the case, then I *should* go.

EXERCISES

A. Point out the errors in tense in these sentences, finding the correct form of the verb in your dictionary if necessary.

1. While I had been working in the kitchen, he is going to the movies. 2. They hung Danny Deaver in the morning. 3. He set the books down on the table. 4. I should have liked very much to have had them visit us. 5. I am finding the work exciting, even though I was working extremely hard. 6. They found old Spot, the hound, laying out there in the middle of the street. 7. They worked hard because they will have been looking forward to the finished result. 8. If cavemen would have been reasonable, they would not have sought for a way to make fire. 9. You most certainly will admit your guilt when you have testified in court tomorrow. 10. If you were to be there, I will appreciate seeing you.

B. Revise the verb form or mood to make these sentences more effective.

1. If I was you, I would listen to your teachers. 2. If you be interested, I shall call tomorrow. 3. I asked him to set down when he come in. 4. He has laid there all day in bed like a lummox. 5. You wish that I will go also, don't you? 6. They hanged the picture by the large window. 7. I suggest that all of you will resign from the club when you will receive the bill for dues. 8. It is the judge's wish that you are taken from this place and placed in prison.

30c.   Problem Verbs

Verbs like *lie* and *lay, sit* and *set,* may give you trouble — they are easy to confuse.

The verb *to lie* means to recline. It can fit only into the subject-verb pattern.

> S V
> I *lie* (I am lying) down on the couch.
>   S V
> This morning I *lay* down on the couch.
> S   V
> I *have lain* down on the couch for a rest.

The verb *to lay* means to place, and fits into the subject-verb-object pattern.

> S V   O
> I *lay* (I am laying) the football down.
> S   V   O
> I *laid* the football down on the ten-yard line.
> S   V   V   O
> I *have* often *laid* the football on the goal line.

Substituting a form of *lie* for *lay,* or the other way around, is a very strong and widespread habit, and many think it illiterate.

NOT:	BUT:
The crash victim *was laying* in the middle of the street.	The crash victim *was lying* in the middle of the street.
The crash victim *laid* there, a spectacle for the morbidly curious.	The crash victim *lay* there, a spectacle for the morbidly curious.

Set and *sit* are sometimes mistaken for each other too. *Set* once meant both "cause to sit" and "put." A hundred years ago you were free to ask a friend to "set down" but the prescriptive grammarians have so effectively squelched it that today we must *sit* down. *Set* is so hard for some people to use that Bergen Evans suggests (*A Dictionary of American Usage*) that we substitute *stand* for it: "He stood the jar on the shelf, and there it stands." Mr. Evans tells us that the anonymous farmer settled the *lay-lie* question for good: "I don't care whether she's sitting or setting. I want to know when she cackles whether she's laying or lying."

31.   Making Subject and Verb Agree

Just as pronouns and their antecedents must agree in number, so must subject agree with verb. So long as the verb comes directly after the subject, educated people don't often get into trouble. In these sentences the number of the subject clearly foretells the verb's number:

NOT:	BUT:
John *love* Mary.	John *loves* Mary.
Captain Cook's men *has* often *seen* a Polar bear.	Captain Cook's men *have* often *seen* a Polar bear.

The subtler kinds of agreement, not these gross errors, make writing harder for most of us. In this sentence the plural subject needs a plural verb:

NOT:	BUT:
War and stories of violence *fascinates* some young people to an undue degree.	War and stories of violence *fascinate* some young people to an undue degree.

But some compounded subjects may seem singular, not plural: "Love and hate is what holds humanity in thrall." You can only weigh such subjects again and again until you find which they are: If the compound subject refers to the same (singular) person or thing, however, the verb is singular.

NOT:	BUT:
My *husband and provider* return again.	My *husband and provider* returns again.

When something comes between subject and verb, look closely.

NOT:	BUT:
I believe that the fascination people seem to have for stories of crime and violence *stem* from a natural curiosity concerning emotions or situations usually foreign to most people.	I believe that the fascination people seem to have for stories of crime and violence *stems* from a natural curiosity concerning emotions or situations usually foreign to most people.
The cowboy stories which take up so much TV time, fill so many movie theaters, and result in so many books *tends* to give the viewer an escape.	The cowboy stories which take up so much TV time, fill so many movie theaters, and result in so many books *tend* to give the viewer an escape.

Singular subjects take singular verbs even when phrases come between them. An adjective phrase that starts with *as, together with,* or *with,* and modifies the subject, may make you think the subject is compound.

NOT:	BUT:
The Army *as well as the Navy* are opposed to escalation at this time.	The Army *as well as the Navy* is opposed to escalation at this time.

In correlative constructions (*either . . . or; not only . . . but also*), the verb can take its number from the number of the noun closest to it.

NOT:	BUT:
Either the boys or the girl *are* ill all the time.	Either the boys or the girl *is* ill all the time.
I suspect either the boys or the stranger *are* guilty.	I suspect either the boys or the stranger *is* guilty.

The singular verb goes with a noun that has singular sense, which isn't always easy to tell; some nouns look plural but are really singular and take singular verbs. *Acoustics* is one; others are units of time (*two years*) and some book titles.

NOT:	BUT:
The acoustics in the theater are poor.	The acoustics in the theater is poor.
Two years are a long time.	Two years is a long time.
Words and Things tell clearly how ideas grow in the mind.	*Words and Things* tells clearly how ideas grow in the mind.

Collective nouns (*group, corporation, mob, family*) often make you so doubtful about their number that you have to let the context guide you and decide arbitrarily what the number should be.

NOT ONLY:	BUT ALSO:
The family *are* in agreement that the traffic is a menace.	The family *is* in agreement that the traffic is a menace.
The mob of race rioters swiftly *move* toward the liquor store.	The mob of race rioters swiftly *moves* toward the liquor store.

31a.   Linking Verbs and *There Are, It Is*

Use *there is* and *there was* when the subject is singular; *there are* and *there were* when the subject is plural.

> *There is* a chair in the closet.
>
> *There are* many elements required for consideration.

When the subject has no more than two compound elements, the verb usually takes the plural:

NOT:	BUT:
There *is* a murder and robbery every day.	There *are* a murder and robbery every day.

When the compound subject has more than two elements, number may be determined by the first noun in the series:

NOT ONLY:	BUT ALSO:
There *is* a reporter, some police-men, and a sheriff's posse outside.	There *are* tanks, a squad car, and a fire truck in the street.

It is usually takes a singular complement.

NOT:	BUT:
It is the *boys* that count.	It is the *boy* that counts.

31b.   Problem Pronouns

Indefinite pronouns such as *each, everybody, anybody, everyone* are especially hard to bring into agreement. *Each* is fairly clearly singular, but the others go from singular to plural in different contexts. "To each his own" is easy; "to each their own" can't be logical. Don't ever tie *each* to a negative verb:

NOT:	BUT:
Each has not rec·ived his share.	None has received his share.

Everybody and *anybody* are harder than most pronouns because they sometimes take a *singular* form of the verb *to be* but a *plural* pronoun.

NOT:	BUT:
Everybody *are* angry.	Everybody *is* angry.
Everybody *is* angry about *his* pay-checks.	Everybody *is* angry about *their* pay-checks.

Intervening elements may make trouble:

NOT:	BUT:
Each of us *are* using TV dramas as a crutch against reality.	Each of us *is* using TV dramas as a crutch against reality.

A rare nuisance is the subject that needs a singular verb but a plural pronoun:

NOT:	BUT:
Because every one of the soldiers was cheering, I ordered *him* to be quiet.	Because every one of the soldiers was cheering, I ordered *them* to be quiet.
	EVEN BETTER:
	Because all the soldiers were cheering, I ordered them to be quiet.

You'll have to choose for yourself when you face "Everybody carries their own luggage" and "Everybody carries his own luggage." The conservative chooses the latter. Antecedents sometimes make the choice easier.

NOT:	BUT:
When one of the canvassers goes among strangers, *they* should be careful.	When one of the canvassers goes among strangers, *he* should be care-ful.

31c.   *None*

A substitute for "no one," *none* can be either singular or plural, but today the plural is preferred. Write "None of the committee members *agree* with you," not "None of the committee members *agrees* with you." *No one* goes better with the singular: "No one agrees with you." When the pronoun refers to things, not people, *none* can be singular or plural. Write either "None of the cars *was* shipped last week," or "None of the cars *were* shipped."

EXERCISE

√A. Correct the agreements in these sentences.

1. Hearing about the problems of the Indians are enough to make people sit up and think.   2. Hatred and malice toward fellow men is everywhere in today's world.   3. I think that the obsession many young people have for motorcycles account in large measure for juvenile delinquency. 4. Either the pilots or the stewardess are constantly smiling nervously at the passengers.   5. The pilot along with the rest of the crew are seen up forward strapping on parachutes.   6. Athletics are the mainstay of any university, providing not only a source of funds but also the main reason for the school's existence.   7. Neither the bishop nor the clergy of the diocese is going to do one single thing about the excommunication of Peter from the church.   8. *Bugles and Drums,* the novel by Rebecca North, show how the troops of General J. E. B. Stuart brought a glow of pleasure to the heart of every Confederate girl.   9. The news that came over the wire last night about the school track team have excited everyone.   10. There is a boy and a girl involved in this matter.   11. She is one of the girls who finds social work exciting.

32.   What Are Problems in Reference?

A pronoun must always refer clearly to its antecedent, the word it takes the place of.

32a.   Antecedents

Make sure the pronoun has only *one* antecedent.

NOT:
For example, Jack Ruby shot Lee Oswald after *he* became so emotionally involved *he* could not control himself. [Both *he's* might refer to either Ruby or Oswald.]

BUT:
For example, Jack Ruby became so emotionally involved that, losing control of himself, *he* shot Lee Oswald.

The Higgins boy met the ambassador when *he* first arrived in town.
[Does *he* refer to Higgins boy or the
ambassador?]

The Higgins boy met the ambassador when *the ambassador* first arrived in town.

Pronouns must agree in number with their antecedents.

NOT:
Anyone who realizes this is likely
to become a successful speaker if
they are able to act upon this principle.

BUT:
Anyone who realizes this is likely
to become a successful speaker if
he is able to act on this principle.

When one pronoun antecedent is singular and the other plural, make the pronoun agree with the closer of the two.

NOT:
Neither the drivers nor the pilot
find their way.

BUT:
Neither the drivers nor the pilot
finds his way.

ALSO:
Neither the pilot nor the driver find
their way.

Constructions like these are so clumsy that you'd do better by recasting
the sentence.

BETTER:
The pilot and all the drivers lost
their way.

The pronoun shouldn't be far from its antecedent.

NOT:
When Von Heckle turned to the
problem of adolescent boys who
find solace in gang companionship,
the response from at least one soci-
ologist was heartening indeed, for
he too felt that boys and gangs were
something of supreme interest. *He*
nevertheless refused to apply conventional methodology. . . .

BUT:
When Von Heckle turned to the
problem of adolescent boys who
find solace in gang companionship,
the response from at least one soci-
ologist was heartening indeed, for
he too felt that boys and gangs were
something of supreme interest. *Von
Heckle* nevertheless refused. . . .

32b.   *One, You, and It*

Shifting your point of view illogically will lead you into too many pronouns (*one, you, it*). And *it* can often be overworked.

NOT:

One sees the Officer of the Day approach the guardhouse. Meanwhile *you* find the Sergeant of the Guard turning out the old guard. The band, gleaming in the sun, appears from the west side of the parade ground. *One* simply never tires of the colorful ceremony of Guard Mount.

It is interesting that *it* is again apparent that *it* is spring.

BUT:

The Officer of the Day approaches the guardhouse, as the Sergeant of the Guard turns out the old guard. The band, gleaming in the sun, appears from the west side of the parade ground, ready for the colorful ceremony of Guard Mount that most of us never tire of watching.

Spring has come again.

32c.   Relative Pronouns

Relative pronouns don't work with vague and broad antecedents.

NOT:

Some historians deplore the attempt of General Bernard Montgomery to draw supplies and equipment away from the army of General Patton to the south, and they argue that Patton could have won the war alone. This is erroneous. [What is erroneous?]

BUT:

Some historians deplore the attempt of General Bernard Montgomery to draw supplies and equipment away from the army of General Patton to the south, and they argue that Patton could have won the war alone. This assumption that Montgomery "drew supplies away" from Patton is erroneous.

An antecedent can also be lost in a complex sentence:

NOT:

He then came to see me, which I did not desire.

BUT:

He then came to see me, a visit I had not desired.

32d.   *Who, Which,* and *That*

The relative pronouns need precise use. Remember that *who* refers to persons, *which* to things, and *that* to persons and things.

NOT:

Hamlet greeted the traveling players, which arrived at the castle in Elsinore.

BUT:

Hamlet greeted the traveling players who [or that] arrived at the castle in Elsinore.

Many good stylists reserve *that* for restrictive clauses (clauses not set off by commas) and *which* for nonrestrictive clauses (clauses set off by commas).

RESTRICTIVE:
The situation *that they encountered* was one of indescribable squalor.

NONRESTRICTIVE:
The situation, which they had expected, did not come up at all.

EXERCISE

A. Resolve the problems in reference in these sentences.

1. The teacher met the Jones boy, and he pulled a switchblade knife.

2. Nobody we ever knew in that crowd got their money back.

3. Mary Stuart and Queen Elizabeth were bitter enemies, especially after she became a part of the Roman Catholic plot against the Crown of England.

4. Neither the tailbacks nor the end were in a position to make the play.

5. This is the question that I have raised before.

6. I recollect that she called the police, which took up the matter with the neighbors.

7. He argued for adoption of the Wentworth measure, which I was strongly opposed to.

8. You cannot tell if it is true that it is gold or silver.

9. Each of the boys asked for their money back when the theater closed.

10. Either the trackmen or the football coach are going to win the lion's share of the athletic budget.

33.   What Is Mixed Point of View?

Shifting person, voice, or tense without warning the reader you're doing it is unfair and confusing. If you start with the first person, shift midway to second, and finish with an impersonal construction, you'll have a distracted reader or none at all. (See also 32b).

33a.   Consistency of Person

Be consistent about person.

NOT:
We feel very sorry when *we* read certain articles, but *you* still feel relieved to know the truth.

The best example *you* can give to show that Americans are fascinated by sports is by the type of literature *they* read and the newspapers *they* buy.

BUT:
We feel very sorry when reading certain articles, but *we* still feel relieved to know the truth.

The sports stories and sports sections in newspapers that Americans love give a hint of the national love for athletics.

God gave us *each* a mind so *we* could choose between what *we* dislike and like.

God has given *us* minds to enable us to choose between what *we* like and dislike.

33b.   Consistency of Voice and Tense

Switching from one voice (from active to passive) or tense to others also is likely to confuse and remove readers.

NOT:
The book *was published* in 1961, and *it received* unanimous denunciation at the hands of critics.

BUT:
The book *was published* in 1961 and *was* unanimously *denounced* by the critics.

NOT:
They *came* that September to the woods and much foliage *was seen* around the lake.

BUT:
They *came* that September to the woods and *saw* much foliage around the lake.

Also keep one tense through all parts of the sentence (see also Tense, 30). The perfect tense (*have seen*) implies action still going on all the way to the present; the past perfect (*had seen*) implies action that was finished at some time in the past. The two are easy to mix up.

NOT:
The principal spoke last year to the seniors about what they *have done* during spring semester.

BUT:
The principal spoke last year to the seniors about what they *had done* during the spring semester. [What the seniors accomplished could not now be continuing after one year.]

Starting out in one tense and then shifting into another is not helpful.

NOT:
I *saw* John on the street and I *greet* him.

BUT:
I *saw* John on the street and I *greeted* him.

33c.   Consistency of Subject

Readers can be badly disrupted when you change subjects in the second clause of a compound sentence without warning.

NOT:
Jones wrote the definitive treatise on juvenile delinquency and *much of his time* went into the project.

BUT:
Jones wrote the definitive treatise on juvenile delinquency and he put much of his time into the project.

33d.   Equating Falsely

Do not use linking verbs to join two ideas that aren't equivalent. People try to get out of the trap by joining a subject with an adverbial clause and get stuck with the awkward *is when, is because, is what* — any of them a bad solution.

NOT:
A chair is *what* people use to sit on. [*What people use to sit on* is not a grammatical or logical equivalent to the subject, *chair*.]

The reason for the delay *is because* the truck is blocking the road.

BUT:
A chair is a piece of furniture *to sit* on.

The delay was caused by a truck blocking the road.

The same awkwardness comes from substituting a prepositional phrase for an infinitive.

NOT:
The team's strategy was by passing for a winning game.

BUT:
The team's strategy was to pass the ball to win the game.

33e.   Mixed-up Sentences

Occasionally an instructor will get a sentence that is permanently tangled by ill-advised combinations of unrelated ideas and by befuddled syntax. The sentence has to be taken apart and rebuilt to make any sense.

NOT:
When a person is being criticized by his speech teacher, eyes light up and others titter and make a few comments about his speaking ability.

We think of love and friendship as someone who sends us flowers.

The meeting that year in Switzerland when Professor Bauer described his work with the boys and the gang in Kansas City you have never seen such an uproar at a convention of social workers.

BUT:
The meaner members of the speech class take sadistic pleasure in hearing a fellow student criticized by the teacher.

Sending flowers makes us think of love and friendship.

That year at the meeting in Switzerland, Professor Bauer's description of his work with the boys caused an unprecedented uproar among social workers.

EXERCISE

A. Correct the illogical points of view in these sentences.

1. When you are underground in a fallout shelter, one cannot tell what his reaction will be.   2. The troops march into the capital today when they have received the signal from the general.   3. The city was surrendered to the general at noon and the city fathers handed the keys over to the general.   4. The general told them over a year ago about

what they have not done to deserve the respect of their people.   5. A surrender is when one army hands over its weapons to another army. 6. Soldiering has always been the main safety valve with which he let himself off in another's shoes.   7. Another reason most of us enjoy war stories is because of our curiosity.   8. They welcomed us to the villa and a cake was gotten out at once to serve us, with some wine.   9. Few sociologists then wrote as well as Von Heckle and they make this fact plain by the bitterness of their statements.   10. When he first reads Blake's book on *Street Gangs in Feudal Switzerland,* one can see how Blake covers the subject completely.

33f.   Omissions and Obscurity

Superfast writing, impatient proofreading, relaxing your attention even for a word or two can wreck a sentence. One or more slow, meticulous proofreadings will fix it, though.

NOT:	BUT:
The ship dropped anchor in the harbor week.	The ship dropped anchor in the harbor last week.
Actually, the term "hippie" is misused as any freek on the coast will tell you because hippies don't go school.	Actually the term "hippie" is misused, as any freak on the coast will tell you, because hippies do not go to school.

34.   How Do I Make Complete Comparisons and Constructions?

To compare things accurately you need to know something about logical errors in thinking. Things that aren't alike in details or as a whole, or relationships that are there but badly unbalanced, can't be compared. Comparing unrelated *parts* of whole things that are related doesn't help, either.

NOT:	BUT:
The football team at Prairie U. is as good as any other university.	The football team at Prairie U. is as good as that of any other university.

34a.   Using *Like* and *As*

The notorious cigarette commercial ("like a cigarette should") that began to liberate us from the rule that *like* is not to be used as a conjunction joining clauses has let the crusaders down. Purists never stopped shuddering at the tastelessness of it all, and the rest of us may as well recognize that in formal speaking and writing *like* shouldn't be used as a conjunction when it is followed by a clause with a verb in it.

NOT:
He told me how to do it like I didn't know.

He acts like he were the boss around here.

BUT:
He told me how to do it, as though I didn't know.

He acts as if he were the boss around here.

When no verb follows, *like* is a legitimate preposition.

He looks like a million dollars.
My love is like a red, red rose.

34b.   Comparisons

Finish all your comparisons.

NOT:
I dislike the boys more than the stranger.

BUT:
I dislike the boys more than I dislike the stranger.

OR:
I dislike the boys more than the stranger dislikes them.

Give the reader the reason for each comparison, not keeping half of it to yourself. The advertising industry's "copywriter's comparative" touts the product as "bigger than . . ." and "better than . . ." and leaves *what* it is bigger and better than to the innocent public's lively imagination.

NOT:
The team is much better this year.

He is a bigger person now.

BUT:
The team is much better than the junior varsity this year.

He is a bigger person now than little Tom.

EXERCISE

A. Complete or patch up all comparisons in these sentences.

1. Our team is better.   2. The girls can sew better than any other schools.
3. He made me do it like I was a child or something.   4. I find the situation more provoking than the boys involved.   5. He is better liked than any of the team.

35.   How Do I Use Modifiers?

Any phrases or clauses that you convert into adjectives and adverbs have to be clearly related to the noun or verb they modify. If you misplace them you give the reader misleading, ambiguous, or foolish information. In this sentence there is some confusion about who or what got shot: "The film *Zonk* used an expert technical crew, which was shot in Chicago." Logic calls for a transposition of the adjective clause: "The film *Zonk,* which was shot in Chicago, was made by an expert technical crew."

35a.   Dangling Modifiers

A word, phrase, or clause that isn't clearly connected to a word in the main clause makes a *dangling* (disconnected) *modifier.* The error is easy to make and exposes you to unkind spoofs.

NOT:	BUT:
Coming home from the party, the lamp post reared up in front of me.	Coming home from the party, I found a lamp post rearing up in front of me.
Barking like fury, Sally was frightened by the dog.	Barking like fury, the dog frightened Sally.

35b.   Dangling Elliptical Clauses

The elliptical clause turns on itself and never reaches the point you are trying to make. It is as disconnected as the dangling modifier. It has no verb and not much connection to the clause that follows it.

NOT:	BUT:
When a young professor, the king awarded Martin Muber a distinguished service wrist watch, inscribed with the letters M.M.	When Martin Muber was a young professor, the king awarded him a distinguished service wrist watch, inscribed with the letters M.M.

35c.   Dangling Infinitive Phrases

Sometimes the dangling modifier is set off by an infinitive phrase.

NOT:	BUT:
To complete the task properly, a report must be submitted by the student.	To complete the task properly, the student must submit a report.

35d.   Squinting Modifiers

The squinting modifier looks both forward and backward at the same time, losing the reader, who can't tell what it modifies.

NOT:	BUT:
The boys were told frequently to avoid the pitfalls of life.	The boys were frequently told to avoid the pitfalls of life.
The German High Command ordered its troops fearlessly to march into Belgium.	The German High Command ordered its troops to march fearlessly into Belgium.

35e. Placing Modifiers

Modifiers are made to dangle by putting subordinate parts of the sentence in the wrong place. A great peculiarity of English is that you have to get the words in the right order or you throw away the sentence's meaning. These sentences show what wrong word order can do:

NOT:
Mrs. Wharton, the Junior League representative at the settlement house, greeted the boys as they entered in a warm and friendly manner.

BUT:
Mrs. Wharton, the Junior League representative at the settlement house, greeted the boys in a warm and friendly manner as they entered the settlement house.

NOT:
The ship was christened by Mary Carroll as she skidded down the ways.

BUT:
The ship skidding down the ways was christened by Mary Carroll.

Clauses must also be close to the subject they modify.

NOT:
Because of what she had been told, the meeting with the committee did not frighten Annie.

BUT:
Because of what she had been told, Annie was not frightened by meeting with the committee.

Usually, put the adverb before the word you want it to modify: "He *eagerly* bought the painting." When the sentence has auxiliary verbs, the adverb normally follows the first of them: "He would gladly have bought the painting." The adverb can also follow the completed idea: "He brought off the whole performance *well*." If you don't follow these rules, you won't be wrong but you may make the reader strain uncomfortably trying to catch your meaning. Writing "He *gladly* would have bought the painting" takes the emphasis from *bought* and gives it to *he;* and if you say "*Gladly* he would have bought the painting," *gladly* modifies the whole sentence, not just the verb. One thing you shouldn't do: Never put the adverb between a verb and a direct object.

NOT:
S V O
He buys *gladly* the painting.

BUT:
S V O
He *gladly* buys the painting.

35f. Sequence of Adverbs

When several adverbs modify a verb, the usual order to put them in is *manner* first, then *place,* and then *time:* "They argued violently in the summer house every afternoon." But no one will say you shouldn't write "They argued violently every afternoon in the summer house that year." Your judgment, not rules, settles where the adverbs should go. Choose the shade of meaning you want and move the adverb around until it says what you want it to.

35g.   *Only* and *Almost*

These adverbs seem to fit almost anywhere you put them, but moving them can change their meaning drastically. What differences in meaning do you see in these sentences?

> He *only* gave me a dime.
> He gave me *only* a dime.
> He gave me a dime *only*.
> *Only* he gave me a dime.

> The man was *almost* overcome with tears.
> The man *almost* was overcome with tears.
> The man was overcome with tears, *almost*.
> The man was overcome *almost* with tears.

35h.   Split Infinitives

The ancient rule, rooted in a mindless imposition of Latin on English, says you mustn't split an infinitive by putting an adverb between *to* and the verb, as in "to *slowly* walk." Following the rule blindly leads to constructions far more awkward than, a knowing, careful split: "He decided to privately continue the project." Don't fall over backward to keep from splitting infinitives just because it's bad to do so — look at the meaning of your sentence before and after splitting, then decide.

EXERCISE

A. Correct the errors in modification in the following sentences.

1. Coming slowly through the fog, the harbor was suddenly there off the port bow of the *U.S.S. Skipjack*.   2. He had an air about him all that day of quiet ferocity.   3. That information known to her, the judge would certainly hear the case.   4. He would very much like to slowly drop out of sight.   5. Having been there myself, Arcadia is well-known to me.   6. Like most such men, a matter of principle was something he would fight fiercely for.   7. Having put the dog to bed, the cat was next put out by the sleepy professor.   8. The athletic board arranged under cover of night to fire the coach.   9. Being that I am a senior majoring in business administration, the world will find me a welcome addition.   10. Not known to anyone, the world only could find one place for the young actress.

This letter, written by a friend of ours,
Contains his death, yet bids them save his life.
                                    [Reads.]
"Edwardum occidere nolite timere, bonum est:
Fear not to kill the king, 't is good he die."
But read it thus, and that's another sense:
"Edwardum occidere nolite, timere bonum est:
Kill not the king, 't is good to fear the worst."
Unpointed [unpunctuated] as it is, thus shall it go,
That, being dead, if it chance to be found,
Matrevis and the rest may bear the blame."
                    CHRISTOPHER MARLOWE,
        The Tragedy of Edward II V. iv. 6–15, 1592

10 Problems in Usage:

Punctuation and Mechanics

PUNCTUATION

Punctuation marks are no more than arbitrary signals meaning "pause here," and telling the reader how the author meant to divide his thoughts into sentences, clauses, phrases, and how he meant them to be read, with the right emphases and breaks in thought. Do you remember that *grammar* has to do with *connecting* words into a sentence so they will make sense? Punctuation *disconnects* words within the sentence so that the parts will make sense. Punctuation marks and the spaces between words govern sound and sense. They tell us where to put the *stress* (loudness) in the sentence, how to *pitch* our voices (vibrate our vocal chords), and where the *junctures* (pauses) should fall. Couldn't this system be followed in speaking as well as writing, using the same symbols? A short pause would mean a comma, a longer one a semicolon, and a still longer one a period. A sustained loudness would make an exclamation point, and why wouldn't a reversed subject and predicate mean a question mark? But because

229

playing punctuation by ear can't be any more than guesswork, we need rules to tell us how to break sentences.

"What is that on the road ahead?" could just as well be said "What is that on the road, a head!" if we had no rules. A fine play on misleading punctuation is in Nicholas Udall's comedy, *Ralph Roister Doister,* which was written about 1540. Matthew Merrygreek, mischief-maker, deliberately misreads Ralph's amorous letter to Dame Custance, putting stresses and junctures at precisely the wrong places. Matthew's reading (left) is as thunderously offensive as Ralph's original is romantically flattering and winning.

[MATTHEW]	[RALPH]
Sweet mistress, whereas I love you nothing at all,	Sweet mistress, whereas I love you — nothing at all
Regarding your substance and riches chief of all,	Regarding your riches and substance, chief of all
For your personage, beauty, demeanour and wit,	For your personage, beauty demeanour, and wit —
I commend me unto you never a whit.	I commend me unto you. Never a whit
Sorry to hear report of your good welfare.	Sorry to hear report of your good welfare;
For (as I hear say) such your conditions are	For (as I hear say) such your conditions are
That you be worthy the favor of no living man.	That you be worthy the favor;

Who made the rules for punctuation? No bureaucratic agency, scholarly academy, or learned author, but they and with them all the editors since publishing began gradually set the practices, which have changed just as gradually.

The remains we have of early writing, mostly in memorial inscriptions, whatever the language (Phoenician, Greek, Latin), were written, usually on stone, entirely without capital letters, word spacing, punctuation — no directions of any kind. That doesn't mean the people speaking those languages didn't start, pause, and stop just as we do, but they hadn't invented the road signs for written communication.

Editors through the years have compiled the rules that most people agree about in handy manuals. The advice you'll find here synthesizes their opinions and brings them up to date. For the full treatment, go to the book many publishers, authors, editors, and writers feel they must have by their sides, the University of Chicago Press *Manual of Style,* twelfth edition. The *Random House Dictionary,* College Edition, has a good small collection of rules and is up-to-date. You'll find fuller coverage (though less than in the *Chicago Manual*), in Edward D. Seeber, *A Style Manual for Students,* second edition (Bloomington:

Indiana University, 1968), and in the 1970 Modern Language Association *Style Sheet,* second edition.

36.   How Do I End?

The symbols we use to close a sentence are almost all decided for us. The few exceptions are listed here along with the rules.

36a.   The Period [.]

1. Periods signal that the declarative or imperative sentence is at an end: "John loves Mary." "Think."

2. They end an interrogative sentence in indirect discourse (a question within a nonquestioning sentence): "He asked how we could do that."

3. They close a deliberate sentence fragment: "Which is what I told him."

4. Use periods to punctuate abbreviations (Dr., Mr., Mrs., Ms., St., Co.) and as ellipsis dots (. . .), which show that something is left out of a quotation (see 38c). Some abbreviated names of agencies that people can be expected to recognize (NASA, UNESCO, USIA) and names abbreviated as *acronyms* (the initial letters of the words when put together make a word: CORE, NOW) do not require periods.

36b.   The Exclamation Point [!]

Any statement that we want to give unusual force to, including exclamations of course, we mark with an exclamation point ("Get out of here!" she said. "Ooops!" "Oh!"). If you tack them onto more than a remote phrase or two you chance falling into a "schoolgirl" style of which Queen Victoria's diary provides an awesome example:

> As for the "confidence of the Crown," God knows! No *Minister, no friend* EVER possessed it so entirely as this truly excellent Lord Melbourne possesses mine!

36c.   The Question Mark [?]

1. Direct questions end with the query sign: "Did the speaker meet with you?" "Are the Smiths back this year?"

2. When you want to hint that you're not sure about a date or a fact, put a question mark in parentheses after it: "The founding meeting of the Episcopal Society was held at Smith's Tavern on Church Street in 1832(?)." *Don't* put a question mark after an indirect question: "I wonder what their mothers would say about their behavior at Fort Lauderdale."

3. But if you rephrase it as a direct question, *do* close with a question mark: "What would their mothers say about their behavior in Fort Lauderdale?"

37.   How Do I Mark Pauses?

The less-than-full-stop symbols are not so rigidly ruled as the periods and other terminal signs. You can come up with an honest disagreement about whether or not a comma should come after an introductory phrase, or whether or not long clauses should be separated by a semicolon or comma. Today most editors feel we should cut down on commas to keep the sentence flowing. If you need crowds of commas to make the sentence clear, you'd better rephrase it; your subordination won't be clear.

37a.   The Comma [,]

1. Set off brief introductory words, phrases, or clauses with commas:

As we all know, business was never better.
In general, avoid people.

But here the comma is optional: "On landing he went home," or "On landing, he went home."

2. Separate dependent from independent clauses with a comma:

Even though the sales manager disagreed, the Boston representative signed the contract.

3. Set off long, introductory participial phrases with commas:

Knowing the danger and sensing that action was needed, I hastened to headquarters.

4. A short phrase or clause that is merely a second thought needs a comma to make it clear:

Shortly after he landed from his trip he became angry with the people on the committee, and shot Jones.

5. A final phrase that is meant to be a contrast takes a comma:

He got back from the trip embittered and frustrated, not full of pleasantness and charity.

6. Commas set off interrupting parts that are in apposition (placed side by side to explain each other):

Larry, a huge man, is the leader.

7. Commas set off interrupting, nonrestrictive clauses or phrases. An

interrupting clause is *nonrestrictive* if you can cut it out of the sentence without making the sentence meaningless — the clause doesn't limit or *restrict* meaning.

RESTRICTIVE

All students who *protested the sacking of the radical political science professor* assembled in the chapel.

To remove the qualification about which category of student assembled would radically change meaning.

NON-RESTRICTIVE

All the students, who ordinarily make their way around campus without a single care, were suddenly confronted with layers of mud from construction work.

The relative clause adds an interesting highlight but does not affect meaning much. Thus it is set off by commas.

8. Commas set off the parts in a series:

The student leaders meet the teachers, the police and fire departments, and the judge.
The dog ran out of the house, sprinted down the street, and jumped into the lake.

9. Separate a day from a year in a date, or geographical units with commas: May 26, 1964; Topeka, Kansas; London, England. In a complete sentence, commas also set off years and places: e.g., "He was born on May 26, 1921, in London, England, where he grew up."

10. Commas mark off a direct quotation from the main clause:

"I love you," she said.

11. Commas set off the salutation in a personal letter:

Dear Mr. Jones,   Dear Jim,

12. Commas separate clauses ("contact" clauses), closely related in thought and in structure:

The boys walked, the men talked, and the women gossiped.

13. Mark off adjectives in a series with commas:

The experience was brief, brutal, and violent; *or,*
The experience was brief, brutal and violent.

14. A comma can stand for an omitted word or phrase in a parallel series:

Mary enjoyed tennis; John, golf.

15. Commas can clear up ambiguous sentences. Put one between two words that are together if they are closely related.

NOT:	BUT:
Generally speaking children are fun.	Generally speaking, children are fun.
As the dictionary says the word "essential" is ordinarily used as an adjective.	As the dictionary says, the word "essential" is ordinarily used as an adjective.
John was the last person to know about the mess to be sure.	John was the last person to know about the mess, to be sure.

If you don't have these guidelines by heart, you may overdo your punctuation. To keep from doing that, simply leave out commas when you are in doubt, especially the ones that come between your subject and the verb.

NOT:	BUT:
The poetry of T. S. Eliot, shows a steady progression toward Christian belief.	The poetry of T. S. Eliot shows a steady progression toward Christian belief.

37b.   The Semicolon [;]

1. Semicolons separate independent clauses connected by adverbs such as *however, therefore,* etc.:

John loves Mary; however, Mary has reservations.

2. Introduce an explanatory statement with a semicolon:

There is much restlessness in the university; for example, the recent student riot.

3. Separate two independent clauses with a semicolon in place of a coordinating conjunction:

The convention convened at noon; that afternoon the delegates confronted the Roberts issue head-on.

4. Semicolons clarify the units in a series containing many commas:

The firms helping us out include Higgins and Sons, Roofers; Felix Stumpf, Plumbing Supplies; Billings, Warhol, and Watkins, attorneys-at-law; and the Simon department store chain.

5. Separate two long and complicated clauses with a semicolon in place of a comma, or use a semicolon to put special stress on a pause between the two clauses:

The riots spread all over the city; and there seems little doubt that the sociological implications of this encounter will reach far beyond the limits of the ghetto and into the lives of citizens everywhere.

37c.   The Colon [:]

1. Colons introduce a series:

Then the police reviewed the charges against Mr. Higgins: (1) breaking and entering, (2) resisting arrest, and (3) driving without a license.

2. They introduce a quotation:

In the final chapter, Feldman moves to the essence of the matter: "The problem of juvenile delinquency remains both perilous and unresolved until the full forces of society. . . ."

3. To introduce the body of a business letter, use a colon:

Dear Sir:
    We have received your inquiry of April 1, and. . . .

4. Colons set off the parts of a citation:

Exodus 4:1; but also Exodus xvi.1.

5. Separate hours from minutes with a colon:

10:30 A.M.

6. Separate the name of a character in a play from his words with a colon:

Ferdinand: Cover her face; mine eyes dazzle; she died young.

7. Use a colon to preface an explanation after an introductory main clause:

The matter finally resolved itself into a question of the king's authority: parliament could respond to the demands of 1623, or the king could find support for his policies only abroad in France or, even worse, in Spain.

37d.   The Dash [—]

Commas, dashes, and parentheses introduce subordinate concepts and information into a sentence. When typewriting, make the dash with two unspaced hyphens (--) to distinguish it from a hyphen or word break.
    Use a comma if the interruption is short.

The students, healthy and strong, attended the rally.

1. Use a dash to signal a major break in thought or syntax:

The Watergate affair has captured the attention of the nation for many months — and I want to say that this has distracted me from my hobbies of gardening and sailing — to the exclusion of all other matters.

2. A dash also introduces a terminating statement that pulls together a complicated series of phrases and clauses:

> The Sixties saw the students riot on the campuses; the missile crisis that erupted over Cuba; the violence surrounding the Chicago Democratic convention; and the climax came in Kent State and Cambodia — all searing events.

3. Use a dash to set up a climactic or anti-climactic statement:

> He turned and there quite suddenly, without warning, stood — the witch doctor.

37e.   Parentheses [( )]

1. Parentheses add a brief note of explanation:

> He was a graduate of the high school in Rochester (Minnesota).

2. They enclose a major parenthetical thought:

> Burroughs then went on to stress the role of the Hungoths in overturning the primitive feudalistic societal structure among the descendants of the Guelphs (elsewhere Burroughs in the fifteen-volume unabridged edition contradicts his own position, first stated here, by pointing out that the Guelphs were essentially an unstructured group).

3. Parentheses enclose numbers or letters in a series:

> He said the term paper was (1) sloppy, (2) poorly researched, and (3) partly plagiarized.

4. Enclose a numerical figure restating a spelled-out number with parentheses:

> The price of the ukulele was thirty dollars ($30.00).

38.   How Do I Use Quotation Marks [" "]?

1. Quotation marks enclose dialogue in narration:

> "You are wrong," he said.
> "No more so than you," Tom shot back, "and I won't change my mind."

2. Mark brief quotations within a sentence:

> "True wit is nature to advantage dress'd," according to Alexander Pope. Wordsworth once said that Newton's face was "the marble index of a mind forever voyaging strange seas of thought alone."

3. Give titles of works not published separately (usually magazine stories and articles, poems, one-act plays, and short stories) in quotation marks:

I am the proud author of "The Case for Captain Bligh" in the last issue of *The Historical Journal.*

4. Quotations indicate names of songs and radio and TV programs:

"The Yellow Rose of Texas"   "Monitor"   "Laugh-In"

5. Enclose a word you are talking about in a sentence in quote marks:

What, then, does "existentialism" mean?

Compare the above sentence with:

Is not the existentialism in his view of life apparent?

6. Quotation marks emphasize irony:

And what results can the Socialists offer after a decade of "free" medical care in the British Isles?

7. Quotation marks can hold up for attention nonstandard, slangy, or other words that for any reason seem out of place:

She was, as "hip" youths might have said in yesterday's jargon, "heavily into the freak scene."

38a.   Single Quotation Marks [' ']

Use single quotation marks to enclose a quotation within a quotation:

"Already by the Middle Ages successive waves of immigrants from eastern Europe had moved into the regions below the Pyrrhic Mountains, mountains which Arthur South has characterized as 'rich repositories of all the culture in Southeastern Asia.' "

38b.   Too Many Quotation Marks

Overenthusiasm for such emphatic devices as italics, quotation marks, and slang is a sure sign of immature writing. No matter how "with it" you may think your audience expects you to be, keep in mind the one reader you most want to impress (your instructor? yourself looking back on your early efforts years from now?). Don't "turn off" that most critical reader by unworthy tricks. In writing, a high standard is the only one that works.

The Jefferson Airplane are real "groovy"! I mean *heavy.* They "turn me on" the way they made "street people" relate to one another.

38c.   Leaving Out Words

Ellipsis points (three spaced periods) show where you have shortened a direct quotation for some reason (usually because the removed material was irrelevant to your context):

> . . . when they saw what had happened . . . and recognized the truth. . . .

When you cut the end of a sentence off, use four points to take care of the period.

38d.   Where Do the Quotation Marks Go?

1. Keep quotation marks *after* the comma and the period:

> "I shall not do it," he said.
>
> He quoted the immortal words of Johnson that "a bad boy is really a bad parent."

2. The marks always go *before* a colon or semicolon.

> The judge called Williams a "menace"; he declared that the man should be jailed for being so irresponsible.
>
> It was no exaggeration to call Williams a "menace": he had completely disrupted the life of the community.

3. Terminal punctuation (periods, questions marks, exclamation points) go *before* the quotation marks when they are part of the statement you've quoted.

> He said, "What regiment do you belong to?"
> They said, "You are a fool!"

Place question marks and exclamation points *after* the quotation marks when they are not an integral part of the quoted statement:

> How do we know that you really said, "I do not choose to run"?
> What impertinence for a stranger to come into our town and say, "I am one with you"!

38e.   Quotations

Quoting others in your writing can make it more informative, colorful, deeper, broader, and more convincing. Plan your quoting carefully, though. Pick quotes because they get much into little and because their authors phrase it well, not just because you think (1) they say it better than you can; (2) they are authorities, you aren't; (3) it's easier to fill a page with borrowed words than to put together your own. "Filler" quotes are painfully obvious. Balance quoted matter with text and select each for a definite reason or you'll end with a patchwork — too little of you and too much of someone else.

1. Set off a verse quotation (two lines or more) with a colon and indent all the lines:

> Without any question, Alexander Pope more than any other poet of the early eighteenth century captured the essence of the neoclassic spirit:
>> True wit is nature to advantage dress'd
>> What oft was thought but ne'er so well express'd.

Set apart from your own text in this way, the quotation (prose or poetry) doesn't need quotation marks around it.

2. Run a short verse quotation (two lines or less) into your text, starting with a colon:

> Without any question, Alexander Pope more than any other poet of the early eighteenth century captured the essence of the neoclassic spirit: "True wit is nature to advantage dress'd / What oft was thought but ne'er so well express'd."

3. Set off a long prose quotation (five lines or a hundred words) with a colon:

> Very often a writer comes close to the heart of what the Tonganoxie group stood for. So it is with Beveridge Grundage:
>> Out there where the wind blew hard over the desolate land, something came to life that none of us had foreseen. It was the hard soil, the hard wind, the hard rain — all of these things. And yet it was something else again, something that came back at every sunrise and at every sunset. It was nothing less, I think, than the revelation of certainty. Mere survival had brought us that.

4. Run a short prose quotation into your sentence after a colon:

> Hospital administrators may wish to recollect the words of Sir Thomas Browne: "For the world I hold it to be an Inn not an Hospital; a place not to live in, but to die in."

Other examples of quotations include:

5. Quotation with introductory phrase:

> According to Alexander Pope, often spoken of as "the Wasp of Twickenham," "true wit" is "nature to advantage dress'd," an expression that epitomizes much about the eighteenth century.

6. Quotation as narrative:

> "The silence of these empty spaces terrifies me," said Blaise Pascal, the celebrated French philosopher of the seventeenth century.

7. Partial quotation (with ellipsis):

It was Bacon who wrote that ". . . this was the justest sentence ever passed in England."

8. When you run the quotation into your own sentence, you needn't capitalize the first word even if it had a capital in the original:

Of Alexander Pope, George Seevers writes that "he was primarily a man of intellect and precision."

Introduce it with a colon, though, and you must capitalize and punctuate it just as the original was:

Of Alexander Pope, George Seevers writes: "He was primarily a man of intellect and precision."

38f.   Using Brackets [[ ]]

1. Brackets indicate errors in a quotation. When you quote directly and when the quote has an obvious error, [*sic*] in brackets immediately after the error will tell the reader that the fault is in the quotation and not in the quoter:

"Columbus then sailed for America in 1493 [*sic*], finding there ideal conditions for a new colony," says H. J. Belwether.

2. Brackets introduce interpolated remarks within a quotation:

"In 1946 [at the annual meeting in June], Harrison was elected chairman."

3. Enclose nouns or pronouns that are not a part of the original quotation but that are needed for syntactical reasons in brackets:

". . . [They] then examined the basis for the decision."

4. Brackets set off comments made about a speech:

Chairman Williams:
Americanism is the highest duty of the citizen [applause].

5. Brackets stand in the place of parentheses in material that has already used parentheses.

[1] See "The Wage Cycle" (R. F. Killigrew, *Economics Today* [New York: Pell, 1967]).

39.   How Do I Use the Apostrophe? [']

The apostrophe can mean either that the noun with apostrophe attached owns something (possessive case), or that it is shortened, a contraction. Form the *possessive* by:

1. Adding an apostrophe and *s* to singular and plural nouns that do not end in *s*: leopard's tail; men's club.

2. Adding an apostrophe and *s* to one-syllable nouns that end in *s* or *z*: Keats's poems; Yeats's lyrics.

3. Adding an apostrophe only to a polysyllabic word ending in *s* or *z*: Kansas' tax structure; to a monosyllabic noun whose plural is formed by adding *s*: The boys' shoes; or to a noun whose plural is formed by adding *es*: The witches' curse.

4. Some unusual cases: in a hyphenated word, add the *s* to the last word: my *mother-in-law's* visits; when ownership is joint, put the *s* after the last name: McKinley, Brown, and *Harrison's* propery; when ownership is individual, give each person his own apostrophe: *Tom's* and *Dick's* boots.

5. For numbers and letters, add an apostrophe and *s* to form the plural: *p*'s and *q*'s, 1880's; to contract a date, place the apostrophe before the digit: class of '08.

Be careful not to confuse contractions and possessive forms of personal pronouns that do not take an apostrophe:

CONTRACTIONS:	POSSESSIVES:
it's number	its number
they're problem	their problem
who's father	whose father

MECHANICS

40.   What Are the Mechanics of Writing?

The larger things in composition — paragraphs, sentences, words — are the most important for you to learn about. But you have to give the details great care, too — hyphens, numbers, capital letters, abbreviations, and italics — making them consistent throughout the piece you're writing. Creativity takes care of itself once you can control the little things mechanically. The dictionary can be helpful too.

40a.   Hyphens [-]

1. When you break a word at the end of a line because it won't all fit, the hyphen shows more is to come. See the dictionary for the correct place to divide the word:

NOT:	BUT:
can-al	ca-nal
neg-oti-ate	ne-go-ti-ate
somn-o-lent	som-no-lent

2. Compound words used as adjectives must be hyphenated:

the seventeenth-century mind   sixty-four-dollar question
a straight-laced person

3. Attach a prefix to a proper noun with a hyphen:

un-American statement   non-Christian eschatology

4. Form a compound noun with a hyphen: teacher-coach; author-explorer. There is a recent trend however, toward the demise of hyphenated words, as in neofascist and filmmaker. Put a decade into words: nineteen-thirties; seventeen-sixties. Write out a fraction: one-half gallon (however, if the fraction is used as a noun, the hyphen is optional: "One half of the class went" or "Half the class went").

5. Do not hyphenate a compound modifier that includes an adverb ending in *ly:* "a widely known author," not "a widely-known author."

40b.   Numbers

1. Numbers that you can't spell out in one or two words should be expressed in Arabic numerals: 10,258 miles; a $10,365,232 deficit. But numbers that can be expressed briefly may be written out: "ten million dollars"; "thirty dollars."

2. Always spell out numbers that begin a sentence; or recast the sentence so that it doesn't begin with a number: "Three hundred and seventy-five men died at the pass" or "At the pass, 375 men died that day."

3. Be consistent. Do not spell out "three hundred and seventy-five" and use figures ("625") right next to it.

NOT: BUT:
The stockholders voted five thou-   The stockholders voted 5,608 to 85
sand six hundred and eight to 85   against the bill.
against the bill.

4. Use figures for street addresses, measurements, page numbers, percentages, dates, time, and statistics: 39 Kirkland St., Apt. 104; 6″ x 8″; pp. 6–10; more than 30 per cent voted; May 26, 1921; May 26th; 10 A.M., but 10:15 A.M.; Net loss was $525,432 compared to $232,532 last year.

40c.   Capitals

When you feel doubtful about whether or not to capitalize, go to the dictionary. Keep thinking consistently. Don't capitalize the *Jacksonian Era* on page 3, and shift into the *Jacksonian era* on page 13.

1. Capitalize geographical areas: the North, the South; but do not capitalize when the geographical reference describes only part of an area: southern Vermont, western Kansas.

2. Capitalize the first word of a sentence, or any words that stand alone as independent elements: "He welcomes us aboard the ship." "Nonsense!" "There is no basis for such a statement."

3. Capitalize the first word in a line of verse:

How vainly men themselves amaze
To win the palm, the oak, the bays. . . .
ANDREW MARVELL

4. Capitalize the first letter in abbreviations: Mr., Mrs., Ms., Dr., Prof., St., Rd. All letters in academic degrees and professional titles: D.D.S.; M.D.; LL.B. (but note Ph.D.).

5. Names of persons, streets, ships, public buildings, geographic locales are capitalized: Cordelia Street; Hudson River; Park Place; The Empire State Building; *U.S.S. Iwo Jima.*

6. Use capitals for titles before proper names: Prof. Gottfried von Heckle (without given name *Professor* should be spelled out: Professor Von Heckle); Dr. Ernest P. Hollaway; Judge Thomas Bribewell; The Hon. George Smith.

7. Capitalize government organizations: Department of the Army; Senate of the United States; Department of State.

8. Capitalize periods and episodes in history: Renaissance; Baroque; Middle Ages; Battle of Bull Run; Jacksonian Era.

9. Days of the week, months, holidays take capital letters: Monday, Christmas, Labor Day. But not seasons: spring and fall, not Spring and Fall.

10. Titles of newspapers, books, plays, and poems (except for internally placed articles and prepositions) are capitalized: *The Decline and Fall of the Roman Empire; Of Mice and Men;* "Mending Wall"; *A Funny Thing Happened on the Way to the Forum.*

11. Some other things require capitalization: the pronoun *I*; exclamations standing by themselves: "Oh!"; expressions of time: 10 A.M. (may also be written 10 a.m.).

12. Foreign names may give special problems: German *van* or *von* is not capitalized (Wernher von Braun) unless the surname appears alone (Von Braun). French *de* as in Chavannes de Giraudiére is dropped when the surname stands alone, Giraudiére.

40d.   Abbreviations

1. Abbreviating too much in informal prose makes the text look bumpy. When in doubt, spell out:

NOT:	BUT:
Prof. Black teaches the English lit. seminar that everyone avoids.	Professor Black teaches the English literature seminar that everyone avoids.

2. Many titles are properly abbreviated: Mr. John Jones; Dr. Harrison Little; M. P. Higgins, M.D.; Hon. H. Pullham Jones.

Titles such as Governor, General, and Honorable may be abbreviated when followed by a given name. If only a surname follows, spell out the title:

Maj. Samuel Williams	Major Williams
Gov. Morris Higgins	Governor Higgins
Prof. George J. Worth	Professor Worth
Rev. Harrison Peabody	Reverend Mr. Peabody (note *Mr.*)

Some other abbreviations acceptable in formal writing include academic degrees (B.A., M.A., Ph.D.); some foreign expressions (e.g., i.e., ibid.); the authorized names of companies (Samuel Jones, Inc.); and except in very formal contexts, the names of states (Mich., N.Y., Miss.).

3. Conventionally, letters used as symbols and chemical formulas are not punctuated with periods:

Let X and Y stand for the first set of variables. . . .

H_2SO_4 $C_6H_{12}O_6$

4. Keep the ampersand (&) out of formal writing.

5. Be sparing of *etc.*; it is an obvious cover-up for the inability to think of more examples.

40e.   Italics

Italics are indicated in typescript by underlining each word separately: English Literature in the Sixteenth Century (not English Literature in the Sixteenth Century). But they show up in print as *English Literature in the Sixteenth Century*.

1. Italicize the title of a ship, book, or periodical: *Titanic, College Handbook, Playboy.*

If the title is italicized you don't have to put before it the explanation *book* because the italics mean that a book is being cited:

NOT:	BUT:
In the book, *Decline and Fall,* Evelyn Waugh has cleverly injected some symbolism.	In *Decline and Fall* Evelyn Waugh has cleverly injected some symbolism.

2. Use italics for foreign language expressions: *horrible dictu, persona non grata, ne plus ultra, in medias res.* But style manuals now recommend that i.e., ibid., and e.g. be unitalicized (or roman). *Sic,* however, is always italicized.

3. Italicize a word being used in some special sense: "The word *semantics* needs special definition."

Italics are sometimes interchangeable with quotation marks. Too many italicized (underlined) words give your writing an immaturely overemphatic look (see 38b).

41. How Do I Prepare a Manuscript?

Some of the mechanics you are expected to follow when you prepare a manuscript depend on where and to whom the material is going. A graduate school's style sheet may specify "Cordelia St." but your local newspaper may insist on "Cordelia street." Instructors ask for different things; most would rather have compositions typewritten, though some prefer to have them handwritten in ink. Be sure you know just what you're expected to do. The rules here are more or less standard.

41a. Paper

Typewritten compositions are welcomed *if* they are typed with a reasonably fresh ribbon, double-spaced, with 1½-inch margins on all four sides (for your instructor's comments), on good-quality white (not "erasable") 8½ by 11-inch bond paper. Make a carbon because papers do get lost. If you're expected to hand in a handwritten paper, use lined paper of the same size as if you were typing it, and write with black or blue-black ink. Your writing will be much less harshly received if it can be read easily by eyes that must read many papers every day. If you were an instructor and had to face a scrap of any old kind of paper scribbled in pencil you'd feel as cordial toward the writer as the mailman toward the owner of a house surrounded by killer-trained dogs. Neatness is a practical precaution in anything that someone else is going to read and criticize. If you do have to make a few last-minute corrections on your final draft, do it in ink between the lines. See the chart of proofreader's marks on the inside covers of this book.

41b. Long Quotations

If you use a quotation of five lines or longer (a hundred words or more), set it off from your own writing by *double*-indenting it, double-spaced, without quotation marks around it (because by indenting it you make it clearly a quotation). See 38e and page 280.

41c. Title

If your composition has a title, capitalize the major words in it and center it at the top of your first page, without a period.

41d. Local Customs

Follow all the rules in getting your paper ready even if some seem arbitrary. If you're asked to fold the paper neatly down the middle and write your name, the class time, and your instructor's name, it's just to make sure that your work, which is after all one among many, gets credited to you and doesn't lie unidentified, wasted. Some schools specify a standard, purchasable format for all papers, which makes your job a little easier. Asking for conformity in writing papers is simply a practical matter. Our civilization stands on a pillar of words and almost everyone has to present something written at some time in life.

41e.   Polish

No matter how good you feel at having finished a writing job, it isn't ready for anyone else to see until you've found and fixed every last typographical error (typo). Because everyone makes mistakes in typing, the least you can do is neatly correct every error, with ink if you can't do it with the typewriter. Corrected copy should look something like this:

> **by**
> The bitterness brought on ∧the conference continued to
>   **hastiness**
> remind the settlers for years to come of the ~~hastinos~~
>
> of their decision.

A decision to begin a new paragraph should be indicated by a ¶ in the margin and an underlining of the opening words, in this fashion:

> ¶   the settlers for years to come. |__Although the colony often found

If you write the paper by hand, use your most legible penmanship, not your fanciest.

Proofreading isn't just reading. A thorough reading will make you concentrate on every letter in all the words in your paper. The typewriter, if you treat it right, will make all the letters evenly dark, giving a clean, easy-to-read page. It also hides even the most obvious typos. Watch for mistakes in spelling, punctuation, grammar. Errors in names of people or books and foreign words stand out more than most. Look again at all dates, quotations, and bibliographic citations, thinking as you come to each: what could have gone wrong with this one?

When you chase errors that intently, few are likely to escape. Read the whole paper aloud if that's the only way that will force your eyes to see what they don't want to see — errors. If the paper is long and you can't find a fellow-sufferer to read it aloud to you from the carbon copy while you read the original seeking faults, a tape recorder will help. Accuracy is troublesome but it's at least as important as originality during your training.

While you're inspecting, check paragraphing, construction of sentences, and wording. How many paragraphs are on each page? Too few? Too many? Unbalanced lengths? Papers consisting only of one immense paragraph aren't as unusual as you might think. And they're not read with pleasure. Are your paragraphs in logical sequence, keeping the idea recognizable from one paragraph to the next? You may have to do some cutting and pasting if they seem far out of order. Do the first sentences of your paragraphs sound alike? Or do you repeat yourself justifiably? Have you amplified the paragraphs fully?

Are your sentences nicely varied in length — not all long or short? Does the syntax have variety? Are your sentences varied enough in complexity? Have you built in a rhetorical turn here and there? Are you sure you've looked hard enough for gross errors in usage and mechanics? Have you checked all difficult and unusual words for spelling and capital letters? Have you repeated words or groups of words without noticing? Have you illustrated your ideas with quotations or paraphrases? Is your diction appropriate to the topic? Have you kept slang and clichés out? Have you varied your introductory, transitional, and summarizing devices enough? Is your ending logical and does it flow smoothly from the text? Would you feel confident enough about the paper's quality to read it aloud to the class? Would it hurt if you were stranded somewhere for a year with nothing but the paper to read and reread?

EXERCISE

A. Correct the following passage for errors in usage, punctuation, and mechanics.

1. Most people remember William Cullen Bryant 1794–1878 as the gentle nature poet who they heard about when children in grade school. All of we boys and girls listened politely while Miss Stritch our fifth-grade teacher told us about Mr. Bryants growing up during the early nineteenth century in Massachusetts at Cummington in the foothills of the berkshires. Then her reading aloud of Thanatopsis and To a Water Fowl her moist eyes glittering with emotion i have often thought since that miss stritch had a special place in her heart for Thanatopsis although she often commented on the sadness of this poem about death and the graveyard she sometimes seemed happiest when contemplating the joys of the cemetery. We learned from Miss Stritch that mister Bryant began writing verses when he was 9 years old when he was only 14 his father sent to a boston publisher a poem called The Embargo about President Jeffersons trade restrictions against the english. When telling us about Mr. Bryant youthful genius Miss Stritch always seemed a little annoyed that none of the boys nor i, the only girl in the ellwood heights fifth grade were equally talented. Certainly however, I could understand how each of the citizens in little Cullen's home town for as Miss Stritch assured us everyone called him Cullen was proud to see their local prodigy write "Thanatopsis" at 17 and publish it at twenty-four. A prominent literary critic even told the young Bryant that he was the greatest genius in America. They all said that what William Wordsworth was to England, the young Williams College man from Cummington was to America.

After leaving the fifth grade years later I learned that William cullen Bryant was not merely a poet but also a successful newspaperman, the fighting editor of the New York Post. Struggling hard always for freedom of speech and religion, the opponents of Cullen Bryant even once went so far as to loot and raid his newspaper office. Did James Russell Lowell the famous New England poet who wrote A Fable for Critics do justice in his description of Bryant, then at the peak of his powers. William Cullen Bryant is as quiet, as cool, and as dignified as a smooth, silent iceberg whose only flame reflects the chill northern lights said Lowell in 1848 and he was destined only five years later to become Smith Professor of Modern Languages at Harvard. Despite Lowell's opinion, Bryant remained to the very end of his days a dominant leader in literature, in politics, in society, in journalism.

Part Three   The Writer in Action

The first task is to search books, the next to contemplate nature. He must first possess himself of the intellectual treasures which the diligence of former ages has accumulated, and then endeavour to encrease them by his own collections.
DR. SAMUEL JOHNSON, Essays from the Rambler, No. 154, 1751

11 Research Papers

42. What Is Research?

Wherever you do your research — in the laboratory, in the library, or out among the people — you are collecting facts, truths. You may be after old truths or new ones, but your ways of collecting them will be much the same wherever you look. The way to start is by getting some knowledge of the subject, finding and reading one or more works all the way through and skimming others, short and long, that look close to your subject. Your first big job is getting to know "the literature" well enough to find your way around among the important writers. Before you can do any research you'll have to learn how to use all the sources of information in the primary place where literary research is done, the library. The library's resources, when you know them well enough to feel familiar with them, can not only bring you deeper knowledge about your subject, but also help you to know truth when you see it, balance opinions, judge attitudes. While you gather knowledge, even on a subject as narrow as most undergraduate papers cover, you learn how to survey whole departments of learning, recording information so that it will be easy to use later.

The goal of library research, however, is not so much to collect as to distil the accumulated information, and then make use of it to write a fresh

251

restatement, or synthesis, of the subject. Everything you say may not be completely original, but the way in which you put it together can be.

Research takes the seeker of knowledge to two kinds of wells of information in the library. *Primary* sources are original documents, which most people never see: legal records (wills, deeds, records of legal proceedings, parish registers, state papers), diaries, letters, literary texts, contemporary newspaper accounts. Add to these direct evidence (statistical or verbal) you may gather. Many primary sources aren't available to undergraduates and are useful only to a specialist. *Secondary* sources are easier to get at, though — libraries are full of them. Most are books written by people who did go to the primary sources. Shakespeare's First Folio, printed in 1623, the first publication of all his plays in one place, is a primary source. Most of the hundreds of books about Shakespeare and his works that have been published since are secondary sources. The Declaration of Independence is a primary source document; anything written about it is secondary. Almost all primary sources are in special archives and libraries, and only specialists can get at them easily, though historical and genealogical societies, regional history rooms in public and school libraries, and town or college archives do have some that you can look at. If you could go to the London Public Record Office, the Library of Congress, the British Museum, the Houghton Library at Harvard University, the Berg Collection at the New York Public Library, or the Folger Shakespeare Library in Washington, D.C., you'd find as much as you could use about Shakespeare's plays. But most school or public libraries have enough secondary sources: books, and articles in journals and magazines.

Because primary sources can be hard to find, and secondary sources don't always give the best information, controlled research pamphlets are sometimes used for composition courses. Whole documents and pieces of sources of all kinds are gathered into one volume to be used by students as their only (or main) source of research material. That is not a way of training people to use the library, of course, but it does get them out of leisurely data-gathering, note-taking, and compilation directly into interpretation of materials. But to learn the footwork and techniques of doing research you must use libraries — their reference rooms, stacks, microfilm rooms, rare book rooms — getting help from reference librarians and learning how to use reference tools. Research is a little like detective work, starting with a general idea of the goal and following it for traces of deeper, more fruitful sources. Any library will eventually run dry of material you can use, possibly before you have all you need; some extra material can be taken from other libraries, near or far, by interlibrary loans. Working with the reference librarian, the card catalog, and the books in the reference room will teach you short-cuts that make your research faster, more efficient, and much easier. Why go through a whole section of the stacks to find nineteenth-century reviews of Jane Austen's *Pride and Prejudice* when you can find all the important ones listed in Moulton's *Library of Literary Criticism*? Reference rooms are filled with such labor-saving devices.

42a. How Do I Choose a Topic?

Your instructor may choose a topic for you or may let you be inventive in creating one. In a more advanced course your topic may come naturally out of the subject. If you do the choosing, you'll find quickly that some subjects that suggest themselves with effort on your part also cancel themselves instantly because they are repetitive or impossibly huge. Don't think of writing a biography of someone prominent — even a partial biography would call for resources far greater than you're likely to find, and besides one probably has already been written. It might be easy to summarize a published biography, but that would give you practice in summarizing, not in research — you'd profit about as much as if you invested in a black-market prewritten paper. Political issues and events covered in newspaper and magazine articles are fine subjects for learning how to do research and will encourage you to write with feeling because if the stories are recent enough no one else has had time to gather all the materials and publish a book on them telling the whole story. The challenge in writing about such a subject is clear, but it calls for restraint. Don't shoulder something you'd need years to handle properly. You won't get far into a subject like "A History of the Arabs in Palestine" before you see how futile it would be to cram the subject into a half million words, much less a thousand. "The Arabs in Israel" is a little more within reach, and narrowing still more would be even better. The narrow topic keeps your paper from becoming elephantine, and exercises your research muscles by getting you to survey current journalism. You could also pick a subject so small and obscure that no material shows up when you start research. Be ready to change topics then. Whatever the subject you choose, be sure to generate some enthusiasm over it. The more you get into it, the more you know about it, the more you will be attracted to it. With that attitude you can breathe life into any topic whether it is the oral epic in eastern Europe, the British naval mutiny of 1797, or the tax troubles of Spiro Agnew.

42b. The Card Catalog

Like any tool of the mind, using the catalog may seem difficult at first. It is just a clearly (but not simply) arranged instrument for helping people find facts.

Once you've found a topic, put together your bibliography. You can start by reading an article in an encyclopedia, which will list some basic books by the authorities. Then go over the books and articles listed in the card catalog, which should give you far more sources than the encyclopedia article has room for.

Card catalogs can be surprisingly rich in the information you need,

though of course they tell only about the books and articles the library has —
the bigger the library the more you'll find. All catalogs are much alike: cases of
drawers with 3-by-5-inch cards arranged in alphabetical order, printed and
typed on one or both sides with a description of the book and a code telling how
to find the book in the library. Each book has three cards filed in different places
in the catalog: a card for the author, another for the title, and a third for the
subject of the book — this gives you three ways of finding which book you want
and where it is. The catalog cards shown here are subject, author, and title cards.
The printed information is the same on all three because the Library of Congress
in Washington sends several identical cards for each book; your librarian adds
to these and files them in the catalog. The library's own code is the first information you see in the file drawer of the catalog. Many books are listed under several
subjects, which also helps you find something that may not be under the obvious
heading.

Arnold Fertig, the author of the research paper on Israel's Arabs that
is fully reproduced on pages 277–84, began his work by examining a subject
entry: Arabs in Israel. Under that heading he located several relevant books,
though D. R. Elston's *Israel: The Making of a Nation* proved most valuable.
Here is the way that the three Elston Library of Congress cards look:

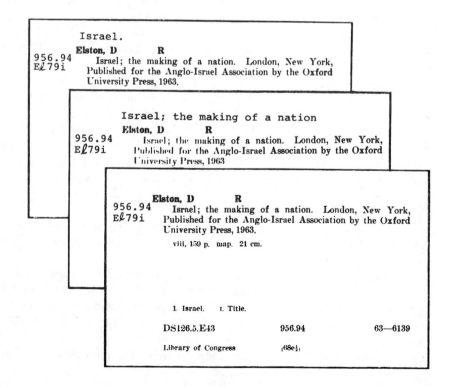

All cards are filed alphabetically except that initial articles *(a, an, the)* don't count on the title cards. Cards contain the following information:

Elston, D. R.	Name of author. Library of Congress cards may give authors' dates of birth and death.
956.94 *Eℓ 79i*	The Dewey Decimal Classification, or Call Number, is typed on the card locally, though the classification is suggested by the Library of Congress (see below). The number 956.94 shows this book is a subclassification of the 900 group, which is reserved for geography and history. The Middle East is represented by the subdivision 956. Eℓ79 is called the author notation. It is a numerical expansion of the number of positions in the alphabet, and *i* is the initial letter of the book's title. These symbols are primarily devices for locating a book in the library stacks and vary from library to library.
Israel; the *making of a nation*	Title of the book. Titles on library cards are often capitalized differently from normal practice.
London, New York	The place or places of publication (and edition number, if subsequent to the first).
Oxford University, 1963	The name of the publisher and year of publication.
viii, 159 p. *map., 21 cm.*	The book has 8 prefatory pages; 159 pages of text; a map; and is 21 centimeters high (shelf height).
1. Israel *I. Title*	The card can be found elsewhere in the catalog under the subject heading *Israel*, and it is cross-listed under its title.
DS126.5E43 *956.94* *63–139*	This information is for the library cataloger. The first number is the Library of Congress call number, which is different from the Dewey number. The second number is the Dewey classification suggested by the Library of Congress. The last number is the Library of Congress card order number, used when a librarian requests cards for newly acquired books.
Library of Congress	The book has been cataloged by the Library of Congress.
64c2	The printer's key to the card.

42c.   The Encyclopedia

The first place to go for the general knowledge you need when you start research is a recent edition of a good encyclopedia. Subject articles give you enough information to protect you from the embarrassment of overlooking elementary facts or a basic study in the field. Academic life is full of horror stories about graduate students who spent years researching a doctoral dissertation only to discover a week before defense of the thesis that an obscure Bavarian had published on exactly the same subject in 1889. The article may also discourage you from pursuing an obviously unmanageable topic, and encourage you to look for another.

For someone like Arnold Fertig, who plans a career as a rabbi and is particularly interested in the Palestinian Arabs, the *Encyclopedia Americana* article on Israel (which appears in volume 15, page 538) is exceptionally helpful. In eight subsections, it covers the people, land, economy, education, culture, mass communications, government, and history. It has a supplemental bibliography of more than a dozen books, including Don Peretz, *Israel and the Palestine Arabs* (which eventually will be a major source of information for Fertig's paper). For most subjects, the Index to the *Encyclopaedia Britannica* also gives solid data, though on this topic Fertig found the *Americana* more helpful. The annual supplements to the encyclopedias, as well as periodic revisions, also give updated information on topical events and world affairs.

These are the important general encyclopedias:

Chamber's Encyclopedia. 4th ed. 15 vols. New York: Pergamon, 1967.
   An incisive British encyclopedia.

Collier's Encyclopedia. 24 vols. New York: Crowell-Collier, 1972.
   Somewhat journalistic in tone and appearance, this reference work is nevertheless a source of information that cannot be overlooked.

Columbia Encyclopedia. 3rd ed. New York: Columbia Univ. Press, 1963.
   A useful one-volume reference work for a quick insight into hundreds of topics.

The Encyclopedia Americana. 30 vols. New York: Americana, 1972.
   Kept up-to-date with annual supplements and revisions, as are many other reference works, it has a good reputation for reliability and thoroughness.

Encyclopaedia Britannica. 24 vols. Chicago: Britannica, 1971.
   In the early Sixties the *Britannica* underwent a flurry of criticism for having allegedly failed to revise and update its great eleventh edition of 1910 with sufficient rigor. Until a similar analysis is made on other encyclopedias, however, it would be impossible to substantiate the charge. The *Britannica,* though slightly battered, retains its status as the grey eminence of the reference field.

The World Book Encyclopedia. 20 vols. Chicago: Field Enterprises, 1971.
An excellent reference work for high school students, this encyclopedia is
not suited entirely to the needs of college students. On the other hand, the
most recent edition of the *World Book* lists as authors some people who
are leaders in their fields, like G. E. Bentley, who writes on Elizabethan
drama.

42d.   Specialized Indexes

The reference room has a third productive source of material: the
subject indexes to periodicals and to collections of material (anthologies of
essays, short stories, plays, etc.). These may lead you to writings directly on your
own subject. For example, if Fertig were curious about how the world viewed
Israel a century ago, he could consult the *Nineteenth-Century Reader's Guide to
Periodical Literature,* and find such a prophetic title as "Are the Jews Returning
to Palestine?" in the 1896 *Review of Reviews.* His next step is to fill out and
turn in a call slip requesting the *Review of Reviews,* hoping that the library still
numbers this defunct journal among its treasures. Some of the major indexes are:

Social Sciences and Humanities Index. New York: Wilson, 1965.
Formerly known as the *International Index,* and dating back to 1907, this
index is a "guide to periodical literature in the social sciences and humanities." Most periodicals indexed are specialized and scholarly, including
such journals as *American Slavic Review, Germanic Review,* and *Middle
Eastern Affairs.*

Nineteenth-Century Reader's Guide to Periodical Literature. 2 vols. New
York: Wilson, 1944.
This index supplements *Poole's* (see below) index to nineteenth-century
magazines and adds the handy feature of classifying by author entries.

Poole's Index to Periodical Literature. 6 vols. New York: Smith, 1938.
Indexing articles published between 1802 and 1906, *Poole's* makes a useful guide to the periodical literature of the past century. It cites articles
published in *American Almanac* (Boston, 1830–61); *Catholic Quarterly*
(Philadelphia, 1876–81); and *New Eclectic* (Baltimore, 1868–71). Entry
is unfortunately by subject only. Despite their bulk, *Poole's* and *Nineteenth-Century Reader's Guide* do not provide a complete index to all
the periodical literature of the nineteenth century.

Reader's Guide to Periodical Literature. Minneapolis and New York: Wilson,
1905–.
The most frequently consulted index, the *Reader's Guide* covers such
popular magazines as *Atlantic, Hot Rod, The New Yorker, Time, Ebony,*
and *Yachting,* not only by author and subject but also by title.

Searching for periodical articles on the Arabs in Palestine, Mr. Fertig
found volume 30 (1970–71) of the *Reader's Guide* extremely helpful. Under the

subject heading of *Arabs,* he is directed to the heading *Palestinian Arabs,* where more than twenty articles are listed:

```
PALESTINE-Jewish-Arab relations. See Jew-
    ish-Arab relations
PALESTINE refugees. See Refugees. Arab
PALESTINIAN Arabs
    Algeria, Israel and the Al Fatah. R. W. Fox.
        Commonweal 92:184-5 My 8 '70; Discussion.
        92:331+, 475+; 93:83+ Jl 10. S 25, O 23 '70
    American innocent in the Middle East; Jor-
        dan. M. Frady. Harper 241:104-6+ N '70
    Arab guerrillas v. Arab governments. il por
        Time 95:22-3 Je 22 '70
    Arabs their own worst enemy. America 122:
        604 Je 6 '70
    Emerging realities. il Newsweek 75:48+ Mr
        23 '70
    Eretz Israel, or historic Palestine? America
        122:666 Je 27 '70
    Explosion in Jordan. il por Newsweek 75:34-5
        Je 22 '70
    Fire and steel for Palestine. J. M. Mecklin. il
        Fortune 82:84-9+ Jl '70
    Hidden leader of the Arab guerrillas; inter-
        view, ed. by O. Fallaci. Abu Lotuf. il
        Look 34:24-6 Je 30 '70
    Lull in the madness. il Newsweek 75:35 Je
        29 '70
    Palestine: a case of right v. right. il Time
        96:28-9 D 21 '70
    Palestine Arab commandos; with report on
        the Gaza Strip by P. Young and interview
        with G. Habash, ed. by O. Fallaci. il Life
        68:26D-34 Je 12 '70
    Palestine's Arabs. D. Peretz. il Trans-Action
        7:43-9 Jl '70
    Palestinian refugees. G. A. Geyer. New Re-
        pub 163:15-18 N 21 '70; Reply. E. Cooper.
        163:30-1 D 12 '70
    Palestinians and Israel. S. Avineri, bibliog f
        Commentary 49:31-44 Je '70; Discussion.
        50:6+ S: 30+ N: 18+ D '70
    Palestinians: refugees or a people? M. C.
        Bassiouni. il Cath World 211:257-62 S '70
    Shoring up a shaky calm. il por Time 95:24+
        Je 29 '70
    Synagogue council head rebukes "Christians
        for Palestine"; Pro-Arab Christian confer-
        ence. Chr Cent 87:783 Je 24 '70
```

Fertig notices that most articles on this list appear in news magazines like *Time* or *Newsweek,* as well as in such journals of national opinion as *Commonweal* and *Christian Century.* The article in *Trans-Action* by D. Peretz catches his eye because Peretz has already surfaced in the card catalog as the author of a book on Israel. Finding an author's name in several places suggests that he might be an authority. According to the code, the Peretz article appears in volume 7 of *Trans-Action,* pages 43–49 in the issue for July of 1970. The abbreviation *il* means it is illustrated. The key to abbreviations for other periodicals, such as *Cath World* and *Chr Cent,* appears in the front matter of the volume. The card catalog, or the rotating file on the librarian's desk in the periodical room, will quickly tell you if this volume of the periodical can be found in the local library. Many libraries microfilm journals and keep them in small cartons in a micro-reader room so that no one has to wait for last year's copies to be bound. You can even reproduce a page from the microfilmed journal, though these reproductions are often blurry. Finding nothing else here of immediate interest, Fertig decides to move on to volume 31 for the next year, under the same heading, *Palestinian Arabs*. There he records an unsigned article in *Newsweek* titled "Second-Class Citizens," which he will eventually quote in his finished paper (see page 283). He elects then to follow up the cross-reference to *Jewish-Arab Relations:*

```
JEWISH-Arab relations
  As Arabs see it. J. P. O'Kane. il America
    124:67-8 Ja 23 '71; Reply. R. Gordis. 124:
    161-2 F 20 '71
  Four ways to break the Arab-Israeli stale-
    mate. M. J. Kubic. il Newsweek 78:31 Ag
    9 '71
  Israel vs. the Arabs. il Sr Schol 99:16-17
    D 13 '71
  Martin Buber: friend of the court. D. J.
    Moore. il America 124:231-4 Mr 6 '71; Re-
    ply. J. M. Oesterreicher. 124:301 Mr 27 '71
  Middle East: frozen. Nat R 23:1100 O 8 '71
  Mideast: unstable as water. Time 98:21 Ag 2
    '71
  My Jewish problem, and ours. S. Stern. il
    Ramp Mag 10:30-40 Ag '71; Discussion. 10:
    68-71 O '71
  Permanent war; symposium, discussion.
    Trans-Action 8:4+ N '70
  Talk with Golda Meir; interview. ed. by M.
    Clark. G. Meir. por Time 98:29 Ag '30 '71
    See also
  Israeli-Arab war. 1967- —Peace and media-
    tion
  United Nations—Israel
JEWISH art. See Art, Jewish
```

For the moment he disregards the tantalizing subheadings listed under *see also,* as ones to be mined later on — the heading *Israeli-Arab War* might well reveal new facts. Instead he records the Kubic article on "Four Ways to Break the Israeli-Arab Stalemate" in *Newsweek,* volume 78, as of potential value. He also records that Stern's article in *Ramparts* (*Ramp Mag*), volume 10, pages 30–40, August 1971, has special interest because Fertig happens to know about *Ramparts'* New Left orientation. Gathering varied political opinions is important in this kind of research. The *Newsweek* article under *Palestinian Arabs* later proves most relevant to his needs (see page 283). But this search for the literature has already given him new insights into the subject.

Besides these major indexes, many other specialized indexes are helpful. From these indexes you can find the museum that owns a famous painting, the collection of short stories that contains a half-remembered tale, the review of a musical production presented many years ago or only last month, and news stories on both past and current events. Here are some of these indexes:

INDEXES[1]	SAMPLING OF PERIODICALS INDEXED
The Biological and Agricultural Index	*American Florist; Market Growers*

---

[1] All these indexes are published by H. W. Wilson Company, New York, except the last two.

Applied Science and Technology Index, 1958–. This and the *Business-Index* have replaced the old *Industrial Arts Index*, discontinued in 1957.	*Analytical Chemistry: British Plastics*
The Industrial Arts Index, 1913–57.	
The Art Index, 1929–.	*Advertising and Selling; Food Industries; Safety Engineering*
	American Academy in Rome; St. Louis Museum Bulletin
Biography Index, 1946–.	Biographical information from 1500 periodicals; the first volume [1946–49] gives 40,000 biographies
The Education Index, 1929–.	*Educational Method; Teachers College Record*
Essay and General Literature, 1900–.	A guide to essays in periodicals and books. The latter are particularly hard to find without some aid such as this index.
The Book Review Digest, 1905–.	*Atlantic; The New York Times; The New Yorker*
Monthly Catalog: U.S. Government Publications, 1960–.	"Pascagoula Harbor, Miss.: Letter from Chief of Army Engineers"; "Conference on Research in Progress on Tungsten"
The Music Index. Detroit: Information Service, 1949–.	*Down Beat; Etude; Music Educators Journal*
The New York Times Index. New York: *Times*, 1913–.	Published semi-monthly, this index is a prime source of information about events, past and present.

If you take an hour to browse in a large reference room you'll be impressed by the many kinds of information available there. It helps to know your way to the different kinds of sources, and a paperbound guide will do almost as well as a personal tour with the reference librarian; read *Reference Books, 7th ed.* (Baltimore, 1970), edited by M. N. Barton and M. V. Bell, or at least skim over it. There are specialized dictionaries such as *Dictionary of American Folklore,* ed. Marjorie Tallman (New York: Philosophical Library, 1959), and *Dictionary of Underworld Lingo,* ed. H. Goldin, F. O'Leary, and M. Lipsius (New York: Twayne, 1950). Yearbooks such as Fodor's *Holland* (New York: McKay, 1972), *The International Yearbook and Statesmen's Who's Who* (London: Burke's Peerage, 1970), published annually, and Keesing's *Contemporary Archives* (London: Keesing's, 1931–) give information about everything from trade statistics to tourist routes. Biographical works include *The International Who's Who,* 36th ed. (London: Europa, 1972) and the massive 63-volume *Dictionary of National Biography* (London: Oxford Univ. Press, 1885–). Various professions list their personnel in such works as *American Men and Women of Science,* 12th ed. (New York: Cattell-Bowker, 1971–).

Specialized fields of study have their own reference works. Art has the *Encyclopedia of World Art* (New York: McGraw-Hill, 1959–68). Business has the *Handbook of Business Administration,* ed. Harold B. Maynard (New York: McGraw-Hill, 1967), which gives the basic information for operating one's own enterprise. The theater has the valuable *Oxford Companion to the Theatre,* ed. Phyllis Hartnoll, 3rd ed. (London: Oxford Univ. Press, 1967). The literary scholar has *The Cambridge History of English Literature,* ed. A. W. Ward and A. R. Waller (New York: Putnam, 1907–17), and engineering and science have *The International Dictionary of Applied Mathematics* (Princeton: Van Nostrand, 1960). For psychology, there is *The Encyclopedia of Mental Health,* ed. A. Deutsch (Metuchen: Scarecrow Press, 1970), and for religion, such works as *The Abingdon Bible Commentary* (New York: Abingdon, 1929) and the various editions of *The Catholic Encyclopedia, An International Work of Reference,* published in New York. The social sciences are also well served by such tools as *Monthly Catalog of U.S. Government Publications* (Washington, D.C.).

For the world of entertainment, consult the *American Film Institute Catalog of Motion Pictures,* ed. Kenneth W. Munden (New York: R. R. Bowker, 1971). And for sports, *The Baseball Encyclopedia* (New York: Macmillan, 1969). If you want to find out more about Maginley & Co.'s Museum, Circus, and Trained Animals, look at the multivolume Odell's *The New York Stage.*

EXERCISES

A. With this bibliography of reference works, go to the reference room of the library and make a chart showing where each book can be found. An afternoon spent becoming familiar with the reference room can make the task of doing research both pleasant and efficient. The good student carries a map of the reference room in his head. In some libraries the reference works in the greatest demand are shelved behind the reference librarian's desk to discourage theft. The librarian should therefore be consulted before assuming that a book is missing.

B. What reference books would you go to first for answers to these questions?

1. Was criticism of Melville's *Moby Dick* in the nineteenth century favorable or unfavorable?

2. What were the best techniques for growing roses in 1950?

3. How did reviewers receive Hervey Allen's novel *Anthony Adverse* when it was first published?

4. Who was Timothy Dwight?

5. How can you find an article on teaching English to high school students in the University of Kansas *Bulletin of Education*?

6. In what collection of essays did George Orwell's "Politics and the English Language" first appear?

7. Which index would be most likely to cover articles written by experts on the language of Geoffrey Chaucer?

8. What was a "virginal"? Did a spinet precede or follow the harpsichord?

9. How many reels were in the Gotham Productions 1926 film *King of the Pack*?

10. What is the meaning of the word *chovan*?

11. Could you find a first-hand contemporary account of the parliamentary debate in 1776 about the American rebellion?

12. What were John Dobson's outstanding contributions to architecture?

13. How did the Shaker religious sect construct furniture?

14. What are the best methods of accounting?

15. What is a "credit union"? "crop dusting"?

16. How should a real estate broker go about selling a house?

17. What does the technical term "confirmed credit" mean when used by a businessman or a banker?

18. What costumes should be worn for the Restoration play *The Way of the World*?

19. What is a good play, preferably dealing with some ethical problem, for the senior class to put on? Would D. Trumbo's *Biggest Thief in Town* be suitable? Where can you get that play?

20. When a stage manager speaks of a "tormentor" what does he mean?

21. Where can you find a picture of Edmund Spenser's tomb?

22. Where can you find biographical information about Albert Camus?

23. Who were the principal characters in Anthony Trollope's *Barchester Towers*?

24. From what poem, in what collection, is the following line: "Long hath she slept, forgetful of delight"?

25. How many home runs did Tom McBride hit for Boston in the 1945 season?

26. Where could you find a camp skit based on a friendship theme?

27. Which reference work would give an account of the "persecution complex"?

28. What important events happened in America on May 5th over the years?

29. Where is there a brief biography of Robert Sudlow, contemporary American painter?

30. Which encyclopedia might give special attention to anti-Semitism?

42e.   How Do I Put Together a Preliminary Bibliography?

With some packs of 3-by-5's, Fertig assembles his preliminary bibliography. It will be very important later that he get things right the first time, writing down all the information he'll need about books and articles related to his topic. Because he can figure out later which are most valuable, the vital job now is to be complete. He won't want to go back when he's typing the paper just to find important facts he could have jotted down at the beginning. First he must get the call number and the exact title. Was it Northrop Frye's *The Anatomy of Criticism* or *Anatomy of Criticism*? Was the title of John G. Neihardt's epic *A Cycle of the West* or *The Cycle of the West*? And does *Northrop* have a *u* instead of an *o* and does *Neihardt* really have a *d*? Small lapses from accuracy can cause massive bother later, when research goes on for days and weeks.

The notations on the bibliography card include (1) the call number of the book; (2) the name of the author, surname first; (3) the title, and if it is not the first edition, the edition number — 2nd, 3rd, revised, or whatever; (4) place of publication; (5) name of the publisher; (6) date of publication; and (7) a code number in the upper right corner keying the bibliography card to the relevant note cards, and the author's surname for convenient alphabetizing. You're sure to need the call number, especially if you haven't written it down, when the time comes for verifying your sources. An accurate record of author, title, place of publication, publisher, and year of publication is clearly indispensable to keep your references useful. If your book is a first edition (as in the card reproduced below) then don't record that information. If you use a subsequent edition, however, that information can be vital, for later editions may be trimmed, revised, and expanded, altering the pagination. Finally the code number gives you a quick cross-reference to the note cards for this bibliographical entry. Recording a number rather than an entire bibliographic reference on each card avoids much irksome repetition.

The sample bibliography card on page 263 and the list below are ways for handling bibliographical data problems.[2] The note cards themselves should be arranged so that when alphabetized they will provide the final form for the bibliography.

The bibliography appears in an appendix of the completed paper and includes (1) the author's name, surname first; (2) the title, in italics; (3) place of publication; (4) name of publisher; and (5) the year of publication. The samples below have been set up for entry on bibliography cards, and they would appear in the same form in typescript (see page 264).

Study the punctuation carefully. Titles of books are underlined, meaning that if they were set in type they would be in italics. Only the words of the title, not the spaces between them, are underlined (The Day of Doom, not The Day of Doom); a period separates title from place of publication; a colon, place of publication from publisher; and a comma precedes the date of publication. The whole citation ends with a period. Finally, lines following the author's name are indented to keep the alphabetical order uncluttered.

Book with one author	Bowra, C. M. From Virgil to Milton. London: Macmillan, 1945.
Book with two authors	Amberson, William R., and Dietrich C. Smith. Outline of Physiology. Baltimore: Williams & Wilkins, 1948.
Book with an editor	Literature in America: An Anthology of Literary Criticism. Ed. Philip Rahv. New York: Meridian, 1957.
Book with author and editor	Spenser, Edmund. The Complete Poetical Works. Ed. R. E. Neil Dodge. Boston: Houghton Mifflin, 1936.
A translation	Homer. The Odyssey. Trans. E. V. Rieu. New York: Penguin Books, 1946.
A multivolume work	Hutchins, John. History of the County of Dorset. 2 vols. London: Bowyer and Nichols, 1774.
Book with more than one edition	Cronbach, Lee J. Educational Psychology. 2nd ed. New York: Harcourt Brace Jovanovich, 1963.

---

[2] For detailed treatment of scholarly documentation, see such leading style sheets as *The MLA Style Sheet,* 2nd ed. (New York: MLA, 1970); Edward D. Seeber, *A Style Manual for Students,* 2nd ed. rev. (Bloomington: Indiana Univ. Press, 1968); and James D. Lester, *Writing Research Papers: A Complete Guide* (Glenview: Scott, Foresman, 1971). The most comprehensive treatise on this subject is *A Manual of Style,* rev. 12th ed. (Chicago: Univ. of Chicago Press, 1969). But in this book the needs of undergraduate students have been considered first.

Essay in a collection	Baldwin, Hanson W. "The Epic of D-Day." <u>Background</u> and <u>Foreground</u>. Ed. Lester Markel. New York: Dell, 1963.
Periodical article	Perkinson, R. H. "The Epic in Five Acts." <u>Studies</u> <u>in</u> <u>Philology</u>, 43 (1946), 465–81. [Omit pp. when you can cite a volume number; you may also give month (March 1945)].
Newspaper article	"Superstitions of May Day Are Worldwide." <u>University</u> <u>Daily</u> <u>Kansan</u>, 30 April 1965, p. 1, col. 2.
Unpublished manuscript	Bryant, William Cullen. Letter, 12 April 1868 to Parke Griswold. Special Collections, Columbia Univ. Library.
Unpublished thesis	Simonson, Harold P. "A Study of the Correlation between Intelligence and Verbal Fluency." Diss. The Midwestern Univ., 1923.
Other sources	Personal Interview with John W. Sassoon, Manager. 5 August 1968.

42f.   What About Taking Notes?

When recording ideas, opinions, facts, dates, impressions, anything that comes out of your research, notes are only a means to the end you are after — writing the paper. Spending all your time taking notes is wasteful because you need a lot of time to turn them into a paper. It is discouraging at the last minute to have an impressive mound of notes and too little time to do a good job of digesting them. Be warned that it's easy to fool yourself when you're transcribing material from the sources. It may feel as if you're doing constructive labor but too much can be nothing but busy-work. The note-taking doesn't get as much into your head or onto paper as it seems — the facts are just being moved from one place to another.

All the time you're doing research, keep going back to your outline, which will steer you directly toward your goal, putting new and fascinating side interests into their peripheral place, saving a lot of wasted work, and telling you the outline should be changed if a minor topic seems worthy of turning into a big one. If you've chosen to write about Arab and Israeli military confrontations in Gaza, don't branch out and gather pages of information and quotations about Jordanian border fighting. Informative parallels may appear but keep them in your head and don't cloud your argument with them in the paper. If you've practiced speed reading, it may help you run through your reading in less time, retaining more facts about the subject. But reading cover to cover all the books that look or are pertinent can be sheer waste. In each book that may become part of the bibliography, read the table of contents, the beginnings and endings of chapters (for the summaries that authors often put there), and look in the index for words that have to do with your subject. After surveying the bibliography like this, you can throw out many cards; all those left over will be the heart of your paper. By now the important sources will stand out clearly and you can get most notes from them.

Write your notes on 5-by-8-inch cards, which hold enough words to make their size worthwhile. Or cut sheets of paper to that size if you'll be carrying the notes around much; paper takes up less room than cards. Unless by the time you read this the Congress of the United States has enacted a new and stringent copyright law forbidding the practice, use the Xerox machine for pages in your sources that are full of information; but don't copy everything in sight — it's expensive and makes the task of boiling down harder. If you find an illustration that should go into the paper, the librarian can get you a photostatic copy, for a price. And typewriters usually are nearby to make the notes compact and easy to read.

Your notes should fall into the four usual kinds: the direct quotation from the source; the paraphrase; the précis; and your own reactions and comments. Most cards will have hybrid information on them, though, combining direct quotations, paraphrases, and your own ideas on the subject, with your comments on the quotations. To get the material on paper, you can use complete sentences (take them from the original or make your own, using phrases from the original); or your own kind of shorthand may be handy. But keep the source's wording and your own strictly apart — it can be confusing to figure out which ideas are yours and which theirs. When your notes are complete, you should be able to tell just what each author was talking about without having to go back to the source, which is the worst waste of time. It should also be clear what the author was talking about, how he handled the subject, how that material might fit into one of the subdivisions you've broken the topic into, and what you thought at the time about the author's ideas. The card reproduced on page 267 shows how Arnold Fertig digested a page from Ben-Porath's *The Arab Labor Force in Israel.*

This note card shows one way of taking notes. The number in the upper left corner refers to the bibliography card, which saves writing out the names of authors and the titles all over again. The catchline in the upper right corner, "History of Economy," shows that the book's author connected Jewish-Arab relations with nineteenth-century economics. Fertig may find in later research that other authors write about this relationship, which will start building a larger pile of cards with the same catchline for this subdivision as the others; he may decide to add a section on this subject to the paper.

With some system in your work like this, you'll find that the research itself takes over from any preconceptions you may have had, and gives the paper

③   History of
Economy

During 19th century Porath sees separation of
Jewish-Arab economics -- but
a) sale of farm prod by Arabs to Jews [how much?]
b) employment of Arabs by Jews
c) land purchase by Jews

Creation of Jewish state gave power "... to pursue
whatever policies it chose" but [and here is a
crucial point for the Arabs] "...responsibility of welfare
state toward a minority group." [relate to 1971
conditions in Time article].

Porath seems knowledgeable.

(p.1)

its shape. If you're lucky, you may find you can take your final outline directly from the catchlines on the cards.

The card shown here shows how paraphrases, direct quotations, and comments on the source are worked together. Fertig has put his own comments inside brackets to keep from confusing them with Ben-Porath's words. He has corrected his own errors in spelling and has written down some of his early judgments on the book's worth, which will be useful reminders later. Finally, he has put the exact page reference in the lower right corner of the card, finishing his careful though tedious job of putting down anything he'll need later just where it's easiest to find. It may not be obvious now but you'll see later that going over the same ground twice to patch up omissions left by hurried note-taking is twice as tedious as getting it all down the first time. Carefully engineered notes make successful papers.

42g.   When Do I Footnote?

If you understand and remember what footnotes are for, you're not likely to misuse them. Use the footnote to show where you get ideas that aren't your own. Of course it's easy to fill up the pages of a paper with footnotes, but they will look like an attempt to impress the reader with your research. It takes experience to know just what to footnote, but in general document only specialized information, not commonly known facts such as Columbus' voyage in 1492. There was a time when the intricate footnote was considered the scholar's bra-

vura display of intellectual prowess, but times change and today there is a tendency to understate the footnote. One efficient way of citing sources is to give
the author's name in parentheses, right in your text (Ben-Porath, p. 69), putting
the full citation in the bibliography. If you've used material from two books by
the same author, you can list them separately in the bibliography by year of publication and match the text reference to the bibliography (Ben-Porath, 1969, p. 16).
This method can get rid of footnotes altogether, though you should know that
many teachers and style manuals still insist on a complete citation following
a first reference to a book or article.

     If you do use footnotes, keep them down to three or four a page at
most. And work for a consistent style in those notes. Every manual of style differs
a little in suggesting how to handle them. The 1970 Modern Language Association *Style Sheet* is most useful for undergraduates. If you have a good reason for
leaving the style recommended there, stick to the style you choose, treating each
element in the same way from beginning to end of the paper. Consistency is the
rule that supersedes all others. And if you're asked to follow some other system
(by your instructor, for example), that way of course takes precedence.

     The first footnote reference for a *book* needs: (1) the author's name,
first name first; (2) the book's title, *underlined;* (3) the name of the editor or
translator, if any, with *ed.* or *trans.* to identify them; (4) the edition (if it's the
first edition then don't mention the edition); (5) where the book was published,
name of publisher, and when it was published; (6) the volume number, if any,
with a Roman numeral; (7) page numbers in Arabic numerals, with p. or pp.
unless the book has more than one volume (then you don't need p. or pp.).

     Your first reference to an article in a *periodical* should have almost the
same information: (1) author's name, given name first; (2) title of the article in
quotation marks; (3) title of periodical, *underlined*; (4) volume number in
Arabic numerals (the numbers get too big for Roman numerals, which are hard
to read); (5) the issue number (Fall 1974) or (June 1974); first and last page
numbers of the article, without p. or pp. unless it comes from a weekly magazine.

     Footnote punctuation is different from that of bibliographies, the aim
being to punctuate them like complete sentences, rather than isolating segments
as in a bibliography. The place, publisher, and date are put in parentheses to keep
them apart from other material, and the entries are indented like a regular paragraph. The number of the footnote (in both text lines and the note itself), should
be in the "superior" position, a half space above the line. Look at these samples
instead of studying rules. They are set in type, so that titles are not underlined as
they would be if you typed them:

Book with one author	[1] Albert Keiser, *The Indian in American Literature* (New York: Oxford Univ. Press, 1933), p. 72.

Book with an editor

[2] Edmund Spenser, *The Complete Poetical Works,* ed. R. E. Neil Dodge (Boston: Houghton Mifflin, 1936), p. 52.

Book with two or more authors

[3] R. L. Sutherland, J. L. Woodward, and M. A. Maxwell, *Introductory Sociology,* 4th ed. (New York: Lippincott, 1952), p. 107.

Selection with author and editors

[4] Sir Thomas More, "The History of King Richard III," in *The Golden Hind,* ed. Roy Lamson and Hallett Smith (New York: Norton, 1956), p. 29.

A translation

[5] Karl Wintersdorf, *The Post-Medieval Crisis,* trans. Henry Williams (New York: Blake, 1967), p. 167.

A multivolumed work

[6] Glynne Wickham, *Early English Stages* (New York: Columbia Univ. Press, 1959), II, 398.

Book with more than one edition

[7] Henry Leffingwell, *New York in the 1880's,* 2nd ed. (Boston: Wendell, 1936), p. 98.

Essay in a collection

[8] Donald C. Bryant, "Rhetoric: Its Function and Scope," in *The Province of Rhetoric,* ed. Joseph Schwartz and John A. Rycenga (New York: Ronald Press, 1965), p. 5.

Periodical article

[9] William O. Scott, "Seasons and Flowers in *The Winter's Tale,*" *Shakespeare Quarterly,* 14 (Autumn 1963), 411.

Newspaper article

[10] "French Demand More Gold," *Kansas City Star,* 11 May 1965, p. 1, col. 2.

Unpublished manuscript

[11] William Cullen Bryant, Letter (12 April 1868) to Park Griswold. Special Collections, Columbia Univ. Library.

Unpublished thesis

[12] G. K. Grigsby, "The Modern Long Poem: Studies in Thematic Form," Diss. Wisconsin, 1960, p. 4.

Simplified first reference to a passage in a long poem

[13] *The Faerie Queene* I.ii.25.2. This and subsequent quotations are from *The Complete Poetical Works,* ed. R. E. Neil Dodge (Boston: Houghton Mifflin, 1936).

[The numbers following the title of the poem stand respectively for Book, Canto, Stanza, and Line numbers.]

Simplified first reference to a
passage in a play

[14] *Romeo and Juliet* III.ii.5. This and subsequent quotations are from William Shakespeare, *Romeo and Juliet,* ed. George Lyman Kittredge, rev. Irving Ribner (Waltham, Mass.: Blaisdell, 1966).

[The numbers following the title of the play stand for Act, Scene, and Line numbers.]

Watch the punctuation — no one will notice it unless you get it wrong.

When you refer to a publication more than once, you can shorten the citation to the author's last name and a page reference:

[7] Ben-Porath, p. 1.

This short reference is better if you keep it right in the text. You'll still run into the old-fashioned "ibid." (the same) and "op. cit." (the work cited) in learned journals. They are much less useful than giving the author's name plus a shortened title if it's needed.

Keep from confusing authors who have the same name by repeating the titles of their books.

[2] Scott, *Shakespeare's Life,* p. 10.
[3] Scott, *The Globe Playhouse,* p. 11.

After the first reference to the source of a long poem, a play, or another literary work, make the reference short:

[4] *Hamlet* I.ii.25. (Read Shakespeare's *Hamlet,* Act One, Scene Two, line twenty-five.)

When you really must cite a work often (once a page or so), you can use a short title for parenthetical documentation,[3] as with Shakespeare's plays:

[5] *MV* IV.iii.6–12. [*Merchant of Venice.*]

Some standard abbreviations for Shakespeare's plays follow: *Ado; Ant.; AWW; AYL; Cor.; Cym.; Err.; Ham.; 1H4; 2H4; H5; 1H6; 2H6; 3H6; H8; JC; LLL; Mac.; MM; MND; MV; Oth.; Per.; Rom.; Shr.; TGV; Tim.; Tmp.; Wiv.; WT.*

References to Scripture are conventionally handled with an abbreviated and unitalicized title, chapter number, and verse:

[6] Gen. xii. 6. or [6] Gen. 12:6.
[7] Mark xvi. 2. or [7] Mark 16:2.

---

[3] The 1970 *MLA Style Sheet* also permits Arabic instead of Roman numerals: *Merch.* 4.3.6–12; *F.Q.* 1.1.10.

When the citation is short, some instructors would rather have you run it into the text, as the Modern Language Association suggests:

Walter Steen, *Late Medieval Sculpture* (New York: Blake, 1921), p. 10, states clearly that . . . ,

John Enton (*Early Carolingian Tapestries* [New York: Blake, 1937], p. 314) writes . . .

The same point is also discussed by Thomas Bridewell, *Medieval Iconography* (Edinburgh: McCain, 1940), p. 11.

As already mentioned, you can economically cite passages in literary works by running them into your text (after you mention them the first time):

"Upon her eyelids many Graces sate" (*F.Q.*II.iii.25.1).

The parentheses come between the quotation mark and the period.

If you use a footnote but introduce the quotation by mentioning the author's name (or another part of the citation) in the text, don't repeat it in the note:

As William L. Barton has said, the current tendency to make the study of language into a science is fundamentally wrong-headed and misguided.[8]
[8] *The Old Grammar* (Boston: Jones, 1968), p. 7.

Over the centuries a language of abbreviations (conventional literary symbols), has been made up by scholars. Most of them used to be italicized in type but if they are used today they are not italicized. Because some scholars still find them serviceable, here they are:

anon.	anonymous
cf.	*confer* (compare)
et al.	*et alii* (and others)
f., ff.	the following page, pages
fn., n.	footnote
Ibid.	*ibidem* (in the same place). Capitalize it as the initial word in a footnote.
i.e.	*id est* (that is)
introd., intro.	introduction, introduced by
l., ll.	line, lines
loc. cit.	*loco citato* (in the place cited)
MS, MSS	Manuscript(s). The *MLA Style Sheet* calls for a period when the abbreviation is used with a specific manuscript: Cheltenham MS. 45.

n.d.	no date. Used when a book does not have a date of publication.
n.p.	no place. Used when a book does not have a place of publication.
op. cit.	*opere citato* (in the work cited). Many style manuals, including the *MLA Style Sheet,* are quietly campaigning against this abbreviation. The author's name is simpler and clearer.
p., pp.	page, pages
passim	throughout the work, here and there
rpt., reprint	Increasingly needed because of the flood of reprints of older books on today's market. Without it an older book may misleadingly appear to have been published quite recently, e.g., John Hoer, *The Boer War* (1911; rpt. New York: Sullivan-Harris, 1970), p. 126.
trans., Trans.	translated by, translator, translation by
vol., Vol., vols., Vols.	volume, volumes

42h.   Plagiarizing, Paraphrasing, Précis

Footnote (or run-in) references in your text are your way of telling the reader that something you've put in your work isn't your own. The difference between stating ideas that you put together (usually some at least were not your own) and plagiarizing sometimes is hard to describe. You're a plagiarizer if you copy someone else's words or thoughts as if they were your own. If you owe something to another writer, make it totally clear where it came from. *Plagiarize* originally meant "to kidnap." This kind of theft, in school as well as out of it, has its degrees. The worst kind in the student world is buying a ready-made paper from an agency or another student. Such traffickers in sloth, after years of profiting by others' laziness, now find the courts backing up those in the academic community who don't like to see some people buying their way to a diploma without working for it. Not so obvious but just as dishonest is the direct copying of a sentence, paragraph, or page written by someone else without acknowledging it. That kind of plagiarizing is often badly done — the plagiarizer usually betrays himself:

SOURCE	STUDENT VERSION
Keats's commitment to a world of sensory data looms larger and larger in the reader's mind, its presence being apparent everywhere in the lyrics and in the longer poems as well.	Keats's commitment to a world of sensory data looms larger and larger in the reader mind, it's presence being apparent everywhere in the learicks and in the longer pomes also.

What if the writer changes the words a little? Doesn't that make the work the copier's not the copied's?

> John Keats, the English poet, was committed to a world of sensory data, a fact that looms larger and larger in the reader's mind, its presence being everywhere apparent in the lyrics as well as in the larger poems.

The copying here isn't word-for-word, but the essence of the idea is still there and the copier hasn't identified the source — it's still plagiarism.

Can't you ever use someone else's ideas without being blamed? If that weren't possible, many great books would still be in manuscript; all you have to do is identify your source, either in the text or a footnote:

> According to William L. Fullerton, Keats's commitment to a world of sensory data "looms larger and larger in the reader's mind, its presence being apparent everywhere in the lyrics and in the longer poems as well."
>
> "Keats's commitment to a world of sensory data looms larger and larger in the reader's mind, its presence being apparent everywhere in the lyrics and in the longer poems as well."[1]
>
> [1] William L. Fullerton, "The Ordeal of John Keats," *Romantic Review,* 6 (1960), 651.

If you copy (without admitting it) only three words in a five-hundred-word paper you're still plagiarizing — it isn't quantity that counts but intent. Mere carelessness can lead you to borrow words, of course; that's still blameable though not quite so heinous. Identify all quotations in your notes so that you won't later mistake theirs for yours.

The paraphrase is one way of using others' ideas legitimately, as long as you tell who it is you're paraphrasing and where the material came from. Restating ideas to fit them to your own can bring knowledge together in new ways. But you *must* acknowledge those ideas. Say you found this material in *Time* (March 1, 1963, page 73) and wanted to weave it into a paper:

> Despite this improvement in the businessman's mood, many executives paradoxically are not yet willing to gamble their funds on expansion and modernization. Capital spending is barely above the level of 1957, and a rise of only 3 per cent is predicted this year (to $38.2 billion) — far less than the increase economists figure is necessary to give the economy the kind of growth it needs. Businessmen are just now beginning to show signs of restocking their inventories, and President Lawrence A. Harvey of Harvey Aluminum grumbles that the basic manufacturing companies have been forced into "maintaining inventory for all the rest of business down along the chain." The economy needs more companies that are willing to put their money where their confidence is.

A lot of information is packed into this paragraph. You *should* quote it directly, mentioning its source in the text or a footnote, but you could carefully paraphrase the essential argument and the supporting data:

> According to *Time* (1 March 1963, p. 73), the present mood of businessmen remains unfavorable to expansion and modernization. With capital spending barely above that of 1957 and with only a 3 per cent increase in growth rate predicted for this year, President Lawrence Harvey of Harvey Aluminum rightly complains about his overstocked warehouses. As the *Time* writer says, more companies need "to put their money where their confidence is."

Another way of getting these facts into your paper is the précis. Making a précis, you compress the source, trying not to lose any essential ideas. Practice in writing the précis is a healthy way of learning economy in writing. You prune until you have a miniature of the original, keeping only the most vital facts. This is a précis of the *Time* paragraph:

> Despite prosperity, capital spending is predicted to rise only 3 per cent (to $38.2 billion). Harvey Aluminum's L. A. Harvey complains that more companies must match confidence with money.

43.   How To Prepare a Research Paper: Rough Draft to Final

Once the bibliography is done and your ideas look as if they can be put in fairly solid shape, you're almost ready to type the first draft. Organize the notes until they form meaningful categories, clearly related groups of ideas, then read through them, analyze and break them down further, looking, like Henry James, for "the design in the carpet." Some cards will be easy to throw out, once you've thought about all the notes; others are worth only setting aside for a future project. But the rest should now be in clear order — they might almost make a paper if you typed directly from them. The catchlines at least will give you the large divisions in the outline.

Now, look back at pages 22–23 for help in making your outline final. Don't plunge into the writing hoping that all you've learned will take form by itself as you write, like a sail filling in a breeze. It won't. Your constantly revised outline will tell you where you are in your argument all the time and will make you take one logical step at a time.

Start typing. For the first draft, triple-spaced lines will leave room for corrections and additions. Where a quotation will have to be documented and verified, number it with red pencil, keying it to the bibliography card it belongs to. Sort and alphabetize your bibliography cards, making sure that every book you've referred to or quoted from shows up in the bibliography. Read the draft, paying attention to organization — see if it's all there, and if anything else needs fleshing out with more research. Read it again to see that your sentences are polished and won't need big changes later. Then get ready to type the final draft.

Make your final draft as close to perfect as you can. Very few instructors will be happy to hunt for glimmers of your genius through slovenly pages in a murky typescript. Follow the specifications in section 41. But type a separate title page; leave an inch margin on all sides of the page except the first (sink that two inches from the top of the page); indent the paragraphs eight spaces from the left-hand margin; type the page number at the top right corner of every page (but center it at the bottom of the first page).

If your instructor doesn't say the footnotes should go on the same page as their references, you can group them at the end of the paper under the heading "Notes," which is the arrangement the Modern Language Association prefers. If you do put the notes at the end, paper clip your pages together instead of stapling them; the instructor can then put the notes beside the pages and won't have to flip pages back and forth to see each one. Type footnotes at the bottom of the page (if that's where they are to go) single-spaced, because they look better that way; but if you group them at the end, double-space them. For either kind, use a superior footnote number a half-space above the line.

Put your bibliography at the end of the paper with the title "Works Cited" or "Works Consulted," or both, if you list the two kinds of books separately. Follow the bibliographic form you used in preparing the cards (if you did them correctly, you'll just have to copy them exactly; see page 284). If the bibliography runs to more than two pages, separate the items into books, periodicals, documents, and other sources. Compare footnotes against bibliography so that they won't disagree; at the same time you'll spot anything left out of the bibliography by mistake.

EXERCISES

A. Explain the information in these footnotes. Why are some abbreviated? Are the citations to books or periodicals?

[1] *The Myth of the Eternal Return* (New York: Pantheon Books, 1955), p. 10.

[2] Ibid., p. 12.

[3] Sacvan Bercovitch, "New England Epic: Cotton Mather's *Magnalia Christi Americana*," *A Journal of English Literary History,* 23 (Sept. 1966), 337–350.

[4] Roy Harvey Pearce, *The Continuity of American Poetry* (Princeton, Princeton Univ. Press, 1961), p. 111.

[5] Quoted in William Bradley Otis, *American Verse, 1625–1807: A History* (New York: Moffat, Yard, 1909), p. 24.

[6] Pearce, p. 12.

[7] Ernst Curtius, *European Literature and the Latin Middle Ages,* trans. Willard R. Trask (New York: Harper & Row, 1953), p. 100.

[8] Walt Whitman, *Leaves of Grass,* ed. Harold W. Blodgett and Sculley
Bradley (New York: New York Univ. Press, 1965), p. ix.
   [9] Edmund Spenser, *The Faerie Queene,* V.iii.68.
   [10] Gen. xii.6.

B. Develop research papers on the following topics, further limiting and re-
fining the topic whenever necessary.

1. The fighter pilot in World War I.   2. The wreck of the airship *Hinden-
burg.*   3. The sinking of the *U.S.S. Dorchester.*   4. The sinking of the
U.S.S. Reuben James.   5. The making of a Hollywood film.   6. Sinclair
Lewis and Edith Wharton.   7. The strange case of Gaston B. Means.
8. *The Red Badge of Courage* and the real Civil War.   9. Jane Austen's
debts to the city of Bath.   10. Shakespeare's Hamlet in the early nineteenth century.   11. Ben Jonson and Inigo Jones.   12. Contemporary
accounts of Emperor Nero.   13. How General MacArthur left Corregidor.   14. Payment systems to college athletes in eight schools.   15. The
role of SEATO in the 1960's.   16. The U-2 Incident.   17. George Bernard Shaw and the Fabians.   18. Socialized medicine in England.
19. Sartre and the new morality.   20. The America's Cup Race: 1963–
64.   21. Dachau: symbol of shame.   22. Russian foreign policy under
Khrushchev.   23. The fight for women's rights in the United States.
24. The *Pueblo* incident.   25. The 1968 Chicago Riots.   26. Mark Rudd
at Columbia.   27. The Berkeley Park Riot.   28. The Origins of Rock:
Elvis Presley.   29. Vietnam in 1948.   30. The Living Theater movement.
31. The Kent State massacre.   32. The massacre at My Lai.   33. The
Watergate Affair.   34. The Pentagon Papers.   35. Nixon in China.
36. The "de-accession" fuss at New York's Metropolitan Museum of Art.
37. The Agnew Affair.   38. The CIA in Chile.   39. The Fuel Crisis of
1974.   40. The Israeli War.

ISRAEL'S SETTLED ARABS:

AN OVERVIEW

by

Arnold Fertig

April 12, 1972
Anthropology 195
Professor Jones

The anthropologist studying people remote from his own culture tries through a relatively short visit to catch a glimpse of another way of life. Underlying his research is the assumption that the society he investigates has existed in basically the same way for many years. The people of Israel in the latter half of the twentieth century do not, however, lend themselves to such an examination. D. R. Elston writes that the student of Palestine "must be ready constantly to adjust his knowledge to the radical changes that occur at a bewildering rate in almost every sphere of the national life."[1] In this paper I shall look briefly at the traditional people of the area, the sedentary Arabs, and show some of the ways in which their culture is in transition.

To get an overview of the change which has taken place in Palestine, one need only look at these figures supplied by Henry Rosenfeld: "At the end of World War II there were 650,000 Jews and 1,200,000 Arabs in Israel. In 1963 there were over 2,000,000 Jews and only 250,000 Arabs."[2] A more recent study updates the latest figure of Arabs to 400,000 in 1971, and suggests at that time that they made up 14 per cent of

[1]D. R. Elston, Israel: The Making of a Nation (London: Oxford Univ. Press, 1963), p. 149.

[2]Henry Rosenfeld, "From Peasantry to Wage Labor and Residual Peasantry: The Transformation of an Arab Village," in Peoples and Cultures of the Middle East, ed. Louise E. Sweet (Garden City: The Natural History Press, 1970), p. 147.

the Israeli population.[3] The migrations that account for the
greatest fluctuation in these statistics occurred in an
incredibly short time. During the fighting following the
departure of the British from Palestine in 1948 and the
formation of the present-day states in the Near East, thousands
of Arabs fled their homes in Israel to neighboring Jordan,
Syria, Lebanon, and Egypt. By September of 1949, over 700,000
Arabs, representing over one third of Israel's population,
were maintained in Arab refugee camps.[4] Even today this
"nation in exile" remains unassimilated into these countries.[5]

The minority that has chosen to remain on its ancestral
lands in the Jewish state faces special problems. Because
of the vast numbers who fled, both sides view the tenacious
Israeli Arabs with distrust. Brother Arabs regard them as
having "sold out" to Israel, and Israel in turn considers
them as potential turncoats and bars them from military
service.[6] One of the three Arab representatives to the
Israeli parliament describes his people's position as "that

[3]Amos Elon, "Two Arab Towns that Plumb Israel's
Conscience," New York Times Magazine, 22 Oct. 1972, p. 76.

[4]Don Peretz, Israel and the Palestine Arabs (Washington:
The Middle East Institute, 1958), p. 30, n. 2.

[5]Peretz, "Palestine's Arabs," Trans-Action, 7 (July
1970), 48.

[6]Edwin Samuel, The Structure of Society in Israel,
2nd ed. (New York: Random House, 1969), pp. 101-2.

of a lamb between two wolves."[7] It becomes, then, a

political football game for the anthropologist interested in

comparing the Israeli Arabs statistically. Should they be

compared to their present countrymen, the Jews, or to people

of the same ethnic stock and historical ties in bordering

countries? Studies comparing the Israeli Arabs and both

larger groups reveal that though this minority lags behind

the Jewish majority in Israel, it enjoys several advantages

over fellow Arabs.

In the area of education, Ben-Porath points out that

the Israeli Arabs have a lower illiterary rate than other Arab

peoples:

> The rate of 32 per cent among Arab men aged 14+
> compares favorably with 59.5 per cent in Egypt
> (aged 15+) in 1960; 49.9 per cent in Jordan (aged
> 15+) in 1961; 46.5 per cent in Syria (aged 10+)
> in 1960; and 73.1 per cent (aged 5+) in Iraq in
> 1957. In addition . . . in Jordan 64 per cent
> of the men aged 15+ did not have more than four
> years of primary school, compared with only 48
> per cent among Israeli Arabs.[8]

While not precisely the same age groups are being compared,

and the figure for Iraq is hardly comparable at all, one

can see from these figures significant educational disparity

between Israeli Arabs and their counterparts in neighboring

countries. Progress is not so dramatic in the area of

women's education owing to the refusal of Moslem parents to

permit their daughters to participate in co-education.[9]

[7]"Lamb Between Two Wolves," Time, 5 Jan. 1970, p. 27.

[8]Yoram Ben-Porath, The Arab Labor Force in Israel
(Jerusalem: Falk Institute, 1966), p. 9.

[9]Samuel, p. 105.

Eroding this resistance, however, is enforcement of the
current Israeli law providing mandatory free formal education
for all children from age five to fourteen.[10] Ben-Porath's
study indicates greater education among both sexes as age
decreases, showing a degree of success for Israeli
educational programs.[11] By way of prediction then, this
trend suggests great changes as more educated Arab individuals
become mature and predominate within their society.

In the sphere of economics, traditional systems in
the Near East have greatly changed since Israel has become
independent. During the first half of this century, Jews
and Arabs had separate economic communities. Interaction,
according to Ben-Porath, consisted of the sale of
agricultural produce by Arabs to Jews, purchases by Jews of
Arab land, and occasional employment of Arabs by Jews.[12]
The increases in population, industrialization and
urbanization that accompany Israel's growth, however, have
created new economic opportunities for the Arab.

A study of the occupational groupings of mature males
in an Israeli Arab Community shows a great decline of
agriculturists, shepherds and cameleers since the 1920's,

[10]Facts About Israel, ed. Misha Louvish (Jerusalem:
Ministry of Foreign Affairs, 1972), p. 144.

[11]Ben-Porath, p. 10.

[12]Ibid., p. 1.

and in turn an upsurge in manual laborers and village
artisans.[13] In addition, 9.5 per cent of the villagers are
now classified as merchants in contrast to a negligible
percentage in 1920.[14] Among agriculturists, Cohen observes
a shift from subsistence to market farming. He further
states that this "became possible, at least in part when
immediately after the establishment of the state, the
government began to supply the entire population heavily
subsidized imported foodstuffs and clothing on a ration
system. This had a revolutionary significance for Arab
villages . . . ."[15]

The economic climate for Arabs in Israel has obviously
improved greatly with the influx of foreign capital to the
fast-growing Israeli state. The minority is still not on an
equal footing with the Jewish majority, however. Time
notes: "Per capita income among Israeli Arabs is $850 a year
versus $200 for most of the 600,000 Arabs of the Jordan
River's West Bank who came under Israeli control after the
1967 war. The overall Israeli per capita income, on the other
hand, is $1,200."[16] Similar inequities exist in education,
where older Arab students complain that the prescribed

[13]Rosenfeld, p. 155.

[14]Ibid.

[15]Abner Cohen, Arab Border-Villages in Israel
(Manchester; Manchester Univ. Press, 1965), p. 23.

[16]"Lamb Between Two Wolves," p. 27.

curriculum shows "a marked tendency to ignore Arab national
values."[17] The serious charge is frequently voiced that
"in political and cultural terms, the Israeli Arab remains
a second-class citizen."[18]

Because of the life struggle Israel is involved in,
traditional Arab values are necessarily being undermined.
As constituted, however, Israel guarantees "complete equality
of social and political rights" for all its citizens.[19]
Encouragingly, indicators show a slow but persistent growth
toward this goal. Certainly as a subsistence way of life
is being replaced by a marketplace, and educational levels
continue to rise, the Israeli Arab looks forward to a bright
future.

[17]"Second-Class Citizens," Newsweek, 8 Feb. 1971, p. 40.

[18]Ibid.

[19]Facts About Israel, pp. 9-10.

List of Works Cited

Anon. "Second-Class Citizens," Newsweek, 8 Feb. 1971,
    pp. 40-41.

_____. "Lamb Between Two Wolves," Time, 5 Jan. 1970,
    pp. 27-28.

Ben-Porath, Yoram. The Arab Labor Force in Israel.
    Jerusalem: Falk Institute, 1966.

Cohen, Abner. Arab Border-Villages in Israel. Manchester:
    Manchester Univ. Press, 1965.

Elon, Amos. "Two Arab Towns that Plumb Israel's Conscience."
    New York Times Magazine, 22 Oct. 1972, pp. 44 +.

Elston, D. R. Israel: The Making of a Nation. London:
    Oxford Univ. Press, 1963.

Facts About Israel, ed. Misha Louvish. Jerusalem: Ministry
    of Foreign Affairs, 1972.

Peretz, Don. Israel and the Palestine Arabs. Washington:
    The Middle East Institute, 1958.

_____. "Palestine's Arabs." Trans-Action, 7 (July 1970),
43-9.

Rosenfeld, Henry. "From Peasantry to Wage Labor and Residual
    Peasantry: The Transformation of an Arab Village."
    Peoples and Cultures of the Middle East. Ed. Louise E.
    Sweet. Garden City: The Natural History Press, 1970.

Samuel, Edwin. The Structure of Society in Israel. 2nd ed.
    New York: Random House, 1969.

. . . great novels and stories make such sovereign use of their form — indeed, to a large extent, are their form — that any kind of transposition becomes a diminishment. It follows, then, that the greater the fiction, i.e., the more its form and content are indissoluble, the greater the loss incurred by transposition. Here, however, the film comes through with another possibility: it can turn a mediocre novel or story into a fine movie. . . .
JOHN SIMON, Movies Into Film, 1971

The structure of a fiction becomes a world, a meaningful and deeply mysterious pattern, and in that sense it can become, however small and broken by comparison, a creation mirroring the Creation.
GEORGE GARRETT, "Morris the Magician," c. 1969

12 Writing About Literature

HOW DO I WRITE ABOUT LITERATURE?

When you first write about literature you join the very large number of people who have tried their hand at literary criticism.[1] To write criticism you have to *comment* on the literature, not *summarize* the plot. It's tempting at first to retell the story; to keep from doing that, simply don't follow the story's chronological order in your paper. If you're writing about Hemingway's "The Killers," start the paper with something from the middle of the story that fits into your analysis. Don't begin with a commentary on the dramatic opening line ("The door of Henry's lunch-room opened and two men came in."). Instead, pick an entry point well into the story, as "When Nick Adams left the lunch-room to visit Mrs. Bell's rooming house, he sensed that life would never be the same for him again."

---

[1] Extensive treatment of techniques for writing about literature are in B. Bernard Cohen, *Writing About Literature*, rev. ed. (Chicago: Scott, Foresman, 1973); Edgar V. Roberts, *Writing Themes About Literature*, 3rd ed. (Englewood Cliffs, N.J.: Prentice-Hall, 1973); and Sylvan Barnet, *A Short Guide to Writing About Literature*, 2nd ed. (Boston: Little, Brown, 1971).

Make your first job finding a *thesis,* a structure in the literature that helps you start understanding the author's plan. At the heart of almost any piece of literature is an ultimate idea that inspires you to think about birth or renewal, death or finality, voyaging or change, discovery or initiation, or any of the ever-intriguing profound secrets: "Nick Adams in 'The Killers' is a young man going through the initiation of innocent youth into adulthood's mysteries."

Analysis, no matter how deep, won't save you from your most challenging duty — you've got to judge the author's writing. Analysis starts you off. You need to understand the work, and analysis will give you a beginning; it will also help verify your taste. An opinion that grows from experience in reading and analyzing literature, fertilized by common sense, is more than opinion — it is criticism.

Close reading of the text will leave you with a dominant impression of the major theme, or themes, of a story. Love? Hate? Despair? Damnation? And so forth. Once you have an insight into what was uppermost in the author's mind, begin to search for key words, episodes, bits of characterization that support the theme. Write them down on cards. If you were analyzing Shakespeare's *Richard II,* for example, and wanted to show the indecisiveness of the King, you would want to think about the banishment, deposition, and garden scenes — each one a commentary on the problem of the ineffectual monarch. Next arrange the statements (cards) in order of importance. The cards should now become a kind of outline, starting not necessarily at the beginning of the work but at the heart of it, ramifying outward through secondary themes and ending with purely peripheral events, ideas, or people. You can use this outline to build the paper. If it does nothing else it will keep you from being a plot summarizer. And it will help you understand the work, proving to the reader that you *did* understand it because you show how the author related all the parts to the whole.

We assume, of course, that the literary artist either consciously or intuitively put together such a structure, carefully making all references and allusions contribute to the whole design, instead of just inventing pieces and throwing them together. That assumption is almost always safe.

Be objective. Make your argument persuade by gathering and presenting evidence logically, not dogmatically. Opinions don't count unless you back them with facts. Getting originality into the paper takes effort, but try to give fresh interpretations of some things in the work. Your reader ought to feel that you have found something in the work that hadn't been seen in quite that way by anyone else, that it would be a good idea to read the work again to see if your interpretation doesn't make it a little more enjoyable.

Don't forget the audience, which may not have read the work. Even if they haven't read it lately, they won't be helped by a summary of the plot and nothing else. And obviously they will be familiar with at least the broad outlines of it, meaning that you don't have to do any more than refresh their memories about the details in the foreground of the plot, not the whole complicated outline.

Don't be shy about quoting. Meaningful quotations brighten and strengthen your analysis without overwhelming it. Quoting a hundred words in a five-hundred-word essay isn't overdoing it if you weave everything together well. (For the mechanics of handling quotations, see 38e).

Your tenses ought to be consistent throughout the paper. Writing about fiction, think of the characters and events as in a timeless present, which will let you stick with the present tense instead of shifting back and forth from past to present, confusing the reader. If you mention the author's life and behavior, you may have to shift to the past, but that shouldn't make anyone dizzy.

44.   What Questions About Literature Will Help Me Write the Paper?

To make sure your paper does something, keep thinking about a question and work throughout toward answering it. It helps to think of any literary work as belonging in one or more of these phases:

1. The story as an ordering of words — how is it designed and put together?

2. The story as an imitation of nature — how does the author copy the real world?

3. The story as an imitation of art — is it like any others?

4. The story as revelation — what truth about God, man, or the universe does it reveal?

44a.   How Is the Story Designed and Put Together?
The Story as an Ordering of Words

The writer of these paragraphs shows how plot in Hemingway's "The Killers" works toward a definite goal:

> "The door of Henry's lunch-room opened and two men came in. They sat down at the counter."
>
> Surely not many famous tales begin so simply as Ernest Hemingway's "The Killers." With a language as bare and sparse as the plot, "The Killers" would seem to be on the surface a fairly conventional story of guys and dolls who have moved temporarily to a small town. The movement of the plot is from a lunchroom to a rooming house and back to a lunchroom. The surroundings can best be described as sordid, early Nelson Algren. Except for the clock on the wall, a sense of motion is absent. The story first shows the killers, Al and Max, entering the lunchroom; it reveals the dialogue between them and the terrified occupants of the cafe; it shows Nick Adams running in terror to Mrs. Bell's rooming house; it reveals the dialogue between Nick and Ole; it shows

Nick back at the cafe, being told just to "forget it." And that is all. What design is there in this carpet to keep admirers coming back year after year?

The first answer must be that behind the naturalness of the setting, Hemingway has concealed a classic pattern of human activity. The characters are all either searching or learning. The opening episode in the diner shows the searchers, that is the killers, after their quarry. It is, then, apparent that the searchers, the probers, come from the world outside the lunchroom. Inside the lunchroom are stability and security for young Nick Adams; outside, terror, violence, and death. The unstated organizing principle of the story is a movement from the world of the unknown to the known, from the world of questions to the world of no answers. The design of "The Killers" — like that of any great story — turns out to be a scaled-down version of the universe. But it is scaled down only to accommodate the learning capacity of man.

44b.   How Does the Author Copy the Real World?
The Story as an Imitation of Nature

This kind of critical paper is meant to find out if the writer reflects the world around him accurately. This is the way to write about writers thought of as "naturalistic": Theodore Dreiser, Frank Norris, Upton Sinclair, Gustave Flaubert. Those who write exotic romances have to be thought about differently: J. R. R. Tolkien and Robert Louis Stevenson. Some writers of fantasy, such as Franz Kafka, seem to feel that only fantastic stories can capture the nightmarishness of our times. This writer tries to find real-life models for Hemingway's gangsters:

> The real-life models for the gangsters of Ernest Hemingway's short stories dwelt in Kansas City during those years when the author was reporting for the Kansas City *Star*. The sinister Al and Max, who come into the quiet of the well-lighted lunchroom from the darkness outside — Hemingway's repetition of the word *outside* contrasts a world of darkness and a world of light — fit the stereotype of the American gangster. Drawn from the ranks of the foreign-born and the misfits, the gangster-figure has captured the American imagination. It achieved great notoriety with the blaze of tommy guns and the roar of getaway cars in the 1920's.
>
> For a youth from a middle-class background, the first sight of these laconic killers — mean, vicious, serenely sure of their own brutality — must have been traumatic. Operating on the fringe of society, in a world of bail bondsmen, minor political figures, corrupt police, gamblers, and sporting types, the killers rarely cross the path of the average citizen. They live in that "underworld" which is, in Hemingway's word, "outside" the normal experience of a Nick Adams. Without much precedent in literary history, the gangster type owes its existence in large measure to this story by Hemingway. The rash of Hollywood dead-end kids, little Caesars, and Scarfaces of the 1930's, the popularity of the "Untouchables" on television in the early 1960's, and the hysteria over Bonnie and Clyde in the late 1960's owe their origins to Heming-

way's vision. In dramatizing the sordid and ugly in the asphalt jungle, the
gangster makes a perennial appeal to the morbid side of man's nature.

44c.   Is the Story Like Any Others?
The Story as Imitation of Art

Writers copy nature but they also have other writers' works to use as
models, fertilizing their own creativity. When they choose bad models they make
stereotypes like the romances of the Old West. Copying popular motifs isn't
necessarily unsuccessful. Think of the generations of cowboys (or pretend cowboys) who learned how to act and look like cowboys from popular fiction and
the movies. And the motorcycle gangs — did they spring out of Marlon Brando's
caricature on the screen or did he copy them? Stereotypes can be turned into
breathtakingly original characters, though, as Shakespeare did with Hamlet who
originated in the hackneyed "revenge play" of the Elizabethan playhouse. A
legitimate and fascinating line of literary inquiry is finding how an author trans-
forms popular motifs. How does the writer reconstruct conventional materials
to fit his fictional creations? Here is this phase of criticism, again used on Hemingway's "The Killers":

> All fictional work combines the conventional and the inventional in varying
> proportions. Shakespeare was not above copying the worst clichés of the
> Elizabethan revenge play in *Hamlet* but at the same time he was resourceful
> enough to add a philosophical dimension totally lacking in something like
> Kyd's *The Spanish Tragedy.* Similarly Ernest Hemingway's "The Killers"
> offers a rare example in literary history of a new form, a new and fresh char-
> acter type: the gangster figure. But Hemingway's originality is more super-
> ficial than real. The Mafia gangster, remote and foreign to the Anglo-Saxon
> sensibility, traces his ancestry to the Iago-like villain of Elizabethan drama.
> Al and Max, like the Machiavel of the Globe playhouse, come from out-
> side, a place remote and distant from the experience of either ordinary
> subjects of Queen Elizabeth I or of average Americans. They have in their
> behavior the same "unmotivated malignancy" as Iago, a quality that Shake-
> spearean commentators have puzzled over for decades. Seeking all kinds of
> clues for Iago's hatred of the Moor, they always fall back on the explanation
> that Iago's behavior stems from pure evil. So it is with Al and Max, men who
> never before saw George or Nick or Ole Andreson, but who for reasons much
> larger than a few dollars in blood money will always be available to annihilate
> a fellow creature. Such monstrous evil, unthinkable and abhorrent, still ap-
> peals to the latent malice in the hearts of men. From Shakespeare's Iago to
> De Flores of Middleton's *The Changeling,* Malevole of Marston's *The Mal-
> content,* Bosola of Webster's *The Duchess of Malfi,* and to Hemingway's Al
> and Max is not so great a distance as one might think. Hemingway has both
> discerned and created an unsavory type in American life. Until captured in
> words and crystallized in a work of imaginative fiction, human experience has
> no reality. Without the record of literature, men would need to rediscover

these patterns in each generation. Ironically, in sketching his gangsters, Hemingway simply rediscovered one of the most successful stage types in dramatic experience.

44d.   What Truth Does It Reveal?
The Story as Revelation

We can examine the story as the author's attempt to capture the ideal that Northrop Frye called "the total dream of man."[2] Writers periodically abandon storytelling to take up philosophizing, especially in recent years. The antirhetorical novel replaces plot with theme, action with soul-searching. The writer challenges us to ask what he is saying about God, man, and the universe. French Existential writers like Camus, Genêt, and Sartre wrote such novels. Read what critics say of their work and you risk burial by an avalanche of commentary on *Verfremdungseffekt,* or "alienation," or "self-exile," or "being and nothingness." That school of the mid-twentieth century reflects a philosophical tradition in writing by Lucretius, Dante, Milton, and Herman Melville. But do we have to probe all fiction for philosophical or metaphysical subtlety? The superb storytellers, among them Charles Dickens, Anthony Trollope, and Mark Twain, show how silly that would be. This is from a composition on Hemingway as a "revealer of truth":

> Essentially Ernest Hemingway's "The Killers" is a tale of innocence and experience. Throughout the story there is a split between two sides of man's fate: the "clean, well-lighted" world of Henry's lunchroom and the gathering darkness of "outside"; the orderly world of Nick Adams and the disorderly world of Ole Andreson; the timeless world of Max and Al and the timely world of George and Sam, as signified by the clock. The fulcrum, the hinge, for innocence and experience rests in Nick Adams, the young boy who discovers the existence of evil and moves, in fact, from the world of innocence to the world of experience. As though satanic figures from a shapeless void, an unformed chaos, the two killers come into the world of order and time of Henry's lunchroom to throw the arrangements of decent mortals into temporary disorder.
>
> So searing is the impact of this kind of sensibility on the innate goodness of the young and innocent that the capture by Al and Max of the lunchroom must be recorded slowly and painstakingly, the elaborate references to the clock suggesting a special time, longer than ordinary time. The gap between innocence and experience is not so great as Nick might have believed. Only a door in Henry's lunchroom separates the world of evil from the world of good. The tragedy for Ole Andreson is that, locked outside the lunchroom, away in the recesses of Mrs. Bell's rooming house, he is permanently

---

[2] Most of the ideas in this section are popularizations or adaptations of concepts advanced in Northrop Frye, *Anatomy of Criticism* (Princeton: Princeton Univ. Press, 1957).

estranged, alienated, from salvation. Hope must be abandoned for those cast into the outer darkness. Henry's lunchroom, as perhaps Sam realizes, stands as a speck of light in a sea of darkness, a sputtering lamp at best, nothing to be tampered with.

EXERCISES

A. Write a critical essay on one of these topics, each representing a different level on the ladder of interpretation:

1. Describe the main patterns of language in a short story by Edgar Allan Poe, such as "Ligeia" or "The Fall of the House of Usher," showing how at key points in the story Poe achieves heights of tension. (An essay on how Poe made use of the real world around him would be futile.)

2. Comment on Mark Twain's use of life along the Mississippi in *The Adventures of Huckleberry Finn,* concentrating on the episodes about the Shepherdson-Grangerford feud.

3. What elements in James Bond stories grow out of the author's imitation of detective stories rather than real life?

4. What does a novel such as Albert Camus' *The Stranger* say about the existence of man in today's world?

B. Read Arthur Miller's *The Crucible,* making your project four essays dealing with these questions:

1. How is *The Crucible* put together to achieve dramatic tension?

2. What historical events does Miller draw on for the trial scenes?

3. As a play about trial and ordeal, what other great literary productions can it be compared with? Plato's *The Apology*? Shaw's *St. Joan*? The trial of *Job*? The passion play tradition?

4. What does Miller have to say about the ultimate significance of human life? Can we give for nobility of soul a natural or supernatural explanation?

C. Write a thousand-word paper interpreting this story by Hemingway. Concentrate on the phase that you consider most appropriate to the story.

THE END OF SOMETHING

In the old days Hortons Bay was a lumbering town. No one who lived in it was out of sound of the big saws in the mill by the lake. Then one year there were no more logs to make lumber. The lumber schooners came into the bay and were loaded with the cut of the mill that stood stacked in the yard. All the piles of lumber were carried away. The big mill building had all its machinery that was removable taken out and hoisted on board one of the schooners by the men who had worked in the mill. The schooner moved out of the bay toward the open lake carrying the two great saws, the traveling carriage that hurled the logs against the revolving, circular saws and all the rollers, wheels, belts and iron piled on a hull-deep load of lumber. Its open hold covered with canvas and lashed tight, the sails of the schooner filled and it moved out into the open lake, carrying with it everything that had made the mill a mill and Hortons Bay, a town.

The one-story bunk houses, the eating-house, the company store, the mill offices, and the big mill itself stood deserted in the acres of sawdust that covered the swampy meadow by the shore of the bay.

Ten years later there was nothing of the mill left except the broken white limestone of its foundations showing through the swampy second growth as Nick and Marjorie rowed along the shore. They were trolling along the edge of the channel-bank where the bottom dropped off suddenly from sandy shallows to twelve feet of dark water. They were trolling on their way to the point to set night lines for rainbow trout.

"There's our old ruin, Nick," Marjorie said.

Nick, rowing, looked at the white stone in the green trees.

"There it is," he said.

"Can you remember when it was a mill?" Marjorie asked.

"I can just remember," Nick said.

"It seems more like a castle," Marjorie said.

Nick said nothing. They rowed on out of sight of the mill, following the shore line. Then Nick cut across the bay.

"They aren't striking," he said.

"No," Marjorie said. She was intent on the rod all the time they trolled, even when she talked. She loved to fish. She loved to fish with Nick.

Close beside the boat a big trout broke the surface of the water. Nick pulled hard on one oar so the boat would turn and the bait spinning far behind would pass where the trout was feeding. As the trout's back came up out of the water the minnows jumped wildly. They sprinkled the surface like a handful of shot thrown into the water. Another trout broke water, feeding on the other side of the boat.

"They're feeding," Marjorie said.

"But they won't strike," Nick said.

He rowed the boat around to troll past both the feeding fish, then headed it for the point. Marjorie did not reel in until the boat touched the shore.

They pulled the boat up the beach and Nick lifted out a pail of live perch. The perch swam in the water in the pail. Nick caught three of them with his hands and cut their heads off and skinned them while Marjorie chased with her hands in the bucket, finally caught a perch, cut its head off and skinned it. Nick looked at her fish.

"You don't want to take the ventral fin out," he said. "It'll be all right for bait but it's better with the ventral fin in."

He hooked each of the skinned perch through the tail. There were two hooks attached to a leader on each rod. Then Marjorie rowed the boat out over the channel-bank, holding the line in her teeth, and looking toward

Nick, who stood on the shore holding the rod and letting the line run out from the reel.

"That's about right," he called.

"Should I let it drop?" Marjorie called back, holding the line in her hand.

"Sure. Let it go." Marjorie dropped the line overboard and watched the baits go down through the water.

She came in with the boat and ran the second line out the same way. Each time Nick set a heavy slab of driftwood across the butt of the rod to hold it solid and propped it up at an angle with a small slab. He reeled in the slack line so the line ran taut out to where the bait rested on the sandy floor of the channel and set the click on the reel. When a trout, feeding on the bottom, took the bait it would run with it, taking line out of the reel in a rush and making the reel sing with the click on.

Marjorie rowed up the point a little way so she would not disturb the line. She pulled hard on the oars and the boat went way up the beach. Little waves came in with it. Marjorie stepped out of the boat and Nick pulled the boat high up the beach.

"What's the matter, Nick?" Marjorie asked.

"I don't know," Nick said, getting wood for a fire.

They made a fire with driftwood. Marjorie went to the boat and brought a blanket. The evening breeze blew the smoke toward the point, so Marjorie spread the blanket out between the fire and the lake.

Marjorie sat on the blanket with her back to the fire and waited for Nick. He came over and sat down beside her on the blanket. In back of them was the close second-growth timber of the point and in front was the bay with the mouth of Hortons Creek. It was not quite dark. The firelight went as far as the water. They could both see the two steel rods at an angle over the dark water. The fire glinted on the reels.

Marjorie unpacked the basket of supper.

"I don't feel like eating," said Nick.

"Come on and eat, Nick."

"All right."

They ate without talking, and watched the two rods and the firelight in the water.

"There's going to be a moon tonight," said Nick. He looked across the bay to the hills that were beginning to sharpen against the sky. Beyond the hills he knew the moon was coming up.

"I know it," Marjorie said happily.

"You know everything," Nick said.

"Oh, Nick, please cut it out! Please, please don't be that way!"

"I can't help it," Nick said. "You do. You know everything. That's the trouble. You know you do."

Marjorie did not say anything.

"I've taught you everything. You know you do. What don't you know, anyway?"

"Oh, shut up," Marjorie said. "There comes the moon."

They sat on the blanket without touching each other and watched the moon rise.

"You don't have to talk silly," Marjorie said; "what's really the matter?"

"I don't know."

"Of course you know."

"No I don't."

"Go on and say it."

Nick looked on at the moon, coming up over the hills.

"It isn't fun any more."

He was afraid to look at Marjorie. Then he looked at her. She sat there with her back toward him. He looked at her back. "It isn't fun any more. Not any of it."

She didn't say anything. He went on. "I feel as though everything was gone to hell inside of me. I don't know, Marge. I don't know what to say."

He looked on at her back.

"Isn't love any fun?" Marjorie said.

"No," Nick said. Marjorie stood up. Nick sat there, his head in his hands.

"I'm going to take the boat," Marjorie called to him. "You can walk back around the point."

"All right," Nick said, "I'll push the boat off for you."

"You don't need to," she said. She was afloat in the boat on the water with the moonlight on it. Nick went back and lay down with his face in the blanket by the fire. He could hear Marjorie rowing on the water.

He lay there for a long time. He lay there while he heard Bill come into the clearing, walking around through the woods. He felt Bill coming up to the fire. Bill didn't touch him, either.

"Did she go all right?" Bill said.

"Oh, yes." Nick said, lying, his face on the blanket.

"Have a scene?"

"No, there wasn't any scene."

"How do you feel?"

"Oh, go away, Bill! Go away for a while."

Bill selected a sandwich from the lunch basket and walked over to have a look at the rods.

ERNEST HEMINGWAY (1899–1961)

45.   How Do I Write About a Poem?

To understand poetry you must know how words work. Analyzing the highly compressed language of poetry gives you limitless exercise in finding how words can be put together. But to write about poetry you'll need some technical vocabulary, such as the words, *rhyme, imagery, meter, foot, stanza, irony*.[3]

---

[3] For technical definitions, see *A Dictionary of Literary, Dramatic, and Cinematic Terms,* 2nd ed., ed. Sylvan Barnet, Morton Berman, and William Burto (Boston:

Words, though, are no more than tools — insight is the artisan. First feel what the poem is about, then choose the right tools for analyzing it. To compose a philosophical essay on "Mother Goose" would be as wasteful as to overlook the deeper meanings in Andrew Marvell's seventeenth-century poem "The Garden." Use the essay to explain how the poet designed the poem, not to show off erudition. The task isn't easy, of course. What would you do if you were faced with analyzing this epigram by the obscure Elizabethan poet John Weever (1576–1632)?

> Some men marriage do commend
> And all their life in wiving spend,
> But if that I should wives have three
> (God keep me from polygamy!)
>   I'll give the devil two for pay
>   If he will fetch the third away.

Before looking *into* the poem for its inner workings, you look *at* it for its superficial, mechanical devices:

STANZA	RHYME	METER
1 stanza	Couplets:	8 syllables per line
6 lines	commend/spend	4 beats per line
	three/polygamy	
	pay/away	

DICTION	STRUCTURE	OUTSTANDING IMAGES
Restrained and clear	Anticipatory	Lines 4–5

Once you've set up this chart, you can arrange your material into a coherent commentary. What is most important about the epigram? Isn't it the structure, concealing the full meaning until the last line (offering the third wife as pay for fetching the first two away)? Do as the poet did and bring this idea in last. Earlier you could mention the rhymes, which hold the thought together in a memorable way, and the diction, which wrings much meaning out of the simple words. You can describe the poem then by looking at rhyme and meter, diction and structure, embellishing what you say about these by building in other information you picked up in your survey of the poetical effects. Here is a brief example:

A WEEVER'S SONG

As musical as it is epigrammatical, John Weever's brief but pithy stanza on marriage pushes the subject further than most people, especially women, would be willing to see it go. Drawing on the age-old theme of the battle

---

Little, Brown, 1971); and *Literary Terms,* ed. R. Barry and A. J. Wright (San Francisco: Chandler, 1966). A more general book is the perennially useful *A Handbook to Literature,* ed. C. H. Holman, 3rd ed. (New York: Odyssey Press, 1972).

between the sexes, the poet has fashioned a neat hatpin for puncturing romantic illusions about the idyllic bliss of matrimony.

To say that the poem is satirical, however, would be misleading, for the irony is too finely drawn, too mellow for that. Mostly the soft chuckle emerges from the tension of gluing together some sharp thoughts by the agency of simple but clanging rhymes. Particularly noticeable is the shift in the fourth line from a masculine rhyme to the feminine rhyme of "polygamy," a departure from the normal scheme that serves to underscore the position of "polygamy" at the center of the poem. The choice of vocabulary is also simple, deceptively simple. Who can imagine that out of such innocent-sounding words as "marriage," "commend," "wives," "pay," and "fetch" there will be constructed a device of such sharpness? And yet a second glance shows that against the backdrop of simplicity, the key words — the words that inform and point up the direction of the epigram — stand out very clearly indeed, these words being "wiving," "polygamy," and "devil." It is as though the poet wanted as dramatic a contrast between wickedness and amiable innocence as possible.

The best effect of all, however, comes from a structural scheme that guarantees suspension of full meaning until the very end of the stanza. While the rhymes help and the diction is selected carefully, this element of surprise, even shock (so characteristic of the epigram), creates the most fun for the reader. Witty and smart, the stanza shifts in tone from a bumpkinish simplicity to a deft and urbane joke. And yet somehow, despite all these things, no one is hurt; all is in fun. The reason perhaps is that the horrors of polygamy are of far less consequence both to poet and to reader than is the clever turning of a phrase.

A useful trick was used in this version — isolating small parts of the poem instead of writing about the whole poem. Small but meaningful subjects for a paper could be "Keats's love for food: the imagery in 'The Eve of St. Agnes' and 'The Ode to a Nightingale' " or "Meaning of the albatross in Coleridge's 'The Rime of the Ancient Mariner' " or "The dark wood in Robert Frost's 'Stopping by Woods on a Snowy Evening.' "

EXERCISES

A. The same multilevel commentary useful for analyzing imaginative fiction can also be applied to poetry: (1) the poem as an order of words; (2) the poem as an imitation of nature; (3) the poem as an imitation of art; (4) the poem as a revelation of truth. Remember that the poem, not the critic, should determine which phase of the poem you can most profitably study. How should a critic approach these poems?

   1. Anon., "Thirty Days Hath September."   2. Keats's "On First Looking into Chapman's Homer."   3. Whitman's "When Lilacs Last in the Dooryard Bloom'd."   4. Keats's "The Eve of St. Agnes."   5. Shakespeare's

sonnets.   6. Robert Frost's "Mending Wall."   7. Milton's "Lycidas."
8. Spenser's "Epithalamion."   9. Eliot's "The Love Song of J. Alfred
Prufrock."   10. Benét's "John Brown's Body."   11. Williams' "The Red
Wheelbarrow."

B. Analyze the imagery, structural design, and recurring rhythms in these
short poems:

ABSURD CYCLE

The wombed thing
First like a fish
Will become a man
And make a wish
For a peck of apples,
A pint of dream,
And a leaping fish
In a stream.

HYAM PLUTZIK

UPON A CHILD THAT DIED

Here she lies, a pretty bud,
Lately made of flesh and blood,
Who as soon fell fast asleep
As her little eyes did peep.
Give her strewings but not stir
The earth that lightly covers her.

ROBERT HERRICK

THE DELAWARE AND HUDSON

Our shoes would wear and bruise
On the heavy mulch of stones.
Walking the ties takes watching.
They are close enough so taken
One by one, we mince or trip —
But try hitting every other, it's
A masterful stride that tires.
Long boardwalk of crossbeams,
It borders the lip of the lake,
A giant keyboard once booming
Concertos of industry. Though
The trestle is still dangerous,
A fading music of rails tames
The whole metaphor. Already
Nature has been engaged in
Reclaiming this railroad line.
Turtles are sent from the marshes
To storm the gravel embankments

And lay their eggs in the scree.
Today we can see a littering
Of scraped sand and the white
Elfin slippers, vacant shells.
Here's a mission accomplished.
And we hear occasional freight cars
Hustling past in an evening —
As the old men, our neighbors,
Who mismanage their affairs,
Wheeze upstairs after supper,
Asthmatic and anonymous.
We have heard of small wafers
Printed with the ciphers of power
And bastions of memories where
A common magnet is enemy.
What happens is white noise
A stratosphere above our ears,
A technology so silent —
No wonder we place our hands
On the sinuous rails, feeling
For a live pulse of engines,
And wander the shoreline searching
The turtles' route of escape.

MARGARET F. EDWARDS

46.   How Do I Review a Film?

Film has been called the fourth literary genre, a complement to poetry, drama, and prose fiction. How can we doubt that film and literature have grown symbiotically (feeding on each other); early movies drew on stage melodramas, and in the Twenties and Thirties writers like Stephen Vincent Benét and F. Scott Fitzgerald worked in Hollywood. A vignette-like epic poem such as Benét's *John Brown's Body* or Ezra Pound's *Cantos* shows techniques not too different from the film editor's rapid cutting from one scene to another. Nothing has handled the stream-of-consciousness, moment-of-recollection technique derived from James Joyce, T. S. Eliot, and Pound as well as film. Movies of course can, and should be, studied as a pure art, independent of non-cinematic influences, with stress on sight over word. But in the composition and literature class they are usually handled not as an autonomous art form (a whole life's study in itself) but as a development or derivative from a literary source — a drama or novel. The critic searches in the film "for the spirit, tone, and nuance of the original." [4] Your class may read Shakespeare's *Richard III* and then go to see the film ver-

---

[4] Joan Mellen, "Outfoxing Lawrence: Novella into Film," *Literature/Film Quarterly,* 1 (Jan. 1973), 17.

sion by Laurence Olivier; or *A Clockwork Orange, A Separate Peace, Lord of the Flies, Great Expectations.*

How would you go about writing a critical review of Franco Zeffirelli's *Taming of the Shrew* (Shakespeare's play), starring Elizabeth Taylor and Richard Burton? Because the English class is at least as interested in the Shakespeare play as the current film production, you can't judge the film independently of its source. Your approach then will be Drama into Film, not Film as Drama. You'll want to hold the film up against a responsible text of the play to see how *accurately* it interprets the original — if they aren't close, why aren't they? How *effectively* does the director capture all that is vital in the printed text in the language of cinematography? Has the original been transformed or transmogrified? Enriched or impoverished? Or has it been made over into something entirely different, neither better nor worse than its source? These questions are not easy and will demand your best thinking. Is the film an imitation of action, as Aristotle would say, or is it an imitation of an imitation of action? If the latter, how successful is the imitation?

But let's leave theory and try action. I suggest these steps in preparing to write a film review:

1. Begin by knowing the text of the play or novel, as well as you can. You must obviously read it; then, it will be helpful if you understand it. By the time you see the film you should be able to evaluate its cinematic incarnation.

2. If you can, consult *The New York Times Film Reviews* (New York: Arno Press, 1970) in the library's reference room. These reviews contain such vital information as the names of the actors, directors, script writers, cameramen, sound technicians. See also the appendix to Roger Manvell, *Shakespeare and the Film* (New York: Praeger, 1971). Such reviews will also show how someone else approached the problem.

3. Attend a screening of the film amply equipped with several large sheets of blank paper (previously numbered) on a firm backing; and a black felt-tip pen. These will allow you to scrawl productively in the darkness.

4. As the film begins, concentrate very closely on the preliminaries. The Zeffirelli *Shrew* begins with a shot of the countryside near Padua, the university town to which Lucentio and Tranio are traveling. There is then a transition to a wild street carnival with great crowds of extras swarming through the streets. It isolates various types of urban riffraff for closer scrutiny. For a split second, the camera catches a glimpse of a poor wretch in a cage, labeled "Drunkard." And then it passes onto Lucentio first glimpsing the fair Bianca, falling in love, hearing the theme music (which looks forward to the hit theme of Zeffirelli's later *Romeo and Juliet*), and watching her milk-and-honey face respond, giggling, to the attention of the young masquers. The director has combined elements from

the Induction to the play, featuring Christopher Sly, with the first act as written by Shakespeare. The drunkard in the cage is Christopher Sly.

Right away you have enough information for a short analytic paper. Why the cuts? Why the revisions? Are they justified or not? Has anyone the "right" to tamper with Shakespeare's text in this way? What function does the camera perform in this scene that cannot be found in either the printed page or on the conventional stage? Certainly the darkness in the movie theater, the enforced concentration on an image, without distraction, has a hypnotic effect no other medium can offer. Even television carries the distractions of one's home surroundings.

Maybe you also noticed the preposterous slapstick in the garden house scene. The wedding scene that is not in the original script. The downgrading of the subplot about the wooing of Bianca. The extra scenes showing kitchen and bedroom at Petruchio's house. The incredible clutter of details — dishes, tables, hangings, goblets, costumes — which seem to fill nearly every frame. The way in which the camera focuses in close-up on Elizabeth Taylor's eyes. And, most of all, how the director handles the important final scene — the ambiguity in Kate's "submission" to Petruchio, which Shakespearean scholars dispute. You will not have time to establish the ultimate purpose and design in each sequence. You take notes in the theater just to gather raw data. Don't be alarmed if your notes seem incoherent — you can decipher them later.

5. After seeing the film, go back and read the original text, looking for anything your notes bring up. What changes have been made? Has the director made cuts? Revisions? If so, to what end? Do you think these improvisations are useful, or offensive? Do you find Petruchio amusing, boorish, charming, disgusting? (Many critics have complained about Burton's constant "sniggering.") Is Bianca appropriately cuddly and stupid? What do you think of that ending? Is it in the spirit of the original? What is your favorite scene, and how does it fit into the whole film?

6. The technical vocabulary of film studies has now evolved sufficiently to call for a "rhetoric" of its own.[5] Without a good deal of expertise in this area, which I cannot claim, these "filmic" concepts can be readily misunderstood. Even so, many people have at least heard of a "shot," (usually defined as a single, uninterrupted running of the camera), "long shot," "establishing shot" (a group of characters are shown sitting around a table or against a landscape, for example), "medium shot," and a "close-up." A "pan shot" (from *panorama*) has the camera swinging from the right or left, and "tilt" and "crane" shot derive from the

---

[5] For the student who wants to know more about film terminology and theory, helpful texts are Harry M. Geduld and Ronald Gottesman, *An Illustrated Glossary of Film Terms* (New York: Rinehart and Winston, 1973), and Louis D. Giannetti, *Understanding Movies* (Englewood Cliffs: Prentice-Hall, 1971).

camera moving up or down, or backward and forward, A "zoom" shot flings us close to the action. A group of related scenes is a "sequence," and interruptions are called "intercuts." Transitions are made by a variety of methods, including the "cut," "fade-in," "fade-out," "wipe," and the "jumpcut" (a rapid change from one scene to another). Demanding a trained eye to distinguish among them, cinematic transitions need to be studied with the help of a film projector, a collection of stills, and a competent teacher of film studies. How can you tell, for example, whether the transition in Olivier's *Richard III* from the execution of Hastings to the charwoman scrubbing the floor is an ordinary "cut," or "jumpcut," or neither?

7. After doing all this you are prepared to compose the paper. Select a thesis from the many possibilities: (a) the pictorial effects (*opsis*) of the film embellish or distract the audience; (b) the directorial improvisations are effective or ineffective; (c) as Shakespeare, the film is a travesty; as film, it is better or worse; (d) the ending is consistent or inconsistent with the source; and (e) the film accomplishes effects that neither stage nor printed text can achieve. Support your assertions by referring to the film and the text. At or toward the close of the paper, begin to draw some conclusions about how effectively you think the director captured the play on film. Has he succeeded or failed, and if so to what degree and why?

8. Do your final draft, which may look like Scott Whitted's 1972 paper whose negative approach perhaps comes partly from his favoring word over picture.

THE TAMING OF THE SHREW?

Franco Zeffirelli's motion picture version of Shakespeare's play showed how a director can fail in attempting to mold another person's work to his own tastes. In this film, the molding was moldy more often than not. Zeffirelli, however, was saved from his own devices by some slick acting, which partially compensated for some of the directorial flaws.

Unfortunately, the opening panoramic scenes set the pace for much of the movie. The audience was treated to a landscape that looked like it had escaped from a frame in the Louvre, but that added nothing to the plot or the themes of the movie or play. Next, Lucentio and Tranio trotted out of the sunset or sunrise, or whatever, and proceeded into Padua, where some sort of festival was writhing through the city thoroughfares. Here, both Tranio and Lucentio were suddenly taken hold of by love, Tranio for a fat whore (close-up), Lucentio for a beguiling nymphet (neo-Petrarchan sound track). Thus, their heads were properly boggled, as was mine (though for reasons different from love) as Zeffirelli literally got into the swing of things.

The movie was dominated by madcap, undisciplined humor completely different from Shakespeare's witty, controlled comedy. Everyone chased everybody, and shouted, yelled, struck someone or something, or threw objects. Of course, while some of this action took place in the play, much of it was added by Zeffirelli, and much of the addenda flopped.

For example, Petruchio's chase of Kate through house, barn, across roof-tops, and finally into a hay mound did little except obscure the matching of wits of the two characters that was such an integral part of the play, though it must have exhausted the cameramen. Although the wedding scene was well done, particularly the close-ups at the altar, most of what Zeffirelli added turned out like the chase scene.

Elizabeth Taylor delivered a sensitive and stirring portrayal of the shrew, from the first close-up of her baleful eye glaring through a window blind. She opened our eyes wide to the fact that Kate, for all her faults, was a human being, with hopes, feelings, dreams, and disappointments. The scene in which Bianca escaped Kate and leapt into her father's waiting arms illustrated why Kate had a right to be bitter, and Taylor played the scene to perfection as she angrily bit off her words and spat them at her father. Later she portrayed a Kate who appreciated the fact that people were at last admiring and gasping at her when she appeared resplendent for the wedding in gown and jewels. Miss Taylor continued her fine performance throughout the movie (which surprised me), as she was at first browbeaten by Petruchio, and then learned how to handle him. Her portrayal of the "repentant" Kate was properly ambiguous, too. The camera made her motive for departing from the hall after the "submission" speech all the more pointed. She played well the part of the "lusty wench," making Kate the rightful center of attraction.

Zeffirelli, as I have subtly hinted, came very close to wrecking *The Taming of the Shrew*. His interpretation of the play obfuscated the subtle theme of illusion and reality introduced by the Christopher Sly Induction, though Sly remains briefly as a drunkard locked in a cage. Zeffirelli's zany antics and lack of control added the fine quality of confusion; the fact that Zeffirelli tried to adapt Shakespeare to his own tastes isn't disturbing, but the way in which he went about it is. Shakespeare didn't write *The Keystone Cops Meet Don Rickles,* but you'd never know it from this movie. Much of Shakespeare's measured, rhythmic dialogue was obliterated by Zeffirelli's wild, uncontrolled action. Shakespeare's words are not the Holy Writ, but they deserve to stay in the movie more than the stuff that Zeffirelli replaces them with.

Zeffirelli's apology to Shakespeare at the beginning of the movie was ap-propriate, and I was left with the impression that it was one of the few times when he knew what he was doing.

Essay — A loose sally of the mind; an irregular indigested piece; not a regular and orderly composition.
                SAMUEL JOHNSON, Dictionary, 1755

When a right thought springs up in the mind, it strives after expression and is not long in reaching it; for clear thought easily finds words to fit it.
                ARTHUR SCHOPENHAUER, "On Style," 1851

13 Writing Essay Examinations

47. How Do I Write an Essay Examination?

You'll need all the resources you've won in studying rhetoric and usage as you sit down to write an essay off the cuff. This is, in its extemporaneous way, the best test of your ability in writing. The first thing you'll be judged for is your knowledge of the subject. And your judge may already have waded through dozens of essays on similar topics. He may even, by the time your paper reaches him, be in a trance-like state. He offers yet another hazard — he is the expert and you the amateur. How do you impress on such a judge that your ideas and execution are worthy?

An impromptu essay is successful when you take these five steps: (1) know your subject thoroughly; (2) read the question very carefully; (3) make a short outline before you start writing; (4) decide which is the most important part of your argument and gather three or four proofs to make it convincing; (5) compose (write) as quickly as you can without becoming incoherent. And allow time to read through the paper for any wrong or misleading statements.

John Snow is a student in a Shakespeare course. He has read carefully each Shakespeare play assigned to the class. To prepare for this test he has reviewed the characters and plots, going over his notes about outstanding stylistic traits of the plays, and browsing through some scenes he likes. He's sure he wouldn't confuse Dogberry's prose in *Much Ado About Nothing* with one of

Romeo's poetic speeches to Juliet. He takes one more large precaution, studying in detail one comedy, one tragedy, one history, and one romance that he likes best among Shakespeare's plays, and is prepared for both broad and deep questions. The principle is good anywhere — you can't know every subject equally well, but you should know a lot about a few subjects. John is ready to be tested.

He avoids panic in the examination room by looking closely at the question. He knows that some people will answer five out of five essay questions even though instructed to answer only two out of five. And he picks carefully the questions he knows most about because he enjoyed reading the plays, instead of spreading himself thin.

Before touching the paper with his pen, he looks for the direction signals in the questions. He's survived a dozen years in school and knows them by heart: Compare and contrast. Discuss. Evaluate. Analyze. Comment on. Trace (something), through six plays. Classify. He follows directions to the letter.

Because his instructor has combined traditional teaching with film-watching, John chooses a question asking him to compare Sir Laurence Olivier's *Richard III* with Shakespeare's play:

> King Richard III has a historical, dramatic, and filmic identity respectively represented in the Elizabethan chronicle histories, Shakespeare's play, and Olivier's film. Making matters even more complicated is the fact that Richard, Duke of Gloucester, had an identity of his own that perhaps none of these accounts has correctly depicted. Using specific examples from history, play, and film, compare these versions of Richard's life, and explore their relationships.

Snow sees that comparison is the question, though it has to be an awkward, four-way comparison. But the instructor has simplified the work by specifying "explore relationships," which means the student can exercise his ingenuity in further limiting and defining the topic. John does this by designing a theme, a thesis statement, around which he will build the whole essay. He finds the theme in the question itself: The historical Richard has been transformed over the centuries by historians, Shakespeare, and film-makers into a mythical creature. Snow sketches a short outline developing this theme to make sure he knows the main points in the argument and has proofs to support it:

> THEME: Richard has been mythologized first by the historians, then by Shakespeare, and now by Olivier.
> I. Actual Richard: See P. M. Kendall's book. Comparison with run-of-the-mill kings.
> II. Historical Richard: Tudor politics. Pro-Lancastrian bias.
> III. Shakespeare's Richard: Half true and half false.
> IV. Olivier's Richard: Grotesque physical details.
> CONCLUSION: The centuries have transformed him from human being into myth.

Snow now plunges into the writing part of his work. He finds a way in this moment of truth to use everything he has learned about spelling, punctuating, organizing, giving examples, and writing emphatic sentences. His essay ends up looking like this. How would you grade it?

The triplex figure that comes down to us as King Richard III is one who sums up a process of converting a person into a myth. The real Richard existed as an historical reality. Shakespeare's Richard was half-real and half-myth. The Richard of Olivier is nearly the completed product — he is almost entirely myth.

Thesis statement: mythic figure

We know from the work of scholars like Paul M. Kendall that the Richard who actually became king of England in the fifteenth century had no exaggerated manifestations of physical deformity. He was indeed a vindictive power manager but a lion in battle. Other than this, there is little, save his murderous nature, to indicate to posterity that he was remarkably different from other routinely cruel monarchs. Behold Henry VIII!

I. Historical Richard.
1. Proof in works of scholarship

2. His comparison with other kings

To Shakespeare, a century later, the character of Richard had been molded not only by the normal growth of his perversity in rumor and legend, but also by the political reality of Elizabethan England. Shakespeare had to accentuate the cruelty of Yorkist Richard because of his acts of genocide against the Lancastrian line. It was to this end that Shakespeare added the physical deformities to manifest the psychological perturbations which were intrinsic to the character of Richard. With the help of Polydore Vergil, More, Stow, and others, Shakespeare initiated the dramatic tradition of Richard that was to destroy the monarch's historical reality.

II. Tudor Politics.

1. Tudor partiality to Lancastrians, whom Richard fought

2. Shakespeare dramatizes his physical limitations

Along with the major emendation of physical deformity, other significant changes were imposed upon Richard by the Senecan elements of horror and intrigue in Shakespeare's drama. Intrigue and blood-guilt were established conventions that figured heavily in Richard's dramatic identity. To

3. Senecan intrigue elements further colored Shakespeare's portrait of Richard

strengthen the force of the evil of the character, he is made a near psychopath, willing to perform any act in order to win the game of power politics: "Plots have I laid, inductions dangerous."

Shakespeare, however, could not completely transform Richard for the king had too strong an historical impact on the contemporary politics of Elizabethan England. Thus Richard's one respectable characteristic, his valor in combat, was maintained by Shakespeare in frequent battle confrontations particularly in the latter part of *3 Henry VI*.

To Olivier the real Richard had fairly dissipated into a hazy shadow with a questionable crown. The role of Richard in the politics of England had weakened into a semi-significant link in the succession of the crown. It seems that it is in the dramatically warped king that Olivier finds life and a vibrant reality, and it is to this gargoyle figure that Olivier adapts his own portrayal of Richard. Olivier has heightened the sense of deformity of Richard and has added many conventions of the hero-villain. The face of Olivier's Richard is pale; the nose long and narrow and pointed; the eyebrows, dark, and highly arched. These all seem to be modern conventions of villainy mapped onto the already grotesque body of Richard.

The characteristics of intrigue and treachery are again amplified by the film in the many shadowy scenes of Richard skulking in doorways, leering through windows, and eavesdropping on old King Edward.

There now exist two Richards. One, the historically accurate king of England, has all but vanished from mass western culture. The other, the literary figure, has not only survived but increased in depth. The limitations which chronological proximity to the life of Richard placed on Shakespeare's distortions of the character do not apply to Olivier. He has carried each deformity of mind and body to an exaggerated extreme to create a purely

4. Direct quotation bolsters writer's authority as expert

III. Shakespeare retains elements of R's true character

IV. Olivier's conception of Richard

1. Gargoyle figure

2. Details: Physical ugliness of O's portrayal

3. Uses of shadows in film version

Summary and restatement
Then and now
Two Richards: Shakespeare's with some valor; Olivier's with none!

mythic character. He completely destroys any shreds of valor or nobility the Richard of Shakespeare may have had. Richard is not shown in noble combat, but only helplessly overpowered and vulgarly slain. *Honi Soit Mal Qui Y Pense!* His reality is now limited to that of a stage legend.

Subject Index

Index of Quoted Authors and Sources

To the student:

As publishers, we realize that one way to improve education is to improve textbooks. We also realize that you, the student, largely determine the success or failure of textbooks. Although it is the instructor who assigns them, it is the student who buys and uses them. If enough of you don't like a particular book and make your feelings known, the chances are your instructor will not assign it again.

Usually only instructors are asked about the quality of a text; their opinion alone is considered as revisions are planned or as new books are developed. Now, Little, Brown would like to ask you about Kenneth Rothwell's *Questions of Rhetoric and Usage, 2nd Edition:* how you liked or disliked it; why it was interesting or dull; if it taught you anything. Would you please fill in this form and return it to us at: Little, Brown and Co., College Division, 34 Beacon Street, Boston, Mass. 02106. It is your chance to directly affect the publication of future textbooks.

_____

School: _____

Course title: _____

Other texts required: _____

1. Did you like the book? _____

2. CONTENT: Was it too easy? _____

   Was it too difficult? _____

   Did you read it all? _____

   Which sections were most useful? _____

   _____

   Which sections were least useful? _____

   _____

3. FORMAT: Did you like the cover design? _____

   Did you like the organization of the contents? _____

4. Were the exercises useful? _____

   How might they be changed? _____

   _____

   _____

5. Did you like the examples?_____

    How might they be improved?_____

    _____

6. Do you feel the professor should continue to assign this book next year?_____

7. Will you keep this book for your library?_____

8. Please add any comments or suggestions._____

    _____

    _____

    _____

    _____

    _____

    _____

9. May we quote you in our promotion efforts for this book?___yes___no

_____   _____
date   signature

_____
address